AF521839

HOW DOES JEWISH LAW WORK?

HOW DOES JEWISH LAW WORK?

VOLUME 2

A Rabbi Analyzes 119 more Contemporary Halachic Questions

J. Simcha Cohen

JASON ARONSON INC.
Northvale, New Jersey
Jerusalem

This book was set in 11 pt. Century by Alabama Book Composition of Deatsville, AL and printed and bound by Book-mart Press, Inc. of North Bergen, NJ.

Copyright © 2000 by J. Simcha Cohen

10 9 8 7 6 5 4 3 2 1

All rights reserved. No part of this book may be used or reproduced in any manner whatsoever without written permission from Jason Aronson Inc. except in the case of brief quotations in reviews for inclusion in a magazine, newspaper, or broadcast.

Library of Congress Cataloging-in-Publication Data

Cohen, J. Simcha.
How does Jewish law work? Volume II : A rabbi analyzes 119 more contemporary halachic questions / by J. Simcha Cohen.
p. cm.
Includes bibliographical references and index.
ISBN 0–87668–155–0
1. Responsa—1800– 2. Judaism—20th century. 3. Judaism—Customs and practices. I. Title.
BM522.27.03624 2000
296.3—dc20 93–19756

Printed in the United States of America on acid-free paper. For information and catalog write to Jason Aronson Inc., 230 Livingston Street, Northvale, NJ 07647-1726, or visit our website: www.aronson.com

With

Appreciation

Good Friends, Patrons of Torah

Ruth and Robert Epstein

Judy and Solly Joss

Melbourne, Australia

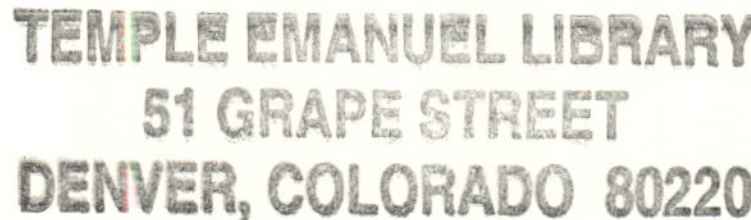
TEMPLE EMANUEL LIBRARY
51 GRAPE STREET
DENVER, COLORADO 80220

Contents

II
CONVERSION

III
SHABBAT, HOLIDAYS, AND *KIDDUSH*

IV
PRAYERS AND SYNAGOGUE RULES

A. Prayers

V
KOHANIM CONCERNS

VI
WOMEN

VII
CIRCUMCISION

VIII
HEALTH ISSUES

IX
SOCIAL AND IDEOLOGICAL CONCERNS

Introduction

No one can foretell the future. We lack such vision. Accordingly, it is impossible to know where a person will be in the future. Here, at the onset of a new century, I am living in Australia, thousands of miles away from my birthplace. I am not a victim of the Holocaust nor of pogroms. It was, rather, the luster of new vistas and greater challenges in the realm of Jewish life that beckoned me to new horizons. It may also be a family tradition.

My family served as rabbinical leaders in Jewish communities throughout the world. In fact, we circled the world of Jewish life. We derive from *kohanim gedolim* in ancient Israel. Eighteen generations ago a forefather was a rabbi exiled from Spain to Solonika. His son moved to Constantinople. His grandsons became *rabbanim* in the metropolitan city of Krakow. Rav Yosef Katz, the brother-in-law of the Rama and the Rosh Yeshivah of Krakow for fifty years, was a famed great-grandfather fourteen generations ago. From Krakow the family resided mostly in Southern Russia and the Ukraine. My paternal grandfather HaRav Shmuel Hakohan was the Rav of Shatava, in Kaminetz Padolslk, Ukraine, and the author of internationally acclaimed halachic volumes. *Minchat Shabbat* (Laws of *Shabbat*) and *Ma'dani Shmuel* (Laws of *Pesach*). Amongst the hasidic *rabbanim* they were deemed invaluable for rendering halachic decisions. My father, HaRav HaGaon Reb Meyer Cohen (*z"l*), emigrated to the United States of America. He served as Rav of Asbury Park, New Jersey and subsequently as Executive Director of the Union of Orthodox Rabbis of the United States and Canada (Agudat HaRabbonim) for over twenty years.

Continuing in the family tradition of eighteen generations, father after son, of being rabbis of Jewish communities, I served as rabbi of an Orthodox community in West Orange, New Jersey and subsequently for approximately eighteen years as rabbi of a congregation in Los Angeles, California.

Torah travels the world of Jewish civilization. In this vein, I assumed the position as rabbinical leader of the Mizrachi community in Melbourne, Australia. This community is a jewel of Jewish life and commitment. Over seventy percent of all Jewish children in a population of about fifty thousand Jews attend a Day School. The Mizrachi community sponsors five simultaneous *Shabbat minyanim*, an elementary and high school for Jewish studies, a *Koshrut* organization, and numerous services impacting the Jewish community at large. I thank God for the privilege of serving as Rav of this magnificent Jewish communal organization.

One essential message must be noted. Torah is eternal. Torah does not become altered by geography. *Torat Moshe* is the same whether one resides in Europe, America, Israel, or Australia.

My *rebbetzen* Shoshana deserves the blessings of God for her kindness, devotion, and constant encouragement to learn, teach, and write Torah. She has faithfully supported my quest with great love.

A *birkat kohen* to our wonderful children and grandchildren. May HaShem bless us with health, happiness, success, and continued devotion to Torah.

Special recognition must be rendered to the Torah mentors of our family: my father, HaRav HaGaon Reb Meyer Cohen and my mother Rebbetzen Henrietta Cohen, Zichronom Livracha; my father-in-law, HaRav HaGaon Reb Yaakov Nayman, the famed disciple of the Brisker Rav; and my mother-in-law, Rebbetzen Chaya Nayman. Their love of Torah molded our personalities and shaped the contours of our lives.

My paternal grandfather, in the introduction to this volume on *Shabbat*, made the following observations that are pertinent, especially in our era. I feel these remarks should preface all volumes dealing with practical halachah and should constantly be placed before the attention of readers. I have taken the liberty of paraphrasing the contents and expanding certain issues.

> Every serious person seeks to impact favorably the world itself; to in some way make a contribution that is lasting (*Tikun Olam*); to perform some action that may have a life of its own even beyond the frail limitation of one's own lifetime. Publishing Torah concepts seems to be a proper vehicle to accomplish this goal; for a quality volume has the potential of influencing future generations. As such, every publication is (in a way) a quest for immortality. Every volume gives an author an opportunity to live, again and again, in future eras. What a *zechut* (a religious privilege) it is to have one's Torah viewpoint discussed, and even perhaps helping to guide future leaders of Jewish people. For such reasons it is definitely understandable why an author seeks to share thoughts by publication.
>
> At issue is that initial common rabbinical reaction to halachic volumes to deflate the egos of new authors by questioning their ability and sagacity or even their impudence to suggest that their works or thoughts should be guides for Jewish life. To such critics, I beg of you, do not dismiss the contents without sufficient analysis and thought. Should, after serious deliberations, it be determined that I erred, please inform me in writing of my errors. This will grant me an opportunity (while I have the ability to respond) to review all charges and defend my position. Moreover, after responding to you should I not satisfy your criticism, then I promise, as strength is within me, that in a future publication (for I will continue to write), I will publicly retract all errors I may have committed.
>
> The Chavat Yair writes that should a Torah volume contain but one good Torah thought, it serves as a guard and spiritual protector over the other parts. Hopefully so will be with this volume. (Mimchat *Shabbat*, Introduction).

Halachah stands at the pinnacle of Torah learning. Yet even this pursuit may be subdivided into two distinct areas of concern. HaRav HaGaon Reb Naftali Tzvi Hirsh Berlin (the Netziv, the Rosh HaYeshivah of Volozon), contends that the highest accolades are to be granted to those involved in halachic creativity; namely, the pursuit of unique creative responses to the problems of the day. The lower level of halachah is the study of existing laws already developed and promulgated by others (Meromai Sadeh, *Berachot* 8a). This volume represents the former pursuit. It is a collection of contemporary creative halachic responses to issues and problems impacting the modern Jew. It reflects my Torah research, knowledge, and logic to questions of Jews entering the twenty-first century.

Part I

Modern Israel

Israel Independence Day and Hallel

QUESTION: What is the halachic basis for the recitation of *Hallel* on Israel Independence Day?

RESPONSE: The Gemorah was concerned with the rationale as to why the Sages enacted the reading of the *Megillah* on Purim. In response, the Talmud notes that logic appears to support its recitation. Indeed, it's a *kal v'chomer*. "Now if the Jews who were delivered from slavery to freedom said a song of praise to God upon witnessing the Egyptians drown in the sea, then certainly we should commemorate our deliverance from death at the hands of Achashverosh and Haman to life with a public reading of the *Megillah*, which is the story of that deliverance." Based upon this citation, the Talmud contends that logic would dictate the recitation of *Hallel* on Purim. Namely, since the Jews were delivered from a potential life-threatening condition, they should be obligated to recite *Hallel*. To this the Talmud responds that there are distinct aspects to Purim that mitigate against saying *Hallel*. One, we were yet servants of Achashverosh even after the deliverance from life-threatening conditions; two, the *Megillah* is equivalent to reciting *Hallel* (*Megillah* 14a).

Based upon the above talmudic citation, HaRav HaGaon Reb Meshulim Rotta ruled that a status transformation from potential death to life merits recitation of *Hallel*. In 1948, the Jews in the land of Israel definitely survived life-threatening conditions. As such, the talmudic *kal v'chomer* is applicable and it is certainly proper to say *Hallel* (Responsa, *Kol Mevaser*, no. 21). The argument that Jews do not say *Hallel* when in servitude to another nation is simply not germane to an independent nation, Israel.

At issue to halachic scholars is whether the status transformation that occurred in 1948 to the Jews of Israel was comparable to the logical argument presented in the Talmud. HaRav HaGaon Reb Moshe Tzvi Neria contended that the *kal v'chomer* had relevance to similar victories only when the status transformation affected or impacted directly the entire Jewish people or the majority of the Jewish nation. In the event that only a minority segment of the Jewish people were saved from potential death the case lacked applicability to all Jews. To the extent that the 1948 victory in Israel related to a minority percentage of the total Jewish population, the Jews of the Diaspora, perhaps, are not under any obligation to recite *Hallel*. The victory becomes comparable to one that took place in a specific area and has no relevance to Jews throughout the world. Moreover, even in Israel the chanting of *Hallel* is not mandated from the Talmud in *Megillah* and, perhaps, should not be said with a *berachah* (HaRav Moshe Tzvi Neria, Chalufai Michtavim Ol Itzumai Shel Yom Haatzmaut, *Shanah B'shanah* 5722, pp. 105–106).

To respond to Rav Neria's probing question it is necessary to analyze the status of Jews who reside in the land of Israel. At issue is whether they are comparable to other residential Jewish communities throughout the world, or are they unique? Do they have a special status, or are they simply like Jewish New York, London, or Melbourne?

The *Sefer HaChinuch* rules that the mitzvah to rebuild the *Bet HaMikdash* is operational only when the majority of the Jewish people reside in the land of Israel (Mitzvah 95). This concept was quite problematic to HaRav Yehoshua Leib of Kutna. It is known that only a small percentage of Jews departed from the Diaspora to build the second *Bet HaMikdash*. In fact, historically, the overwhelming majority of the Jewish population were not living in Israel when the second *Bet HaMikdash* was built. Thus, according to the *Sefer HaChinuch's* ruling, the mitzvah appears not to have been operational when the second *Bet HaMikdash* was built.

HaGaon HaRav Reb Yehoshua of Kutna (Yeshuot Malko)

provides the following response to the above question. The Talmud notes that each person has a potential share in Gan Eden as well as in Gehinnon. Should he be worthy (*zacheh*) he acquires his share as well as the share of his neighbor (*Hagiga* 15a). This principle, suggests the Yeshuot Malko, gives meaning to the mitzvah of the Jews when they built the second *Bet HaMikdash.* Everyone had an opportunity to depart from the *galut* and join those who returned to the holy land. Every Jew had permission to share in the mitzvah of building the *Bet HaMikdash.* Those who chose not to return to the land of Israel forfeited their rights. Their share in Israel was granted to those who did return to the biblical land. Thus, those who did make *aliyah* received a multiple inheritance: their share as well as the share of those who simply refused to return. Accordingly, the Jews that actually built the second *Bet HaMikdash* were entitled to do so. They were the symbolic representatives of *k'lal Yisrael.* They may have been a numerical minority but they represented the totality of Israel. Indeed, the Talmud notes that the *kohanim* of a specific *mishmar* that returned to serve in the second *Bet HaMikdash* were privileged to acquire the rights of those who did not return (see *Ta'anit* 27a, b), again signifying the same concept. Indeed, the Rambam ruled that the sages of the land of Israel have the authority to provide ordination (*Hichot Sanhadrin*, chap. 4). The fact that the sages of the Diaspora are not even considered must be due to the principle that anyone who has the ability to reside in Israel and chooses not to relinquishes authority to the resident sages of Israel. Thus, even though the majority of Jews did not reside in the land of Israel during the building of the second *Bet HaMikdash*, those who did in fact move to Israel served as the surrogates of the entire Jewish nation (see HaGaon HaRav Reb Yehoshua Leib of Kutna, Response Yeshuot Malko, *Lekutai Torah*).

The principle articulated has relevance and contemporary application to the Jews residing in Israel. Jews in Israel represent not just themselves but the entire nation. The Jews in Israel are qualitatively distinct from Jewish communities throughout the Diaspora. Whoever has the choice to return to Israel or reside in the Diaspora and refrains from making *aliyah* relinquishes his right to speak in the name of *k'lal Yisrael.* Only one community in the world has the halachic authority to represent the totality of Jews: Israel. This means that a life-saving action occurring to any Diaspora community is an action impacting but a segment of our people. Should the Israeli community be so involved in a status transformation from potential death to life, the halachic concern permeates the totality of our people. As such, Israel Independence Day is a joyous moment for Jews all over the world. The comparison to the *kal v'chomer* is correct: 1948 was a victory for all Jews, not just those living in the land of Israel.

Israel Independence Day

QUESTION: Does Israel Independence Day contain religious overtones?

RESPONSE: *Yom Ha'atzmaut* commemorates the realization of an age-old dream, an age-old prayer. For thousands of years Jews prayed *Leshanah habah b'Yerushalayim,* "Next year in Jerusalem." Not this year, next year. Always next year. *Hashatah avdai, leshanah habah bnei chorin,* "This year we are slaves." This year we are dependent on the whims, the passions, the hates, the anti-Semitic onslaughts of almost every nation in the world, from the most crude and primitive to the most cosmopolitan and sophisticated. The dream of *Li'yot am chofshi b'artzeinu,* "A free nation in our own land," was constantly pushed into the neverending tomorrows of the future. So on *Yom Ha'atzmaut* we publicly proclaim that the dream is now reality.

The Talmud (*Makkot* 24b) relates that Rabbi Akiva and his

colleagues were walking past the remnants of the holy *Bet HaMikdash* and noted a fox creeping out of the scorched ruins. The rabbis were dismayed. The sight of the depths of destruction to which the holiest Jewish site in the world had evolved depressed them to tears. Look, they said, how low we have become that our holiest site is now a haven for animals. Rabbi Akiva did not cry. Just the opposite, he smiled. He felt the sighting was cause to be happy. It meant that it would once again be rebuilt. The *Meharsha* tells us that Rabbi Akiva was happy that our enemies had not benefitted from our sacred places. A personal interpretation is that the Rabbi was happy that the gentiles of the world did not rebuild Jerusalem and make it into a gentile city. The rebuilding was reserved for Jews. So, too, with the State of Israel. We are blessed. It is our age, our era that has been given the *zechut*, the privilege of rebuilding Israel. We have the privilege of having our nation built in our time, hopefully according to our dreams. Israel is not being rebuilt by the nations of the world: We built it. We greened its lands and refurbished its soil. We make it reverberate with Torah and our culture. It was reserved for our age to crystallize this nation into the stature it now commands. In addition, for thousands of years we have been denigrated as a nation that had lost the favor of God. It has been said that we were once God's chosen people, but lost that status due to our sins. Gentile theologians have substantiated such venomous infamy by citing the fact that we had no nation, no land of our own. They claimed that we were a people destined to roam the cities and nations of the world as punishment for our sins. The establishment of the State of Israel put an end to this canard. It therefore provides a theological refutation of our religious enemies, and has major religious ramifications apart from the mitzvah of settling the land.

Israel is a reality. Many were blessed to be present at its formation. All of us are blessed to be witness to its growth. All of us stand taller because of its existence. May Israel grow from strength to strength. May our children and grandchildren share this *kavod. Am Yisrael Chai.*

Prayer for Medinat Yisrael

QUESTION: The authorized prayer for the State of Israel contains the phrase *Raishit tzmichat ge'ulatainu*, meaning that Israel is "the precursor of our redemption." Does this concept not conflict with the traditional belief that redemption is to be concomitant with the coming of the Messiah? If so, the apparent absence of the Messiah—or any era of world peace—should vitiate against any pragmatic assertion of present-day redemption.

RESPONSE: It may be demonstrated that *ge'ulah* (redemption) has a social and religious context independent of specific messianic manifestations. Israel is a precursor of redemption and not its final stage. An analysis of the ancient Exodus should shed light on this matter.

Jews celebrate freedom from Egyptian bondage on Passover. At the *seder*, on the first night of the holiday, we laud our deliverance and numerous rituals dramatically and symbolically transport us thousands of years to the lifestyle of an ancient past. We act as if we ourselves were freed from slavery.

But were we actually free at that period of time? The Talmud (*Megillah* 14a) notes that the Jews chanted *Hallel* (Praise to the Lord) at their transformation from slavery to freedom. Rashi contends that this occurred by the miracle of the Red Sea. Accordingly, when their enemies were destroyed, the Jews were so elated that they spontaneously sang a song of praise to God. This suggests that the true sense of freedom occurred on the seventh day of the Passover. Only when the Egyptian soldiers were destroyed did the Jewish people really feel free enough to express their joy of thanksgiving. Thus the major ritual celebration of Jewish freedom should take place on the seventh day of Passover, not on the eve of the first day. It is difficult to consider the ancient Jews free prior to the crossing of the Red Sea. They departed from Egypt, but shortly afterwards they were besieged by the Egyptian army. They were confused, bewildered, and frightened. Is this the freedom we celebrate, a one-night elation subsequently transformed into a potential national calamity? Should not the *seder*, therefore, take place on the seventh day of Passover, a time of communal bliss, an era of future-directed action, a period wherein all enemies are destroyed and fear dissipated? This suggests that the *seder* does not necessarily commemorate freedom per se, but something else.

The Talmud (*Berachot* 9a) contends that *ge'ulah* (redemption) occurred the first night of Passover, and the actual exodus took place by day. Rashi defines redemption as "permission to depart."

Thus, three major events took place: (1) redemption (at night), (2) exodus (by day), and (3) freedom (on the seventh day).

The *seder* celebrates not freedom but redemption. Freedom from enemies is not a realistic status; it is messianic in nature. Every generation has its share of anti-Semites. Every era in history has had anti-Jewish pogroms. To be Jewish is to be rooted in reality. Our people revere miracles but do not rely on them to guide our lives.

We celebrate, rather, redemption. The Jew has permission (authority) to depart from his bondage. We may be surrounded by enemies, but we can leave them and "do our own thing." In Egypt, it was a courageous act of faith to depart from the land. The proclamation that we had permission to leave was a psychological form of strength: No one can enslave us; we can leave Egypt. Only God is our Lord. Whether we actually do depart—that is a matter of faith in our future.

For this reason, the Aggadah states that the *rasha* (the nonbelieving son) is told that had he been in Egypt, "he would not have been redeemed." Why? Because he would not have acted upon a mere permission to leave. He would have viewed the might of Egypt, realized the potential danger, and then been paralyzed with fear.

The Jew celebrates redemption each year. He recalls that he possesses the inner ability to seek freedom. It is within him.

No man can give him that right; it is his birthright. He can live in or depart from any nation, he can leave any situation. Any bondage is transitory. He has permission from God, not from man. He celebrates not the annihilation of enemies but the unshackling of bonds. The spirit of tomorrow permeates his presence. He and his people need not fear existing enemies. He is redeemed.

So, too, today. Israel is a reality. The Jew is free to depart from the *galut*. He may move to Israel; he "has permission to depart." For centuries this simply was not feasible. The existence of a Jewish nation that welcomes back its members from the far-flung nations of world civilization is a form of redemption. It simply cannot be denied that Israel is now a realistic option for Jewish living. This option was denied us for centuries. Even those who do not return to Israel feel psychologically secure because that option is available. That is a degree of redemption today. Is this not *Raishit tzmichat ge'ulatainu*?

Yom Yerushalayim

QUESTION: Does Yom Yerushalayim, the day that the Israeli army recaptured Jerusalem, have any religious significance?

RESPONSE: I. The Mishnah reports that "for rain and upon hearing good tidings (*besurot tovot*)," one says (the blessing) "Blessed Be He who is good and bestows good (*Hatov U'maitiv*)," and on hearing bad tidings one says (the blessing) "Blessed Be The True Judge (*Dayan Ha'emet*)" (*Berachot* 59b).

At issue is the extended phraseology of the Mishnah. Why is it necessary for the Mishnah to state that good and bad events need to be heard? The Mishnah could have simply stated that for good one recites one blessing, and for bad another. HaRav

Naftali Tzvi Yehuda Berlin (The Netziv) contends that the term "good tidings" suggests something good happened to *k'lal Yisrael*, even if the person who heard the news may not personally be affected. When one is present and actually sees (good) things happen, this implies that the person himself (or herself) is involved in the event. When the Mishnah mentions that one merely hears "good tidings," it suggests that the person who heard the news has no involvement with it but is, rather, simply happy that his people have such a joyous event transpiring (Meromai Sadeh, *Berachot* 59b). Accordingly, should a Jew hear that Jerusalem, our ancient capital, our holiest city, the *makom HaMikdash*, is within Jewish dominion and access to all our holy places is guaranteed, this is certainly a good tiding (*besurah tovah*) impacting on *k'lal Yisrael*, that deserves a blessing. Being happy that Jerusalem is controlled by Jews is one of the finest expressions of a happy tiding for *k'lal Yisrael* itself.

II. The Talmud reports that the fifteenth of Av was made into a partial holiday for "it was the day when Hosea ben Elah removed the guards that Yerovam ben Nevot had placed on the roads to prevent Israel from going (up to Jerusalem) on pilgrimage" (*Ta'anit* 30b, 31a).

Thus, the inability to go to Jerusalem was not due to the sin of the king, it was the people themselves who refused to make the pilgrimage (Rashi, II Kings 17:2).

Accordingly, mere access to Jerusalem proclaimed by a king whom Scripture overly designates as evil is considered of such importance that the sages decreed a national celebration of joy. Indeed we learn that the establishment of a *Yom Tov* classification has nothing to do with the religious status of those who removed the barriers. Therefore, Yom Yerushalayim—the day Jews gained access to the Western Wall—should definitely be cause for celebration by all. The fact that such access was crystallized through Jewish military prowess and numerous Jewish deaths should heighten our appreciation. It was not an evil king who by fiat permitted access: It was a Jewish army representing *k'lal Yisrael* that captured the *Kotel*. All who pray there should extend gratitude to God and His messengers, the Israeli army, for the privilege.

While it is readily recognized that access to the *Kotel* is not comparable to access to the *Bet HaMikdash*, the option of praying at the *Kotel* is certainly a sacred religious event unparalleled in modern times.

III. Rema rules that common custom is to permit haircuts on Lag b'Omer and that (it is proper) to increase (somewhat) happiness (*marbin ketzat simcha*) on that day (*Orech Chayyim* 493:20). *Aruch HaShulchan* adds the notion that Lag b'Omer necessitates added happiness for it is deemed a (semi) *Yom Tov* (Yom Tov Ketzat) (*Orech Chayyim* 493:7).

Yet, why is this so? Why is Lag b'Omer classified as a partial *Yom Tov*, which necessitates added joy and happiness? The source, says the Vilna Gaon, is the talmudic citation that reports that on the fifteenth of Av the Jews who departed from Egypt and were destined to perish in the wilderness finally ceased dying (*Ta'anit* 26b). The implication of the Vilna Gaon's position may be as follows: The Mishnah reports that to the Jews the most joyous holidays were Yom Kippur and the fifteenth of Av. Yom Kippur was considered a joyful period of time because Jews were granted an opportunity to have their sins forgiven. The fifteenth of Av was deemed a happy time because, on that day, the Jews who wandered forty years in the wilderness and were destined to perish stopped dying (*Ta'anit* 29b). Since the Mishnah designates the fifteenth of Av as *Yom Tov*, it indicates that when large scale communal deaths cease the day is classified as a *Yom Tov*. To the extent that custom has it that Rav Akiva's students ceased to die on Lag b'Omer, that day also may be deemed a partial *Yom Tov*.

This halachic conclusion may be challenged on a variety of levels. The Talmud notes that not just one good thing happened, but a number of happy events transpired on the fifteenth of Av (Chamisha Asar b'Av). Indeed, the following took place: "It was the day on which permission was granted to the tribes to intermarry. . . . It was the day on which the tribe of Binyamin was permitted to reenter the congregation of Israel. . . . It was the day when the generation of the wilderness ceased to die out. . . . It was the day when Hosea ben Elah removed the guards that Yerovam ben Nevot had placed on the roads to prevent Israel from going (up to Jerusalem) on pilgrimage. . . . It was the day when permission was granted for those killed at Betar to be buried. . . . It was the day on which (every year) they discontinued to fell trees for the Altar" (*Ta'anit* 30b, 31a). In other words, six wonderful events took place on that day. As such, its status as a semiholiday may be the result of the convergence of all of these events and not just one. It is evident, however, that the Vilna Gaon rules otherwise. He considers each event by itself as sufficient to merit the fifteenth of Av as a partial holiday. Otherwise, there would be no basis to support the contention that Lag b'Omer is a semiholiday due to the singular fact that students ceased to die on that day.

There is another issue of contention. The ceasing of deaths of those who departed from Egypt implied that the Jewish people were ready to enter the holy land. So, perhaps, the stopping of death by itself is not indicative of a *Yom Tov* status. The holiday classification was due to the fact that *k'lal Yisrael* was ready to acquire the land of Israel. Again, the fact that the Vilna Gaon made no such notation relating to the purpose for the ceasing of deaths suggests that each act by itself, regardless of ultimate purpose, is sufficient to classify a day as a semi- or partial holiday.

Based upon the above consideration, it appears logical to note that Yom Yerushalayim—the day Jerusalem was recaptured, the day the *Kotel* became under Jewish control—certainly merits consideration as a national holiday. Just as the Talmud notes that when obstacles to make pilgrimage to Jerusalem were removed it became a day of rejoicing, so too should Yom Yerushalayim. We do not have any obstacles to prevent us visiting our holy places. Just as the Vilna Gaon selected only one item to merit status as a *Yom Tov*, without concern for ultimate purpose, so too may just the singular, modern removal of obstacles to Jerusalem merit *Yom Tov* classification.

IV. Jerusalem means much more to the Jew than its status

as the capital of the modern state of Israel. It is, moreover, more significant than simply its historical considerations. To the Jew, Jerusalem is an essential component of Judaism and of the Jewish perception of peoplehood.

The Talmud contends that the format and number of blessings of *Birchat HaMazon* (Grace after meals) was a reaction to distinctly different experiences in the life of the Jew. The first blessing (*Hazon*) was enacted in response to the *manna* from heaven that fed the Jews in the wilderness. The second blessing (*Al Ha'aretz*) was ordained to commemorate Joshua's conquest of the land of Israel. The third blessing (*Boneh Yerushalayim*) was established by both King David and King Solomon. The phrase "Be compassionate with your people Israel and with Jerusalem your city" was established by King David. And the phrase "The great and holy Temple" was enacted by King Solomon (*Berachot* 48b).

This talmudic citation suggests that Israel and Jerusalem serve unique roles in Jewish life. Indeed, it appears that the second blessing of *Birchat HaMazon* is essentially a blessing of appreciation for the land of Israel. Thus, the mitzvah of Israel is so important that the sages of the Talmud decreed that after each meal a *brachah* of thanksgiving was to be chanted. It mattered not where a person resided, whether in Israel or the Diaspora; a blessing of appreciation for Israel became a daily practice.

The third blessing of the *Birchat HaMazon* delineates the vital importance of Jerusalem. The city Jerusalem is not noted simply as the ancient capital. The phrase of the Talmud is "for your nation Israel and your city Jerusalem." The implication is that reference to nationhood is intertwined within the fine fabric of Jerusalem. A nation has a homeland. A homeland has a capital. A nation without a capital lacks cohesion, unity, or even the symbol of a unified people. King Solomon subsequently made reference to the Holy Temple. This means that King David's previous ordinance related to concerns of unity and cohesion of our people as a nation and not because of the presence or stature of the *Bet HaMikdash*.

When Jews have Jerusalem they are a nation. Accordingly, Jerusalem symbolizes the totality and glory of our nation.

V. It is interesting to note that the actual text of the third *brachah* of *Birchat HaMazon* appears to have more than one accepted version. Common practice is to state *Boneh berachamav Yerushalayim, Amen,* "We bless God as He Who will rebuild Jerusalem with mercy." Others delete any reference to mercy and, instead, recite *Boneh Yerushalayim, Amen,* namely, "God will build Jerusalem." Why the different versions? What is wrong with rebuilding our ancient capital with mercy or compassion?

The custom of the Vilna Gaon was not to add the phrase relating to mercy (*Maaseh Rav*). Some scholars cite the verse "Zion will be redeemed with judgment," (Isaiah 1:27), which openly demonstrates that redemption will be through the process of law or judgment and not through compassion (*Kol Bo*). Thus, reference to mercy as a component necessary for rebuilding Jerusalem is not accurate.

Yet this contention that Jerusalem will be rebuilt with judgment (not compassion) is rejected by some scholars. Why? It is true that the actual rebuilding will be via the principle of judgment, but its glory, beauty, and distinction to overshadow even the first *Bet HaMikdash* will yet require heavenly mercy (Ateret Zekeinim, *Orech Chayyim* 188:1). Others suggest that the meaning of the phrase "Zion will be rebuilt with judgment" relates to the people themselves. Justice will generate a heavenly response to return Jews to Israel. But the quality of justice will not be sufficient to merit the rebuilding of Jerusalem. For this, God's "mercy" will yet be required (see Be'er Yaakov, *Orech Chayyim* 188:1).

Of interest is the wording of the request for mercy. We do not beseech Jerusalem to be rebuilt "with mercy," but rather "with His mercy." Why such a terminology? The Pri Megadim suggests that mercy is an emotional sensitivity that is somewhere between love and kindness. We therefore request God's special mercy to bring the Messiah, even though we may not be worthy (Be'er Yaakov, *Orech Chayyim* 188:1).

We have been blessed with a renewed and rebuilt Jerusalem, which certainly was the merciful act of God. For this we are thankful.

Yom Yerushalayim: She'hecheyanu

QUESTION: Is it proper to recite the blessing of *She'hecheyanu* on Yom Yerushalayim?

RESPONSE: A negative position might note that halachah does not consider it proper to recite *She'hecheyanu* during Sefirat Ha'Omer. The *Shulchan Aruch* rules that the *brachah* of *She'hecheyanu* should not be recited during the three weeks between the seventeenth of Tammuz and Tisha B'Av (*Orech Chayyim* 551:17). The Magen Avraham notes that the prohibition is due not to a sense of mourning, but rather to the fact that tragic historical events happened to Israel during this period (ibid. 551:42). Since Sefirat Ha'Omer, the time between *Pesach* and *Shavuot*, commemorates the death of Rabbi Akiva's many students, such a time may also be classified as one of the tragic events to Israel (*pur'anuyot*). Indeed, due to the deaths of these students, Jews do not marry or engage in merriment during Sefirat Ha'Omer (ibid. 493:1–3). Yom Yerushalayim falls on the forty-third day of Sefirat Ha'Omer, namely, the twenty-eighth of Iyar. As such, the blessing of *She'hecheyanu* should be prohibited during this period of time.

Two responses: (1) The Talmud reports that in the event a child hears of the death of a parent who bequeathed an inheritance, the son makes two blessings. The first *berachah, Dayan Ha'emet,* is recited over the news of the death of the parent, and the *She'hecheyanu* is recited over the good news of the inheritance (*Brachot* 59b). From this, says the Vilna Gaon, there is proof positive that it is an excessive stringency (*chumrah yetera*) to prohibit *She'hecheyanu* during the three weeks prior to Tisha B'Av. His argument is that if *She'hecheyanu* is permitted during the period of traumatic mourning for a parent, it certainly should be permitted during the time of general historical tragedy (*pur'anuyot*) (see notes of the Vilna Gaon, *Shulchan Aruch, Orech Chayyim* 554:62). Thus, according to the Vilna Gaon, one certainly could recite *She'hecheyanu* on Yom Yerushalayim.

(2) The only reason why *She'hecheyanu* is restricted during the three weeks is that this period of time reflects tragedy to *k'lal Yisrael* (*pur'anuyot*), not joy. Yet, the very fact that the day has been transformed into one of magnificent happiness for *k'lal Yisrael* should offset the rationale for designating the day as one of tragedy. As such, the twenty-eighth of Iyar, Yom Yerushalayim, should no longer be a day of sadness but one of joy.

An added halachic insight is that the restriction relating to reciting unwarranted *brachot* does not apply to the blessing of *She'hecheyanu*. In a discussion concerning the propriety of reciting *She'hecheyanu* on Rosh Hashanah and Yom Kippur, the Talmud notes that anyone may chant the blessing on a voluntary basis, the issue (says the Talmud) being whether it is mandatory to say *She'hecheyanu* on these holidays (*Eruvin* 40b). From this talmudic section, it is evident that there is nothing wrong with saying the *brachah* on a voluntary basis, for it is not deemed to be an unwarranted *brachah* (*brachah she'einah tzirchah*) (see *Tzlach Brachot* 60a). The rationale must be that if a person is happy (over an event), then to that person it is certainly a joy that merits a *brachah*.

Hatikvah

QUESTION: Is it proper for a religiously observant Jew to sing the Zionist anthem, *Hatikvah*?

RESPONSE: Many who subscribe to the yeshivah and hasidic worlds, as well as to halachic orientations, absolutely refuse to sing this song. In fact, they make a point of eliminating it from any program under their auspices. Why? Are they against the State of Israel? Are they anti-Zionist?

A brief review of the history of the *Hatikvah* will shed light upon a view that is oft overshadowed and denigrated by emotional and popular concerns. (The following facts are culled from the *Encyclopaedia Judaica.*)

During the latter part of the eighteenth century, Naftali Herz Imber composed the Hebrew poem the *Hatikvah.* It is suggested that he was influenced by German and Polish lyrics. Subsequently, Samuel Cohen, a resident of Rishon LeZion, set the words to a melody based upon a Moldavian-Romanian folk song entitled "Cart and Oxen."

The song became identified with Zionism at the Seventh Zionist Congress held in Basel in 1905, when all present concluded the program with the singing of *Hatikvah.*

In 1933, at the Eighteenth Zionist Congress in Prague, it was formally declared to be the Zionist anthem. During the Mandate in Palestine, *Hatikvah* was viewed as the unofficial anthem. Indeed, in 1948, it was performed and sung at the ceremony celebrating the formation of the State of Israel. Subsequently, the *Hatikvah* has been considered the anthem of the State of Israel, though there has not been a formal proclamation by the Knesset officially declaring it so.

Who was Naftali Herz Imber? It is reputed that on his visit to Bombay, India, as well as to Palestine, he was "wooed by missionaries and was later accused of apostasy." Even his friend Israel Zangwill believed that he had converted to Christianity to escape starvation. The latter part of his life was spent in America, where he was known to live in "squalor, misery, and alcoholism."

Now here is the issue: The Jewish people is a holy nation. Our history is graced with martyrs who died rather than betray our religious beliefs. Our heritage is adorned with rabbis, scholars, and pious Jews whose lifestyles were models of moral rectitude. We are a nation that identifies with *kedushah*—holy sanctity. We are a people of the Torah.

Should this holy people use the words of an acknowledged alcoholic, reputed apostate, and immoral individual as a theme of its national aspirations? Should a tune based upon "Cart and Oxen" be the song to stir the heart of a religious Jew? As a result, even those who love Israel and will fight to the death for its existence feel that the *Hatikvah* is repugnant to religious sensitivities and beliefs. Jews deserve a more suitable and significant anthem, they say.

Today, the lay leaders of our people cannot tolerate such views. Anyone who refuses to sing the *Hatikvah* is stereotyped as an anti-Zionist. Some have even withheld funds from institutions that do not have the *Hatikvah* sung at their annual banquets. Others have castigated rabbis for not embracing the *Hatikvah* as the national anthem.

I, for one, sing the *Hatikvah* with pride. There are even times when the song evokes great positive emotions within me.

This does not mean that I approve of the composer or would not prefer an anthem written by a *tzaddik*. There are many things that preferably should be altered yet are not forsaken; there are other facts of life that originally were denigrated yet subsequently became venerated.

An example: The Passover *Seder* commences with the phrase "This is the bread of affliction that our forefathers ate in the land of Egypt." Yet Scripture specifically notes that the unleavened bread called *matzah* is a reminder that the Jews were rushing to leave Egypt and the bread had not had time to rise (Exodus 12:39). In other words, *matzah* was not eaten while the Jews were in Egypt. It is a symbol of freedom and deliverance. Accordingly, this contradicts the statement that the bread of affliction was eaten during the slavery.

The Vilna Gaon and others contend that *matzah* was the food provided for slaves throughout the bondage—it was a basic staple food item of the Jews. On the night of Passover the Jews baked bread. They wanted to taste real bread, not *matzah*. However, through a quirk of fate, that very night freedom was proclaimed—the Exodus was to commence; the bread could not be baked, there was no time to tarry. So *matzah*, which was originally denigrated as a symbol of servitude, became viewed as a message of freedom. The same *matzah* eaten by slaves became transformed into the bread of freedom. Today we care not about the origins of *matzah*. To us it is identified with liberty; it is now a Jewish symbol of freedom.

So, too, with the *Hatikvah*. Its roots may be clouded with non-Jewish origins and unholy composers, yet look at what has happened to it! For decades it was the clarion call for statehood. It stirred the emotions of Jews throughout the world. It united our people. Polish, Russian, German, English, Hungarian, Czechoslovakian, and American Jews all marched to its tune. All who envisioned a national homeland, a state, cherished its words—*Hatikvah*, the hope of the Jews. Jewish soldiers died with the words emblazoned in their hearts. It became the spirit of a reborn Israel.

Yes, the basic concern of the religious Jew is not necessarily "to be a free nation in our land." It is for the Messiah. So *Hatikvah* is not the song of our rabbis, but it certainly is the theme of our people. It is the one song that all Jews sing. It is the one song that emotes national pride. It reminds us of the hordes of Arab soldiers, the displaced Jews of Europe, the homeland for the homeless. It is modern Israel. It is our *matzah*. It is freedom. It is identified as our song, so let us sing it with pride.

The Hatikvah *Text*

QUESTION: Do Torah leaders perceive any part of the text of the *Hatikvah* anthem to be objectionable?

RESPONSE: Some rabbis take issue with the following: The anthem notes *od lo avda tikvainu* (we never lost hope), *liyot am chafshi b'artzainu* (to be a free nation in our own land). Some find this contrary to the hopes and the aspirations of the Torah Jew. The fervent dream of the Jew, recorded in all lands and by all ethnic cultures, was not to be a free nation in our own land. It was, rather, that the Messiah should come and the world should radiate the glory of God. Accordingly, some have felt that the text does not reflect the Torah perception of the Jewish people. Others agree that the text does not necessarily articulate a high-level Torah perspective, yet they are not overly concerned for they do not feel that the clause reflects anti-Torah sensitivities. They, therefore, do not consider it objectionable.

Of interest is that a number of rabbis recall that HaRav Dovid Lifshitz, (*z"l*), the late Suvalker Rav and a Rosh Yeshiva of Yeshiva University, had a unique variant of the questionable clause when singing the *Hatikvah*. He was overheard saying, *liyot am daati b'artzainu* (to be a religious people in our land). (Rabbi Michael Broyde, *Issues of Ideology and Identity-Prayer for the State of Israel*, March 1998, RCA). In other words, the text of the anthem was not deemed as sacred or written in stone. The objectionable phrase was simply altered to reflect the Torah viewpoint. This appears to be quite a healthy attitude. All Jews may, therefore, unite in song for Israel. Those disconcerted by a phrase may simply replace it with another that meets their religious standard.

It should be noted that the original text of the anthem differed from the prevailing popular text. The *Encyclopaedia Judaica* records an original text of *Hatikvah*. This version predated the establishment of the State of Israel in 1948. The original version did not contain the phrase *liyot am chafshi b'artzainu* to be a free nation in our land). Instead, the phrase was *lashuv l'eretz avotainu* (to return to the land of our forefathers). In other words, the dream of the Jew that galvanized a love of Zion was simply to return from the *galut* to *Eretz Yisrael*. That's an aspiration all Jews could accept.

The present variant is a modern rendition that echoes the exhilarating sentiments of those who actually experienced in 1948 the establishment of the State of Israel. It was sung by thousands who assembled in the Mograbi Square of Tel Aviv, the fifth of Iyar, 1948, to celebrate the vote in the United Nations and the proclamation by Ben Gurion that *Medinat Yisrael* was a reality. As such, it is understandable why freedom and independence became an integral part of the text of the anthem.

What is clear is that there are a variety of ways to overcome even the concerns of those troubled by the *liyot am chafshi* phrase.

Medinat Yisrael *and the Mitzvah of Living in Israel*

QUESTION: Does the formation of the State of Israel have any impact upon the mitzvah to settle the land of Yisrael?

RESPONSE: The mitzvah of *yishuv eretz Yisrael*, living in the land of Israel, is noted by the Ramban to be a biblical imperative. His basic source is the Scriptural verse "And you shall dispossess the inhabitants of the land, and dwell in it: for I have given you the land to possess it." (Bamidbar 33:53, Koren translation). Commenting on the first part of the verse, *Ve'horashtem* (and you shall dispossess the inhabitants of the land), the

Ramban notes that this is a mandate to not permit the land of Israel to be in the hands of others or to be desolate. In other words, it is a Jewish obligation to conquer the land of Israel. On the phrase *Vi'yeshavta ba* (and dwell in it), the Ramban notes that this is the source of the mitzvah to live in the land of Israel (see *Sefer HaMitzvot L'Rambam*, Positive Mitzvot According to the Ramban, mitzvah four).

The Ramban adds that the mitzvah is operational "even in *galut*"! This suggests that the mitzvah of living in Israel is not related to the building of the third *Bet HaMikdash*. It implies that every Jew in every era must in some way endeavour to observe this mitzvah. Indeed, the phrase "even in *galut*" appears to reject interpretations that contend that the mitzvah is not operational in contemporary times.

At issue is the rationale as to why great sages throughout history did not attempt to observe this mitzvah. Numerous explanations have been presented. Rabbeinu Chaim Cohen, of the Baalai Tosafot, notes that the actual journey to the land of Israel, as well as the economic conditions therein, was difficult and dangerous. In addition, the poverty was so oppressive, Jews simply could not support families or sustain themselves. They could not afford to leave the land fallow in the seventh year. Accordingly, many did not attempt to go to *Eretz Yisrael*. Other rabbis, however, discounted danger and poverty as reasons to forgo the mitzvah of *Yishuv HaAretz* (Responsa Avmai Nezer, *Yoreh Deah*, vol. 2, no. 454; also *Pitchai Teshuva*, *Even HaEzer* 75:3).

A unique theory is presented by Rabbi Yisrael Yehoshua of Kutna. In a responsum to Rav Yisrael of Kotsk in the year 1891, he wrote that even according to the Ramban the mitzvah of *Yishuv HaAretz* is operational only in the circumstance wherein the land of Israel is owned and controlled by Jews. His rationale is that the *yerushah* (inheritance) and *yeshiva* (dwelling) must be in land belonging to the Jews: i.e., under Jewish jurisdiction and control. Should Jews not govern and control the land, then all efforts are in the realm of preparatory endeavours (i.e., a *hechsher mitzvah*; see Responsa Yeshuot Malko, *Yoreh Deah*, no. 66).

As such the mitzvah may not have been fully operational until *Medinat Yisrael* was established in 1948. The fact that Israel was formally proclaimed as a Jewish nation certainly fulfilled the definition of the mitzvah according to the Yeshuot Malko. The new state revitalized the mitzvah, for prior to that period the mitzvah could not be actualized. In other words, the mitzvah of *Yishuv HaAretz* was to dwell in Jewish land that not just historically but pragmatically belonged to Jews. Accordingly, Israel Independence Day enabled the mitzvah to be observed fully in modern times.

Torah Learning Versus the Mitzvah of Living in Israel

QUESTION: Which takes priority: the mitzvah of learning Torah or the mitzvah of living in the land of Israel?

RESPONSE: The Gemorah states, "The study of Torah is greater than the mitzvah of building the *Bet HaMikdash*. For as long as Baruch ben Neriah (Ezra's Rebbe) was alive, Ezra did not leave him to emigrate" to the land of Israel, and join those who actually rebuilt the *Bet HaMikdash*. Additionally, the Gemorah rules that "the study of Torah is greater than the mitzvah of honoring parents. For all the years Yaakov spent in the yeshivah of Ever [fourteen to be exact] he was not punished," even though during that time he failed to honor or provide service to his parents (*Megillah* 16b).

The Meharsha notes that the talmudic citation does not present conclusive proof that the mitzvah of Torah learning is actually greater than either the mitzvah of building the *Bet HaMikdash* or that of honoring parents. Perhaps, he suggests, Torah learning was simply equal to either of the two mitzvot noted. Since, moreover, no one mitzvah was greater than the other, Yaakov was not punished for the lapse of *kibud av* nor Ezra for not building the *Bet HaMikdash.* He contends that the phrase stating that Torah is greater than the other two mitzvot is not derived from the Gemorah in *Megillah* but, rather, from the Mishnah in *Peah,* which makes a general statement that Torah learning is esteemed as a most important mitzvah (*Talmud Torah keneged kulom*).

Of interest is that the brilliant halachic sage Rav Aryeh Leib, the author of the *Turai Even,* argues that the citations in *Megillah* clearly demonstrate that Torah learning is superior to the mitzvot of building the *Bet HaMikdash* or honoring parents. At issue, he notes, is that there are more than two variables to consider. In case one, Ezra decided that the mitzvah of learning Torah with his Rebbe was more important than the mitzvah of building the *Bet HaMikdash.* Yet there was another mitzvah to be concerned with: namely, the mitzvah of living in *Eretz Yisrael.* By remaining with his Rebbe, Ezra withheld himself from the above two mitzvot. The Talmud rules that Ezra was proper to stay with his Rebbe, for Torah learning takes priority. In other words, Torah learning takes priority over the mitzvah of building the *Bet HaMikdash* as well as the mitzvah of living in Israel. Now if Torah takes precedence over two mitzvot together, it certainly takes priority over one of them by itself. This proves that Torah learning is more important than either the mitzvah of building the *Bet HaMikdash* or living in Israel.

The same argument pertains to the case dealing with Yaakov Avinu. Yaakov not only was not able to observe the mitzvah of *kibud av,* but he also missed out on the mitzvah of living in Israel. Thus, the mitzvah of learning Torah was deemed more important than both the above mitzvot. Accordingly, Torah learning is more important than either one of these mitzvot. As such, Torah learning takes priority over the mitzvah of living in Israel.

Of concern, is that Torah learning does not automatically take priority over any mitzvah. Indeed, the *Shulchan Aruch* specifically rules that Torah learning takes priority only over those mitzvot that may be performed by others (*Yoreh Deah* 246:18). As such, Torah learning may only be granted priority over such mitzvot as honoring parents, building the *Bet HaMikdash*, and living in the land of Israel if these mitzvot may be performed by others. The Talmud in *Megillah* does not provide any limitations to the priority given to Torah over, for example, the mitzvah of honoring parents. At issue is whether the service to be provided to parents is always readily available through others? Indeed, a pragmatic response is the recognition that service to parents via others is problematic. As such, one simply may not establish any general principle that Torah learning always takes priority over *kibud av*. Indeed, it would appear that there is no general maxim granting precedence to Torah learning.

HaRav Yosef Rosen, the Rogashover Gaon, provides a brilliant means of harmonizing all the laws relating to priority granted to Torah learning over other mitzvot. He suggests that there are two distinctly different types of mitzvot. One is a personal obligation upon each individual. The basic concern is with the action, the process by which one observes the mitzvah. The other deals with the result, not with the process by which the mitzvah was effectuated. Using this distinction, the Rogashover Gaon suggests that Torah learning takes priority only over those mitzvot wherein the issue of concern is the result, not the process (*Tzafnot Pa'naiach, Mahadura Tenina, Hilchot Talmud Torah* ch. 3, law 3).

This suggests that each Jew may not have a personal mitzvah to actually build the *Bet HaMikdash*. Rather, the concern is that the *Bet HaMikdash* should be built. As such, the mitzvah may be observed by others and an individual need not forsake Torah learning so that he may perform the mitzvah of building the *Bet HaMikdash*. To the extent that the Talmud rules that Torah learning takes priority over the mitzvah of honoring parents implies that the mitzvah of honoring parents also is a concern for the end result. This means that the mitzvah is not an imposition of a personal requirement for a child to actually provide service to his or her parent. The Gemorah states that *kibud av* requires a child to provide such services as food, clothing, and shelter to a parent (*Kiddushin* 31b). Since Torah learning takes priority over the mitzvah of *kibud av*, the child may not be obligated to personally feed the parent. As long as he makes proper arrangements for the service to be rendered, the child observes his mandate.

Of interest is that the Turai Even (*Megillah* 16b) contends that the mitzvah of Torah learning takes precedence over the mitzvah of living in the land of Israel. According to the theory advanced, it would appear that the mitzvah of living in the land of Israel may be comparable to the mitzvot of building a *Bet HaMikdash* and honoring parents. This suggests that the mitzvah of living in the land of Israel may also be a general concern that Jews should live in Israel, but not necessarily an obligation upon each Jew to personally reside therein. This *hiddush* means that as long as Jews do in fact live in Israel, the mitzvah is being observed. This may be a rationale explaining why great sages did not make *aliyah* to Israel.

Modern Israel and Tisha b'Av

QUESTION: Tisha b'Av marks a period of national Jewish mourning. It is a Jewish "bad luck day" as, throughout the ages, numerous terrible events befell our people on this day. It is best known as the time when both the first *Bet HaMikdash* and, generations later, the second *Bet HaMikdash* were destroyed. Common custom is to fast and mourn. Numerous prayers bemoan the utter devastation of the city Jerusalem and the exile of the people.

But Jerusalem is no longer desolate and in ruins. The city

has all the trappings of modern society. Daily, new and elegant buildings are being built. Jerusalem is a thriving metropolis with a vibrant, exciting religious community. Consequently, are not the prayers bemoaning the plight of Jerusalem incongruous with modern reality? Is not modern Israel the answer to our prayers for a rebirth of Jerusalem?

RESPONSE: A partial response.

So says the prophet Amos, "Behold the days come, said the Lord God, that I will send a famine in the land, not a famine of bread nor a thirst for water, but of hearing the words of the Lord" (Amos 8:11). Commenting upon this special famine, Rav Shimon bar Yochai called out, "*Chas v'shalom*—Heaven forbid that Torah will ever be forgotten from Israel; that cannot ever take place." Torah is an integral, essential element that will exist as long as Jews survive. If so, then what is meant by a famine or a thirst of hearing the words of God? To this Rav Shimon bar Yochai responds, "They (the Jews) will not find a clear halachah in one place." (See *Shabbat* 138b–139a.)

Tradition has it that *Yisrael v'oraita chad hu*—Israel and the Torah are one (see *Zohar Parshat Acharai* 73). The MaHaral of Prague says that this means that the status of Torah is impacted by the status of the Jewish people. According to this concept, should the Jewish people be dispersed throughout the world and thus lack unity, Torah should also lack unity. This, then, may be what the Talmud teaches us when it says that a time will come when one "will not find a clear halachah in one place." Namely, there will be divergent halachic opinions. One Rav will permit something; another will prohibit the same item. One religious group will find certain rules beneficial; others will condemn the same laws.

This, then, may be the real *galut* (exile) that we bemoan on Tisha b'Av. We are not mourning physical buildings. We are not crying over architectural ruins. The modern Jew prays for the unity of our religion and the unity of our people. We want a *Bet HaMikdash* that will be the unifying force solidifying all segments. It is the spiritual *galut* that yet needs to end. Buildings and cities may be rebuilt, but the division of our people and our Torah into factions that do not even reasonably talk with each other—that *galut* does not conclude with a new building. The elimination of divisive Torah tactics is the real contemporary rationale for mourning even with a modern Israel. Unity is still a goal for the future. So far, it is not an achievement of the present. Then, *b'ezrat HaShem* this *galut* will become a token of the past. May so be the will of *HaShem.*

Mourning the Bet HaMikdash

QUESTION: Contemporary Jewry still mourns the destruction of the *Bet HaMikdash.* Common custom has it that meat and wine are forbidden during the first nine days of the month of Av. Yet, a mourner is permitted to have meat and wine during the seven days of mourning. To the extent that *k'lal Yisrael* is in a state of mourning for the *Bet HaMikdash* during the nine days, meat and wine should be permitted, for mourning the destruction of the *Bet HaMikdash* should be on a par with the general laws of mourning for a loved one.

RESPONSE: When a person dies, the mourner experiences two distinct halachic categories. Prior to burial, the status is deemed *ani'nut* and one is not permitted to drink wine nor eat meat. Subsequent to the burial, the *availut* of *shivah* commences. This stage permits digesting wine and meat yet galvanizes a number of other prohibitions, namely, not wearing leather shoes, not bathing, sitting on a low chair, etc.

It is apparent that the reaction to the destruction of the *Bet HaMikdash* generated the stringencies of both *ani'nut* and *availut.* Close to two thousand years may have transpired since the *Bet HaMikdash* was set on fire, but to the Jew the shock of the event is comparable to something that just happened. *K'lal Yisrael* is in a stage of *ani'nut.* It is as if a new, contemporary tragedy took place. It's deemed too soon even for consolation. The fire and destruction just took place. Even more so, the event is not buried in Jewish history. The *Bet HaMikdash* is not something of the past. It's not buried or out of sight. For this reason, the custom of refraining from wine and meat may have developed to dramatically and poignantly portray the open, raw wounds of the loss of the *Bet HaMikdash* even for contemporary society.

Israel and the Laws of Mourning

QUESTION: Does the existence of the modern State of Israel in any way mute or nullify any of the talmudic practices set up to mourn the destruction of ancient Israel and Jerusalem?

RESPONSE: *Kri'ya,* the rending of one's clothes, was ordained as a sign of bereavement not only for those who lost a parent or a close family member. The Talmud rules that this must also take place upon witnessing a *Sefer Torah* being burnt or at (the sight of the ruined) cities of Judea, the *Bet HaMikdash,* and Jerusalem (*Moed Katan* 26a). Of interest is that the *Shulchan Aruch* in citing these cases specifically notes that the act of *kri'ya* on one's clothes is operational only if such cities of Judea and Jerusalem are in a state of destruction (*b'churbano*) (*Orech Chayyim* 561:1, 2). At issue is the definition of "a city in a state of destruction." Magen Avraham rules that the term does not refer to whether the area is populated by Jews. Thus, Jerusalem may be halachicly deemed to be in a state of destruction even should Jews reside therein. The main issue is whether the area is controlled by Jews. Accordingly, one must rend clothes upon sighting Jerusalem and the cities of Judea as long as such areas are ruled by gentiles (ibid. 561:1).

Based upon the above sources, HaGaon HaRav Moshe Feinstein (*z"l*) ruled that the emergence of the State of Israel radically changed the status of Jerusalem and the cities of Judea. Such areas are under Jewish sovereignty and may not be classified as being in a state of *churban*. This halachah, says Rav Moshe (*z"l*), in no way relates to our concern for the coming of the Messiah. It is merely a definition that the Jewish State of Israel eliminates the halachic status of destruction (ruin) of Jerusalem (Iggrot Moshe, Volume VIII: *Orech Chayyim Siman* 37:1). Thus, the State of Israel has a major halachic ramification.

Visiting Israel for Yom Tov: *Should One or Two Days Be Observed?*

QUESTION: A man and his wife who live in the Diaspora spend the holiday of Passover in Israel. Are they to observe one or two days of *Yom Tov*?

RESPONSE: From a biblical point of view, the exact date of all Jewish holidays was determined by a proclamation of *bet din* sanctifying the onset of the new lunar month. This process required two witnesses to testify that they personally sighted a new moon, signifying a new lunar month. *Bet din*, therefore, had to formally determine each month whether the new moon was on the thirtieth or the thirty-first day. Confirmation of witnesses was required only for consecration of the thirtieth day as the new month. The thirty-first day would be consecrated even without witnesses, for the moon renewed itself every twenty-nine-and-a-half days. Those who resided in ancient Israel could be informed that the Sanhedrin in Jerusalem had consecrated the new month on either the thirtieth or thirty-first day of the month. The difficulty was that the Diaspora communities could not be so readily informed of this decision. To therefore insure proper observance of the holidays, the Diaspora communities observed all holidays for two days (see tractate *Rosh Hashanah* and *Betzah* for details).

In talmudic times (about the fourth century, C.E.), the process of *bet din* formally sanctifying the new month ceased. The Jewish holiday calendar was set up by Hillel II. Since the calendar was fixed, there was no longer any doubt as to when holidays were scheduled to take place. Thus, there was also no reason for Diaspora communities to observe more than one day of *Yom Tov*. The Talmud was well aware of this concern. It notes that the basis for Diaspora communities to continue to observe two days of *Yom Tov* was simply a tradition implored by the sages of ancient Israel to the Diaspora communities to "give heed to the customs of your ancestors that have come down to you, for it might happen that the government might issue decrees and it will cause confusion" (*Betzah* 4b). In other words, governments may destroy all Torah writings and people would not be able to know when *Yom Tov* should take place. Thus, the underlying mandate for Diaspora communities to observe two days of *Yom Tov* is simply a requirement for Diaspora Jews to continue ancient customs and not to cast them aside. It should be noted that this obligation for Diaspora Jews to celebrate two days *Yom Tov* is operational even in modern times (*Shulchan Aruch Orech Chayyim* 496:1).

A halachic quandary emerges when a Diaspora Jew visits the land of Israel for *Yom Tov* or when an Israeli Jew is in the Diaspora for the holidays.

To resolve this problem, halachah set up a guide for travellers: Namely, all travellers must conduct themselves with the stringencies of their native areas as well as with the stringencies of the communities they are visiting. Accordingly, a native of *Eretz Yisrael* who visits the Diaspora for Pesach, for example, is prohibited to do work on the second day of Pesach (*Orech Chayyim* 496:3). Though the *Shulchan Aruch* does not specifically note that a Diaspora Jew who visits Israel must retain his stringency of two days *Yom Tov*, the Mishnah Berurah does note this fact. He rules that such a Jew who has intention to return to the Diaspora must observe two days *Yom Tov* while in Israel (ibid. 496:13). This means that anyone making *aliyah* to Israel may observe only one day *Yom Tov.* Visitors must still observe two days.

The major criticism of such a practice was articulated by the early eighteenth-century sage HaRav Tzvi Ashkenazi, the leader of the Amsterdam Jewish community. In his response (Chacham Tzvi 167) he argued that anyone visiting the land of Israel for a holiday must only observe one day *Yom Tov.* The general rule that a traveller must assume the stringency of his native area was operational, he contended, only in the event that the custom or stringency could conceivably be applicable in the new area. Should, however, such a stringent custom never be able to take root in the community visited, then it should not be practiced. The land of Israel never had a custom of observing two days *Yom Tov* on Passover. As such, there should be no mandate to practice the two-day *Yom Tov* custom in *Eretz Yisrael.* The two-day custom should even, moreover, be banned in *Eretz Yisrael* as a form of *bal tosef*—the biblical prohibition against adding unwarranted mitzvot.

His argument may be somewhat bolstered by the fact that the *Shulchan Aruch* does not mention any requirement for a visitor to the land of Israel to observe the Diaspora custom of celebrating two days of *Yom Tov* while in Israel. It only notes that should one visit the Diaspora, then it is mandated to observe two days of *Yom Tov* (see *Orech Chayyim* 496:3). In other words, the celebration of one or two days *Yom Tov* is a matter of geography. Should one be located in the Diaspora, then two days are mandated. Should one be in Israel, then only one day *Yom Tov* is required. Yet, as mentioned previously, the Mishneh Berurah specifically disregards this omission and rules that a visitor to the land of Israel must observe two days of *Yom*

Tov (ibid. 496:13). Thus, the Mishneh Berurah simply rules against the position of Chacham Tzvi. In addition, the Mishneh Berurah's ruling appears to be the traditional mainstream halachic position.

Of interest is the ruling of the *Shulchan Aruch HaRav* (HaRav Shneur Zalman of Laidi). He specifically notes that should one travel from the land of Israel to the Diaspora "with his wife, even though he intends to return (to his home in Israel after the holiday) it is deemed as if he has no intention to return" (ibid. 496:10). Of concern is the utilization of the example of a traveller to the Diaspora with his wife. Why did not the *Shulchan Aruch HaRav* provide the other alternative of a visitor to the land of Israel with his wife? It may be suggested that the *Shulchan Aruch HaRav* basically holds a position comparable to that of the Chacham Tzvi. In another section, the *Shulchan Aruch HaRav* says that just like the time for the onset of *Shabbat* and *Yom Tov* differs from place to place, so too is the *kedushah* of places different. "This is the reason why there is a special *kedushah* in the Diaspora on the second day of *Yom Tov*," requiring visitors from *Eretz Yisrael* to observe two days of *Yom Tov*, even though they intend to return (see *Shulchan Aruch HaRav*, *Mahadura Batra*, *Hilchot Hashkamat Haboker* 1:8). The implication is that in the land of Israel there is a special one-day sanctity. Accordingly, it was not necessary to utilize the legal loophole of travelling with one's wife when discussing a visit to the land of Israel to permit a one-day holiday. Yet, on the other hand, even though one was to return to Israel directly after the holidays, the fact that one visited with one's wife was sufficient to require a two-day Diaspora holiday (see also the comparable ruling of the Lubavitcher Rebbe Shaarei Halachah U'Minhag *Orech Chayyim*, Volume 11, 180).

Clarification is yet necessary to establish the halachic significance of the proviso that one who travels to a destination with his wife changes his status. The Mishneh Berurah contends that this clause deals with one who uproots his family to go to another area. The implication is that if the person should find a means of making a living in the new area, the traveller would settle there (*Orech Chayyim* 496: conclusion of 13). Thus, travelling with a wife, according to the Mishneh Berurah, is an indication that the traveller does not intend to return. This would only make sense in a situation wherein a person took all their possessions with them. It also would not be applicable to a person who purchased a round-trip ticket to Israel for the holidays.

The *Aruch HaShulchan*, however, adds a unique rationale to the reason why travelling with one's wife changes the status of a traveller. He contends that when one travels with a wife there is a sense of permanency (a *dira kavua*, a degree of *kevi'ut*). The visitor thus manifests a reasonable degree of involvement with the new area. This has application even though a person will return from Israel directly after Passover (see *Aruch HaShulchan* 496:5). This concern for permanency is used by the *Aruch HaShulchan* to rule that one who is in *Eretz Yisrael* for a year need observe only one day of *Yom Tov*.

Though it must be noted that most authorities do not accept the position of the Chacham Tzvi by itself, in the event, however, when there are additional factors to mandate leniency in Israel, then one may add the Chacham Tzvi's position to permit the observance of a one-day holiday in Israel. Therefore, should one travel with one's wife to Israel for the holidays, one may rely on the rulings of the Chacham Tzvi, the *Shulchan Aruch* HaRav, and the *Aruch HaShulchan* to observe only one day in Israel.

There is yet another consideration, which may be viewed as derived from the Chacham Tzvi's position. The fact that the two-day *Yom Tov* is only observed in the Diaspora brings home the concept that *galut* is different than the *kedushah* of *Eretz Yisrael*. In *galut* we observe two days *Yom Tov* because it's the *galut*. Thus, the two-day *Yom Tov* is endemic to Diaspora life. This is not operational in Israel.

The above analysis provides added clarity to the following ruling of HaRav Shlomo Zalman Auerbach. He contended that a person who lives most of the year in the Diaspora but owns a home in Israel and generally is in Israel for the holidays may observe only one day *Yom Tov*. His rationale is that since that person's mode of residence on holidays is in Israel, he has a holiday status comparable to Israelis who are required to observe only one day of *Yom Tov*. This theory is used together with the Chacham Tzvi's position to bolster his ruling (Responsa Minchat Shlomo 19:7). The concept of permanency, as articulated by the *Aruch HaShulchan*, sheds light on this halachah. Since the person in question is always in Israel during the holidays, he is deemed a permanent holiday resident of Israel (his *kevi'ut* is to be in Israel for *Yom Tov*). It is also interesting that this theory is only used in conjunction with the decision of the Chacham Tzvi.

Of further concern is the issue of whether the owning of a home in Israel qualifies a Diaspora resident to be classified as an Israeli for purposes of observing only one day *Yom Tov*. In the previous responsa, HaRav Auerbach notes that this issue is a matter of debate. Some say that the owning of a home in Israel by itself classifies the owner, when in Israel for the holidays, as an Israeli, to celebrate only one day of *Yom Tov*. Others contend that one must reside in a place for a minimum of six months to be classified as a resident. Accordingly, anyone who spends less than six months in Israel may not consider themselves an Israeli for purposes of observing only one day of *Yom Tov*. Yet, as previously noted, should the person make it a rule to be in Israel for the holidays, that generates a special permanency.

New Israeli Communities and the Second Day of Yom Tov

QUESTION: Are new neighborhoods or communities in Israel classified as part of *Eretz Yisrael* for observance of only one day of *Yom Tov*?

RESPONSE: The halachic geographical dichotomy was that the Diaspora celebrated two days and *Eretz Yisrael* only one day of *Yom Tov*. As such, perhaps the one day observance was limited to neighborhoods or cities known to have had Jewish communities during the period of time that the *bet din* sanctified each new month. This suggests that new areas of Jewish life should perhaps be classified as part of the Diaspora.

HaRav Tzvi Pesach Frank, the former chief rabbi of Jerusalem, reported that such indeed was the opinion of a Jerusalem sage. HaRav Frank, however, disagreed. He ruled that all of Israel, including new neighborhoods, communities as well as the Negev, (including Eilat) are to be considered part of *Eretz Yisrael* for purposes of observing one day of *Yom Tov*.

His rationale is as follows: The Ritva notes that when the original rule was set up for Diaspora Jewish communities to observe *Yom Tov* for two days, it was applicable for all Diaspora communities. This included those few areas that the messengers of *bet din* did reach each month and were aware of the actual date when *Rosh Chodesh* was established. Thus, there were areas in the Diaspora that were required to observe two days of *Yom Tov* even though they knew the exact date of the new month. The reason for setting up a general two-day observance in the Diaspora was to keep the Diaspora observance uniform. The communities aware of the true date of *Rosh Chodesh* were in the minority and were mandated to follow the majority custom of two days (*Sukka* 43). Accordingly, all of Israel should also be uniform in practice. The fact that certain areas may not have been sent messengers in ancient times should not generate a new halachic practice. The majority custom of one day *Yom Tov* should override other considerations and set the rule for all areas. In addition, any extension to a Jewish community has the status of the original area. The final argument is that perhaps a two-day observance in the land of Israel was limited to areas known definitely not to have had Jews in ancient periods of times. Doubtful areas would by tradition follow the general custom of observing only one day of *Yom Tov* (*Mikra'ai Kodesh, Pesach*, vol. II, Siman 58).

National Independence

QUESTION: Does the fact that Israel is an independent nation have any impact upon halachah?

RESPONSE: The Rambam rules that Jews fasted on Tishah b'Av during the era of the second *Bet HaMikdash* (Rambam, Commentary on Mishna, *Rosh Hashanah*, ch. 1: see *Rosh Hashanah* 18).

Of concern is the rationale for such a custom. Why should Jews fast for the destruction of something that has been rebuilt? The fact that God had mercy upon the Jewish nation and enabled the *Bet HaMikdash* to be beautifully rebuilt as well as to flourish certainly is not a cause to mourn or fast. From a homiletical view it may be suggested that those who fasted were not lauded by the rabbis (the Talmud is clear that not all Jews fasted; some did). They represented the psychological orientation of those who are never satisfied with the present while they over-glorify the past. In other words, no present action or edifice could compare with the past. As such, the Jews who fasted during the second *Bet HaMikdash* in a way devalued its glory by negatively comparing it to the original *Bet HaMikdash* built by Shlomo HaMelech. Such people could not appreciate properly the second *Bet HaMikdash.* Those with a similar attitude in the contemporary scene would find it difficult to acknowledge the religious significance of modern Israel.

The Sefat Emet, the Ger Rebbe, provides an interesting explanation of the Rambam's position that has a contemporary application. He suggests that *k'lal Yisrael* fasted even during the existence of the second *Bet HaMikdash* because they were not free. The Jews were subordinate to the political dominion of the Persians and the Romans. This means that Jews cannot be happy as long as they are politically governed by other nations. The Talmud states, "When there is peace these days [the fast days] shall be for joy and gladness, but when there is no peace, they shall be fasts." Rashi notes that peace implies that Gentile nations do not govern the land of Israel. (*Rosh Hashanah* 18b, also commentary of Sefat Emet). Thus, Jewish independence is essential for Jewish happiness. Having a second *Bet HaMikdash* was not sufficient for *k'lal Yisrael* to manifest national happiness, for it lacked the key ingredient of independence. Accordingly, national independence is intertwined within the fine fabric of Jewish national joy. Such may not be devalued nor disregarded.

Rabin's Assassination

QUESTION: Is there an halachic reaction to the assassination of Prime Minister Yitzchok Rabin?

RESPONSE: The prophet declared that "on the seventh" a fast day would take place (Zechariah 8:19). The Talmud contends that this refers to the fast that takes place on the seventh month, namely Tishrai. On the third of Tishrai is when "Gedalia ben Achikan was murdered. Who killed him? [asks the Gemorah and responds,] Yishmael ben Netaniah killed him, and [the fact that a fast was instituted on this day] "shows that the death of the righteous is put on a level with the burning of the House of our God" (*Rosh Hashanah* 18b).

This citation requires analysis. What was so unique about the murder of Gedalia that spurred the sages to institute a fast day? In almost every generation Jews were victimized and murdered. In one era after another Jews were made the scapegoats for economic problems. Accordingly, it was not an uncommon event for Jews to be murdered. Indeed, should fast days be decreed whenever a Jew is murdered, then Jews would probably fast throughout most days of the year. Wherein was the murder of Gedalia so brutally distinct that a national fast day was ordained to take place after Rosh Hashanah? In addition, some rationale must be provided to explain why the Talmud felt the necessity to designate the name of the murderer. Of what significance is the knowledge of the name of the murderer?

The famed P'nai Yehoshua talmudic commentary makes the following astute remarks that give contemporary relevance to the fast day. The Talmud was well aware that in almost every generation and country Jews were murdered. What was unique about the murder of Gedalia was that he was murdered not by a Gentile, but by a Jew. This so impacted the composure and moral pinions of our sages that they decreed a fast day to mourn this immoral act. Jews do not kill Jews. Jews should not kill Jews. The mourning is not only for the man killed, but for the eclipse of morality that shockingly may have justified such a murder (P'nai Yehoshua, *Rosh Hashanah* 18b).

As such, the fast of Gedalia and the reaction of the sages suggests the halachic reaction to a Jewish murderer. Jews do not murder. A Jewish murderer is a violation of the persona of the Jew. The contemporary relevance is clear-cut.

Religious Zionism: Definition and Goal

QUESTION: What is religious Zionism? What does it stand for?

RESPONSE: A religious Zionist is a person with a vision and a quest who views the land of Israel as well as the establishment of the State of Israel as a manifestation of major religious significance. *Yisrael v'oraita chad hu,* "Israel and our Torah are one." Religion is intertwined within the fine fabric of the land of Israel (*Zohar*, parshat Acharai 73).

The basic goal, policy, and orientation of religious Zionism may be summarized by the following terse concept: *Eretz Yisrael le'am Yisrael—al pi Torat Yisrael.* This is our motto. This is what makes us tick. This vibrates our *neshama. Eretz Yisrael le'am Yisrael*—"The land of Israel belongs to the Jewish people." *This* is our national homeland—not Uganda, not any other area in the world. *This* land is our land. It is the land promised to us in the Bible. It was given to Abraham who bequeathed it to Yitzchok, not Yishmael. It was then Divinely promised to Jacob and to his children after him. Deny the Biblical grant to Jews, and the strongest argument for a Jewish inheritance and homeland is lost. Even Ben Gurion, not known for his religious piety, proclaimed the Bible publicly as the strongest, most viable evidence for a Jewish homeland.

Eretz Yisrael le'am Yisrael. Israel is for the *Jewish* people. There must be a Jewish character to the people. Jewishness must permeate its core. Israel is not just another democratic nation, with inhabitants who just happen to be Jewish. Israel is not just a Jewish Australia or America. One cannot do away with thousands of years of Jewish Torah and culture. Israel is not just an answer to anti-semitism as some thought. Israel has existed for fifty years and anti-semitism is still rampant. Israel is unique. It's also not simply a major residence of Jews. It's the land of our forefathers. It was ruled by the Jewish King David and the Jewish wise man King Solomon. Samuel the prophet walked its paths. Yerimayahu and Yesha'yahu preached in locations recognizable even today. The land, the geography is a living seminar of our traditions and culture.

Eretz Yisrael al pi torat Yisrael. Israel has a tradition. There is a religious culture of pride and glory. Israel is marked by the impramateur of Torah not from today or yesterday, but from the ages of history. The religious Zionist will use his/her influence to insure that the Jewish image is not removed for the sake of assimilation or a desire to emulate non-Jews. No leader has the right to alter our religious posture by declaring it irrelevant for today. No member of the Knesset has the authority to radically change Israel into a democratic nation devoid of a Jewish character. The posture of Israel must be as a Jewish nation. The religious Zionist will not sacrifice Judaism upon the altar of democracy. Torah values are not subject to the actions of a majority vote. Israel is not a Jewish Sweden.

Religious Zionists pray to *HaShem* for the strength, the *koach* to inculcate the minds and to penetrate the souls of all Jews, to the right and to the left, with the Torah values of Jewish *mentschlichkeit*—pride in our tradition and tolerance for those who disagree. Religious Zionism serves as the moral conscience of a Jewish Israel, a moral conscience permeated with love of Torah, love of Israel, and love for Jews.

Jericho and Jews

QUESTION: Does the city of Jericho have any religious significance for Jews?

RESPONSE: In the era of the *Bet HaMikdash*, Jericho not only had Jewish inhabitants, but was also a vital, integral component of the process that enabled the *Bet HaMikdash* to function.

The Talmud reports that the *kohanim* and *levi'im* were divided into twenty-four groups (each group of *kohanim* and *levi'im* was called a *mishmar*). When the time came for a specific *mishmar* to serve its allocated service in the *Bet HaMikdash* in Jerusalem, "one half of the *mishmar* went up to Jerusalem and the other half went up to Jericho in order to provide their brethren in Jerusalem with water and food" (*Ta'anit* 27a).

Rabbenu Hanniel notes that the function of the Jericho *mishmar* was to sustain the Jerusalem *mishmar*. Also, to grant everyone equal opportunity to serve, the *kohanim* and *levi'im* would alternate functions—namely, the *mishmar* that had the privilege of serving in the *Bet HaMikdash* would on the next allocated period for service go to Jericho to permit those who were in Jericho to serve in Jerusalem.

Thus Jericho was a regular supply station for the *Bet HaMikdash.* In addition during the year, *kohanim* and *levi'im* from throughout the entire land of Israel were based for a specific period of time in Jericho.

Accordingly, any concern for the emergence of a future *Bet HaMikdash,* must recognize that Jerusalem and Jericho are intertwined within the same fabric.

Praying for Victims of Terrorism

QUESTION: Does halachah mandate any special consideration for victims of terror?

RESPONSE: Yes. This concept may be derived from the following text:

"If at the present time a man comes (desires) to become a proselyte, he is addressed as follows: 'What reason have you for wanting to become a proselyte? Do you not know that (the children of) Israel at the present time are persecuted and oppressed, despised, harassed and overcome by afflictions?' If he replies, 'I know and yet am unworthy,' (see Rashi: "If only I may be worthy" of the privilege to be a member of Israel) he is accepted forthwith and given instruction in some of the minor and some of the major commandments" (*Yevamot* 47a).

This citation demonstrates the necessity for a potential convert to commit himself to share the fate of *k'lal Yisrael* prior to any discussion of any specific mitzvot. The implication is that a commitment to observe mitzvot is not even considered unless it is preceded by a commitment to share the fate and suffer the plight of *k'lal Yisrael* amongst the nations of the world. HaRav HaGaon R. Yitzhak Hutner (*z"l*), former Rosh Yeshivah of Yeshivat Rabbenu Chaim Berlin, made the following comments on this Gemara: "If recognition of the negative status of Israel (with all its pain) is a precondition for conversion to Judaism, how much more is such a recognition essential for those already in the fold?" (*Iggeret* no. 63).

In other words, empathy for Jews is an essential element of Judaism. It is, therefore, necessary for Jews to publicly express their communal feelings of shared pain and sorrow over the plight of those who are innocent victims of terrorism. This suggests that synagogues throughout the world should publicly demonstrate solidarity by offering special prayers on behalf of the wounded victims of terrorism.

There is another consideration to note. The Rema rules that *Kaddish* is to be recited by the son of an apostate who was killed by Gentiles (*Yoreh Deah* 340 and 376:6). The Taz and the Shach both contend that such a death is deemed an atonement for sins. Thus victims of terrorism against Jews may be classified as *kedoshim*, Jews with a special merit (*zechut*). As such, prayers for these innocent wounded victims should be obligatory in every place of worship throughout the world. Not to pray for these victims is comparable to a message that one does not care. That is not and can never be the essence of Jewry.

Part II

Conversion

Commitment at Conversion: Halachic Parameters

QUESTION: What religious commitments are necessary at a conversion to Judaism?

RESPONSE: Conversion to Judaism is a religious status transformation that entails *kabbalat mitzvot*, a commitment to perform the commandments. This essential feature serves as the major obstacle for discouraging numerous converts from ever seeking a halachic conversion and concomitantly looms as the "measuring rod" to assess the validity of conversions actually performed. As such, it is necessary to finely hone the parameters of this rule so that pragmatic guidelines may be formulated.

The basic requirement for commitment at a conversion is derived from the following talmudic citation:

> "If a heathen is prepared to accept the Torah except for one religious law, we must not receive him [as an Israelite]. Rabbi Yosi bar Yehuda says: Even [if the exception was] one point of the special minutiae of the Scribe's enactments." [See Rashi: even a rabbinic stringency.] (*Bechorot* 30b; see also *Tosefta, D'mai,* ch. II:b, wherein the term "heathen" is replaced with the word *ger*—a potential convert.)

To the extent that a commitment to observe all mitzvot with but one exclusion invalidates a conversion, logic dictates that the absence of any commitment altogether certainly invalidates a conversion. Accordingly, some form of commitment must be present at a conversion. This is essential. This commitment, moreover, cannot be restricted to biblical law but must encompass rabbinic decrees. (The assumption is that Rabbi Yosi bar

Yehuda was clarifying the rule requiring total commitment and there is no dispute between his position and the original law.)

Of concern is the means of assessing the integrity of the commitment. A simple reading of the text suggests that a potential convert should be well versed in all facets of Judaism so that the actual commitment would be based upon knowledge, rather than ignorance. How could a commitment to Judaism be meaningful if the potential convert (i.e., *ger*) simply is unaware of the ramifications of Jewish law? Coupled to this is, perhaps, an obligation of *bet din* to specifically question, or better yet interrogate, the *ger* about reactions to various crisis situations to mitigate against any possible exclusionary considerations. Thus, ignorance of Jewish Law by the *ger* or an absence of any investigation to determine the limits of commitment should impair the credibility of the *ger* as well as that of the *bet din* and invalidate the entire process. Indeed, this is the preferred procedure by a number of rabbinic courts. Such a process, however, is not necessarily supported by all halachic scholars. Indeed, it represents a one-sided, stringent orientation that subtly interchanges ideal conditions with essential features. Though *kabbalat mitzvot* is a vital factor in a conversion, there are a variety of less-than-ideal dimensions to this commitment that are sanctioned as legitimate and valid halachic expressions of the religious requirement.

Some examples:

I. The Mishnah (*Shabbat* 67b) discusses the religious culpability of someone who is unaware of any work prohibitions on *Shabbat* (see Rashi). Rav and Shmuel contend that the Mishnah refers to those who never knew that *Shabbat* entails prohibitions. Two examples are presented: a child captured by Gentiles and a convert converted amongst Gentiles (*Shabbat* 68a). Commenting on the first case, Rashi says that the child never knew anything about *Shabbat.* The assumption is that the second case, relating to a convert, also deals with a situation wherein the convert was never aware of *Shabbat. Tosafot* note that the conversion must have occurred in the presence of three men, for otherwise the conversion is invalid (see *Yevamot* 47b). They suggest the case deals with a situation wherein the *bet din* never informed the convert about the mitzvah of *Shabbat* altogether.

The validity of such a conversion certainly should be questioned. A person who is totally unaware of *Shabbat* definitely cannot observe its laws. It is simply impossible to be a *Shomer Shabbat* without some knowledge of *Shabbat* itself. Accordingly, the case is tantamount to a conversion commitment with an obvious exclusion of the laws of *Shabbat.* Yet the Talmud does not invalidate the halachic status of such a convert. Why? Rav Moshe Feinstein contends that there is no contradiction between the two talmudic cases cited (i.e., *Bechorot* 30b and *Shabbat* 68a). He notes that a conversion has halachic validity (*b'dieved*) even if *bet din* failed to inform the potential convert of any *mitzvot* altogether. Even *ab initio* (*lecha'chila*) one need not inform the *ger* of all mitzvot. There is no necessity to teach the *ger* the entire Torah. The crucial issue is commitment, even if such commitment is based upon ignorance. The case in *Shabbat* relates to general commitment to observe "all that *B'nai Yisrael* are obligated to observe" (Iggrot Moshe, *Yoreh Deah*, vol. I, Responsum 159). In other words, as long as there is a total, sincere commitment to observe all that is required of a Jew, ignorance is not deemed an exclusionary condition. (Rav Feinstein also expressed personal qualms over converting women who convert merely to marry Jewish men. His rationale is that in those cases there is an assumption (*anan sadi*) that the verbal commitment will not be followed by observance. Yet, since many rabbis do, in fact, perform such conversions, he refrains from invalidating them because perhaps those women subsequently will, indeed, observe *mitzvot* [ibid.].) As such, as long as the general nondetailed commitment to observe Jewish law is sincere, the commitment is valid and the conversion kosher even if the potential convert is ignorant of the details of the commitment.

II. A corollary from the above discussion is that any *ger* who is aware, at the moment of conversion, of the laws of *Shabbat*, and subsequently violates its laws, provides prima facie evidence that the commitment was invalid for it lacked sincerity.

Yet even in this situation, Rav Feinstein provides a lenient consideration. Assume, he maintains, *bet din* informed the *ger* of the necessity to observe *Shabbat.* Yet, the convert may have believed erroneously that *Shabbat* observance is not essential to being a Jew but, rather, a beautiful custom (a *hiddur*). Thus the *ger* sincerely believed one may be a Jew even without strict *Shabbat* observance. As such, the commitment is still classified as a total pledge to observe all that a Jew is *required* to follow, even though based upon an error (Iggrot Moshe, *Yoreh Deah,* vol. I, Responsum 160).

III. Accordingly, there are two conversion models: (1) The Optimum Method (*lechat'chila*)—a convert is realistically afforded knowledge of halachic Judaism. All major mitzvot are outlined as essential. (See Rabbi Dovid Hoffman, however, who contends that at least the following three mitzvot must be delineated and confirmed: *Shabbat* [and *Yom Tov*], *kashrut,* and laws of *nidah* [family purity]. Malamaid L'Hoel, *Yoreh Deah,* Responsum 88.) Any violation or reservation is detailed as a breach of commitment. The convert who fails to specifically commit to *Shabbat* observance, for example, is not accepted or is told that nonobservance would invalidate the conversion. (2) The Ex Post Facto Method (*b'dieved*)—a convert is not informed, for example, that violation of *Shabbat* invalidates the conversion. The convert merely was required to make a generalized statement in the presence of a *bet din* to observe all required of a Jew without specific delineation of essential observances. According to Rav Feinstein, the second model has validity as long as the convert was not made aware that specific observances are vital to Judaism.

To be explored is a rationale as to whether the *b'dieved* option may ever be utilized *ab initio.* For example, are cases of conversion due to marriage to be viewed as *ab initio* or ex post facto?

HaRav Ben Zion Meir Hai Usiel, former Sephardic Chief Rabbi of Israel, made the following rulings relating to intermarriage:

1. Every effort should be utilized to induce the Jewish mate to leave the non-Jewish spouse.

2. In the event such is impossible or impractical (as most cases are), *bet din* is obliged to convert the spouse even if it is known, in advance, that the non-Jew is converting only for purposes of marriage. This ruling is based on the following considerations: (a) The halachah is that even though *ab initio* one does not convert a person who has ulterior reasons for conversion (i.e., marriage), ex post facto such conversion is valid (see *Yevamot* 24b). (b) It is imperative to save the Jewish mate from the ongoing, constant sin of living with a non-Jew. Such a sin portends the dissolution of our people (Piskai Usiel, *Siman* 63, p. 370). This concept is also derived from the Rambam, who contends that one who is suspected of living with a female slave should free her and marry her. This rule appears contrary to the general halachah that prohibits such a marriage *ab initio*. Yet the Rambam notes that it is preferable "to eat soup rather than *shuman* (prohibited fat) and times dictate such a policy (*et la'asot*)" (Responsa, P'Air HaDor, *Siman* 132). Rav Usiel suggests the following general rule: Whenever a procedure is only prohibited *ab initio*, one should permit such action if the alternative is worse, namely to live constantly with a Gentile wife and have children not deemed Jewish [Piskai Usiel, *Siman* 59, p. 350]. (c) When potential converts are turned away by *bet din*, such people generally become enemies of Jews. Indeed, the Jewish mate may also rebel against his or her people. History confirms such reactions (ibid., *Siman* 65, p. 385).

3. Even should the mother not wish to convert, it is imperative upon *bet din* to convert the children (ibid., p. 386).

According to HaRav Usiel the *ab initio* strictures relating to conversion are not operational in cases of intermarriage.

IV. It should be noted that even if a *ger* is informed of the essential obligation to observe *Shabbat* and it is known at the time of the commitment that under duress the *ger* will violate the *Shabbat*, the commitment is still valid. Rabbi Hayyim Ozer Grodensky, the former acclaimed decisor of halachah in Vilno, officially ruled that an exclusion to a commitment to observe mitzvot exists only when the convert specifically and verbally excludes some religious item from commitment. Such a commitment is definitely invalid. In the event, however, that the *ger* assumes the obligation to observe the Torah in its entirety yet it is known that he (or she) will violate halachah under duress or exacting pressures, such is not deemed as a breach of the commitment (Responsa Ahiezer, Part II, 26).

Based upon the decision of the Ahiezer, Rav Isar Yehuda Unterman, former Chief Rabbi of Israel, ruled that *bet din* should refrain from probing the extent of the convert's commitment. Specifically, they should not seek to ascertain whether the convert would agree to quit his job in the event that his employers would require *Shabbat* work as a condition of employment. To the extent that such violations of *Shabbat* are under duress of employment, they would not invalidate the commitment even if known at the conversion itself. Accordingly, the questions should not even be posed. Indeed, Rav Unterman openly stated that such questions should not be directed at Russian immigrants (Shevet Yehuda, Laws of Converts, pp. 378–379). The Kovner Rav, Rav Abraham Duber Kahana Shapiro, however, takes issue with the ruling of the Ahiezer. He contends that any reservation even under duress is a breach of a commitment. Yet from a practical view he rules that *b'dieved* such a conversion is valid. Though personally he frowned upon the decision, he notes that, perhaps, pragmatically, the power of leniency coupled with the individual case history may be the decisive ruling (Responsa, D'var Avraham, Part III, no. 28).

Rav Unterman (citing Response, Hemdat Shlomo, *Yoreh Deah*, Responsa 29 and 30) overtly rules that a commitment may be invalidated only if (a) a specific mitzvah is orally excluded from observance, and (b) *bet din* is certain that the convert will definitely violate prohibitions of the Torah (i.e., *Shabbat* and *kashrut*) and there is no doubt that the commitment lacked sincerity (Rav Unterman, op. cit., p. 378). Accordingly, he contends, even if it is known that the convert's husband may violate the *Shabbat*, the woman's commitment is independently judged and is not invalidated by his non-observance (ibid., p. 380).

V. There are, moreover, major distinctions between the rituals of *milah* and *tevilah* and the commitment of *kabbalat mitzvot*. Rabbi Shlomo Kluger rules that from a biblical perspective, a conversion is valid even without the preconditions of *kabbalat mitzvot*, which is a rabbinic requirement. Yet, *kabbalat mitzvot* without the other two rituals is meaningless (Responsa, Tuv Taam V'Daat, vol. 2, 111). As such, perhaps qualms relating to the integrity of totality of the commitment may be classified as doubts relating to rabbinic laws that generally are guided by leniency (Safek D'Rabbanan L'Kula). This position, however, is not the majority viewpoint, for scholars dealing with conversion contend that its absence invalidates the entire conversion. Though not explicit, the implication is that even biblically the process is invalid (see Rabbi Yosef Don Soloveitchik, "Besod Hayahid VeHaYahad," notes p. 389). Rabbi Hayyim Ozer Grodensky, however, poses the following question: Is a commitment to observe the Torah with reservation concerning a rabbinic ordinance a valid conversion, at least from a biblical viewpoint? Or, since a commitment to observe the Torah includes a willingness to follow the rules of the sages, is any willful negation of a rabbinic decree tantamount to a reservation relating to biblical law? Rabbi Hayyim Ozer does not resolve the issue and contends it is a matter for further research (*Tzorech Eeyun*) (ibid.). Of need for further research is whether the lenient concerns may be utilized as but additional corroborating factors to validate a questionable conversion.

VI. The Talmud relates three instances in which Hillel converted Gentiles who made specific conditional commitments prior to conversion. One wished to be taught the Written and not the Oral Torah; the second desired to be taught the whole Torah while standing on one foot (i.e., a single formula encompassing the entire Torah; see Meharsha, *Shabbat* 31a); and the third converted on the condition that subsequently he would be made a *kohen gadol* (*Shabbat* 31a).

Rashi's commentary (*Shabbat* 31a) adds a unique dimension

to the concept of *kabbalat mitzvot.* The Talmud relates that Shammai refused to convert these individuals, while Hillel was praised for his actions. Why then did Shammai refuse such converts? Rashi contends that Shammai based his ruling on the talmudic dictum that invalidates a conversion with an exclusionary clause (*Bechorot* 30b). As such, were not Hillel's actions questionable? On what basis did Hillel accept a convert who overtly stipulated reservations? Rashi notes that Hillel's actions were not contrary to the requirement for total commitment in that the convert, for example, did not disbelieve in the Oral Torah; his problem was simply that he did not believe that it was (commanded) from God. Hillel relied on his judgment that through his efforts, the convert's observance would be complete and altruistic.

HaGaon Rav Yitzhok Hutner (*z"l*), Dean of the Rabbi Chaim Berlin Rabbinical Academy, presented the following unique analysis of Rashi's position.

1. The Written Torah makes no reference to the requirement of *bet din* at a conversion. Its source is totally within the oral tradition (see *Yevamot* 46a). Accordingly, if this *ger* did not believe at all in the Oral Torah, then there was no reason at all to seek out Hillel or Shammai to convert him. He could have (or should have) converted himself. To the extent that he did not do so, this is indicative of his basic belief in the Oral Tradition.

2. Of concern is the quality of belief in an Oral Torah not from God. Does such a belief have any merit? Perhaps, reasons Rav Hutner, he believed that the entire Oral Torah was comparable to rabbinic decrees. Though the Written Torah grants authority to rabbinic sages to enact laws, it is accepted that such laws are not comparable to biblical mitzvot decreed by God. The *ger* extended this concept to the Oral Torah.

3. Rashbah rules that anyone who does not believe in the Oral Torah is comparable to an apostate (*mumar*) who disbelieves in the entire Torah. Accordingly, he is declassified as a Jew (see Responsa Rashbah, no. 430; cited also by Bait Yosef, *Tur Yoreh Deah* 119). This appears to be the basis for Rashi's rationale that the potential convert did, indeed, believe in the

Oral Torah, for otherwise the *bet din* would not classify such a person as a Jew due to his disbelief in the Oral Torah. The difficulty with this ruling is that a Kuti (a member of a sect that believed only in the Written Torah but not in the Oral Torah) is deemed a Jew to validate the kosher slaughter he performs (see *Hullin* 3a). Perhaps, suggests Rav Hutner, *kabbalat mitzvot* according to Rashi is radically different than the other rituals of conversion. Conversion lacking *milah* and *tevilah* is comparable to no conversion at all. It's as if no conversion transpired. Should, however, *kabbalat mitzvot* not be total, but contain reservations or exclusions, one simply *cannot* assume that it is similar to an absence of *milah* and deemed as if no conversion took place. A potential *ger* should be no different than a natural-born Jew. "Any violation of mitzvot that does not transform a natural-born Jew into a Gentile does not invalidate the conversion of a *ger*" (Pachad Yitzhok, Iggrot, no 34, pp. 61–63). If so, then what is the rationale for the ruling that we do not accept converts who fail to make total commitments? The reason is that an exclusion is not an invalidation of the conversion process but a restraint upon *bet din.* Basically it is a concern that *bet din* has no right to increase by its action violators of Jewish law by converting people who are known sinners. Indeed, several scholars contend that if *bet din* did, indeed, accept *b'dieved* converts who made commitments with reservations, the conversions are valid. Now, if a commitment with a reservation invalidates the conversion, there would be no rationale to distinguish between a preferred action and an ex post facto validity. As such, the entire issue revolves upon the propriety of *bet din* to formally increase Jewish sinners. Rashi's position is as follows: A person who does not believe in the Oral Torah is tantamount to one who denies the essence of committing oneself to observe *mitzvot.* As such, it's as if there was no commitment altogether. In such a case any presumption of future observance would not validate the conversion. Just as a future commitment to observe *milah* is meaningless, so too is a future commitment to observe *mitzvot.* The conversion must contain a commitment of immediate observance. Should, however, a person believe in mitzvot yet contend that Oral Law is totally rabbinic, such a process at least manifests a basic commitment to observe *mitzvot*. Hillel was aware that *bet din* was not permitted, however, to convert would-be sinners. Yet, since Hillel relied on his wisdom that he would successfully persuade the convert to achieve total observance, he felt that such activity was not prohibited at all (Rav Yitzhok Hutner, Pachad Yitzhok, *Iggrot*, no. 34, pp. 61–63).

[Rav Hutner's theory may be somewhat corroborated by the Talmud in *Bechorot* (30b). The Talmud does not explicitly rule that a commitment with a reservation is halachically tantamount to no commitment at all. Rather, it says *Ayn m'kablin oto*, "We do not accept him." The implication is that *bet din* does not accept such a commitment and consequently does not complete the conversion process. Now, if a commitment with a reservation is comparable to no commitment altogether, then the Talmud should have openly ruled that the conversion, even if rituals were completed, was simply invalid. The terminology suggests that *bet din* is only withheld *ab initio* from validating the conversion.]

The commentary of Rabbenu Gershon (*Bechorot* 30b) provides additional insight into this concept. Rabbenu Gershon presents a rationale as to why commitments with reservations are not accepted by *bet din*. He notes: "Since he [the *ger*] is unable to withhold [violating] one item, it is certain he will not be able to withhold [himself] from [violating] others." Accordingly the problem is one of credibility. The implication is that should *bet din* firmly believe in the integrity of the commitment made, then *bet din* may legitimately validate a conversion even should commitment be with exclusions.

Though Rav Hutner did not present a halachic ruling but only an interpretation of Rashi, his theory has vast pragmatic implications.

First, it provides a guideline for determining minimum obligatory observances. A *ger* is assessed to be comparable to a natural-born Jew. Any violation of Jewish law that does not halachically transform a natural-born Jew into the status of a

Gentile is not deemed an inherent breach of the commitment. This suggests research into the parameters of halachah for declassifying Jewish sinners.

In addition, the propriety of converting sinners is within the judgment of *bet din*. Basically, *bet din* has no moral right to convert would-be sinners. Yet, should some rationale be developed that (in certain cases) the merits of such conversions outweighed the charge of generating sinners in *k'lal Yisrael*, then, perhaps, a case may be made to approve and validate such conversions as a matter of policy.

VII. The Talmud relates that Bet Shammai and Bet Hillel disagreed on a number of family status laws. Bet Hillel contended that Bet Shammai's rulings were erroneously legitimatizing marriage to Jews classified as bastards (*mamzerim*). Bet Shammai considered many of Bet Hillel's decisions a means of validating marriage with persons who had tainted ancestry. Yet, both families (Bet Shammai's and Bet Hillel's) freely intermarried with each other. But how did they permit this? Each should have refrained from intermarriage because of their radically different decisions. The Talmud states they intermarried because they made a practice of "informing each other" of problematic families (*Yevamot* 14a). Each group respected the halachic integrity of the other. No one side felt so certain of its position that it was deemed wrong, embarrassing, or extraneous to disclose problematic cases. The Talmud further notes that the intermarriages between the two groups taught us "that they showed love and friendship toward one another, thus putting into practice the Scriptural text (Zech. 8:19) 'Love ye peace and truth'" (*Yevamot* 14b).

Maharsha comments that even though there is but one real truth, for purposes of *shalom* both interacted with friendship. Consequently, mutual respect mandated that both interact with integrity for full disclosure. Each group, once aware of a family's case history, had the option of refusing marriage without castigating the decision of the Rav who legitimatized the family. Should not this be the practice today? Rabbinic scholars who honestly rule to validate certain conversions because of their perception of halachic parameters should be respected as alternate legal approaches rather than as illegitimate violators of halachah. One may disagree with a halachic decision. One may feel it is totally in error. One may not wish such a ruling to be practiced in his community. One may even publicly attempt to refute the halachic basis for the decision. But if the decision was developed with proper halachic principles and in conformity with Torah guidelines and precedent, then the ruling has validity for those who wish to observe it. Halachah is not monolithic. Jewish family status law must be rooted in halachah. A non-halachic position must be decried. A halachic position must be granted validity. Just as Bet Shammai recognized that Bet Hillel would not marry certain families, so too should the option be made available to differing Rabbis, even with conflicting rulings.

Notes

Rav Yitzhok Elhonan Spector notes that proof may be derived from a talmudic text to demonstrate the absolute invalidity (ex post facto) of any conversion wherein a commitment had a reservation. The Talmud (*Avodah Zarah* 64b) defines a *ger toshav*. One theory presented is that of "others [who] maintain [that a *ger toshav* is a proselyte who] . . . took upon himself to observe all the precepts mentioned in the Torah apart from the prohibition of [eating the flesh of] animals not ritually slaughtered." Now, if a commitment with a reservation is valid ex post facto, reasons Rav Yitzhok Elhonan, the above-cited person should be classified as a true proselyte and not just a *ger toshav* (Bait Yitzhok, *Yoreh Deah*, no. 100). To this Rav Yehuda Gershuni retorts that there is no comparison between the above-cited case (*Avodah Zarah*) and the rule set forth in *Bechorot* (30b). A halachic conversion requires the performance of three essential rituals: *milah* (circumcision) if male, *tevilah* (immersion in a *mikvah*), and *kabbalat mitzvot* (a commitment to observe commandments). Should the first two rituals be performed and the third contain a reservation, the process may be deemed ex post facto valid. A *ger toshav* does not undergo the rituals of *milah* and *tevilah*. His sole ritual is that of commitment. Accordingly, any reservation expressed in the absence of the other two rituals simply cannot make the process valid as a full-fledged conversion (Rav Yehudah Gershuni, "Convert," *Hadarom, Nisan*, 5730 (1970) p. 37).

*May a Jew who Marries Out Be Counted in a Minyan?**

QUESTION: May a Jew who marries out be counted in a minyan?

RESPONSE: I. Recent studies reveal that a majority of American Jews, 52 percent to be exact, marry out of the faith, whereas prior to 1965 only 9 percent intermarried. Thus, in just twenty-five years, intermarriage went from an aberration to the majority mode of marriage among Jews.[1]

As the shocking prevalence of intermarriage became well known, the tendency of the Orthodox Rabbinate has been to face this problem in the same way in which it confronted most types of social turmoil. They bemoaned and condemned the terrible plague of intermarriage, and sought greater intensification of Jewish education to prevent its further spread.

At the core of this response lies the conviction that intermarriage is not really a problem of the Orthodox community, but rather proof positive of the abject failure of nonhalachic move-

---

*Part of a larger paper presented at the *Yom Iyyun* of the Rabbinical Council of America, August 20, 1991. Appreciation to Rabbi Jeffrey R. Woolf for his editorial and research assistance and to Rabbis Marc Angel and Reuven Bulka for their critical review and comments.

ments. The recent intermarriage statistics are deemed, therefore, to be proof of the intrinsic value of concretizing an Orthodox "fortress philosophy" that is impervious to change. Added to this is the recognition that intermarriage constitutes a grave sin.[2] Thus, no Orthodox rabbi may condone or be seen as validating such deviant behavior, and most rabbis write off intermarried couples and their children.

This attitude, however, warrants careful, critical reexamination. It may well be argued that the high incidence of intermarriage among couples presently marrying (and the changed perceptions of the import of that act, which are its byproduct) strongly suggests the entertaining of an alternative reaction, consistent with halachah and responsive to present-day realities. For while we rightly condemn intermarriage, it is equally self-evident that we must respond constructively to the future of *k'lal Yisrael* in the next generation. The entire concept of *arvut* pushes us in this direction. Therefore, if the majority of Jews now marrying are marrying Gentiles, we are morally and halachically bound to explore the full range of possible responses to this phenomenon. We simply cannot ignore the phenomenon nor cast aside a goodly proportion of our people.

II. A key example of this type of shift in attitude is provided by the issue of whether a person who intermarries should be permitted to be a part of a minyan. This question will become increasingly practical as Jews who intermarry seek out synagogues for attendance, and for the observance of *Kaddish*, *Yartzeit*, and other items. Up until now, it has been common practice that such people not be counted in a minyan or enjoy any rights in the synagogue.

This practice is based (most commonly) on a responsum of Rabbi Yechiel Ya'akov Weinburg, author of *Resp. Seridei Esh.*[3] He ruled that an intermarried person could not be considered part of a minyan. His rationale is as follows: The *Shulchan Aruch* states explicitly that "Habitual sinners who transgress communal decrees or whoever commits a sin, may be included within the quorum of a minyan providing they were not formally excommunicated."[4] At the same time, Rabbi Joseph Caro continues, "Anyone formally placed under a ban may not be included in any religious matter that requires a minyan. It is permissible to pray in a synagogue wherein such a person is present unless it was [originally] specified that such a stringency would be applied."[5] *Pri Megadim*,[6] in turn, modified this latter ruling by stating that permission to pray with sinners who were not formally excommunicated relates only to those who violate the Law for personal pleasure or benefit (*letei'avon*). Those who transgress Jewish Law, however, out of hostility to Judaism and/or a desire to incite anti-Jewish behavior (*lehachis*) may not be counted in a minyan, even in the absence of a formal ban.

In light of the above, Rabbi Weinberg suggests that one who marries out of the faith may be deemed to have violated Jewish Law for personal pleasure. To the extent that such a sinner was never formally excommunicated, logic would presume that he may be counted as part of a minyan.

To counter this view, *Seridei Esh* cites a responsum of Zichron Yehudah, who radically alters the thrust and practical application of the halachah under discussion. He contends that permission to include a non-excommunicated sinner in a minyan applies only to an era when rabbis had the authority to issue bans of excommunication. Consequently, anyone not formally banned was, ipso facto, reckoned as a full member of the community. In our day, however, since such bans are[7] prohibited by government statue, the permissive rule of the *Shulchan Aruch* does not apply. As such, anyone who violates a Law that would normally have resulted in the issuance of a ban is categorized as if he were actually excommunicated and therefore may not be counted in a minyan.

Rabbi Weinberg endorsed this position of Zichron Yehudah and concluded by asserting that intermarriage is such a reprehensible transgression—that rabbis, were they able, would definitely excommunicate the transgressor, as a safeguard of Jewish Life. Thus, intermarried persons are not to be counted in a minyan or to receive an *aliyah* to the Torah.[8]

It may be demonstrated, however, that the logic upon which

his decision is based may either not apply to contemporary circumstances or not even be compelling on its own terms.

To begin with, the position of Zichron Yehudah that a presumption of *niddui* is tantamount to actual excommunication is a highly debatable point. Certainly, the major thrust of discussions of *niddui* and *cherem* presume actual enactment of a ban. What is more, it may be shown historically that when bans were restricted or outlawed they fell into obsolescence.[9] But even when granting Zichron Yehudah's contention, it is not at all obvious that in contemporary circumstances rabbis or rabbinical courts would automatically excommunicate intermarried Jews (in the severest terms) even given the opportunity.

This is because it may be contended, in light of recent statistics, that the act of intermarriage does not constitute an outright and conscious attack on the Jewish People and Judaism, as it may have once been. Rather, it is a natural outcome of highly assimilated lives led in an open society. Jews who intermarry, in large part,[10] do so quite naturally. Thus, one wonders whether excommunication with its attendant ramifications would really be the presumed, immediate (if indeed the most appropriate) response to an act whose motive has so drastically changed.[11]

Support for such a reevaluation may be derived from the *Shulchan Aruch* itself. Rema rules in *Yoreh Deah*[12] that a sinner may be excommunicated even if it is known that such a harsh action may drive him away from Judaism altogether.[13] Taz, on the other hand, strongly disputes this finding. He concludes, based upon a variety of sources,[14] that rabbis must refrain from any act of excommunication that might lead to apostasy.[15] Even Shach,[16] who ultimately supports Rema's ruling, does so not out of disagreement with the substance of Taz's argument, but because he rejects the possibility of restricting the freedom of action of any legitimate *bet din*.[17]

Two conclusions may be drawn from this case. The first is that according to both Shach and Taz, the apostasy (or total alienation) of a sinner is a legitimate consideration for any *bet din* in determining how to proceed. Second, and more importantly, each individual case must be judged upon its own merits as to the advisability of issuing a ban of excommunication. Thus no general rule may be developed, in order to preserve the freedom of action championed by Shach. Two individuals may, therefore, violate the same religious law, yet *bet din* may brand only one of them as deserving of excommunication. *In fine*, no presumption of excommunication, as advocated by both Zichron Yehuda and *Seridei Esh*, may exist.

Further vitiating their contention is an explicit statement of the *Aruch Shulchan* that one placed under *niddui* is excluded from a minyan only if this was included as a detail in the actual text of the *niddui*.[18] Thus exclusion from participation in a minyan constitutes a discretionary act of *bet din*. As such, it does not follow that presumption of excommunication would definitely generate exclusion from a minyan.[19]

III. Two objections may well be raised at this juncture. The first is: On what halachic basis does one advocate a serious reassessment of so dangerous a phenomenon as intermarriage? Secondly, even granting our point that formal *niddui* does not result de jure from intermarriage without a *ma'aseh bet din*, it is a fact that this is the accepted way in which rabbis and communities have expressed their revulsion at intermarriage. On what basis, and with what alternative, should that policy be altered?

A response may be derived from the halachah of *mechallel Shabbat b'farhesiah dino k'akum*, i.e., one who publicly desecrates *Shabbat* is to be treated, for most purposes, as a non-Jew.[20] This is a principle that is accepted by all authorities. Nevertheless, its parameters are by no means clear. Indeed, there is a significant group of *poskim* who contend that it may not be applicable to most present-day Jews who, overwhelmingly, do not observe *Shabbat*.

The basis for this socially conditioned understanding of the rule is rooted in its own underlying rationale. As expressed by Rashi,[21] the desecrator of *Shabbat* is singled out by the Torah for such a severe penalty not only due to its legal severity but because of all that *Shabbat* symbolizes for Judaism. As the sign of the covenant between God and Israel, and testimony to God's creation and mastery over the world, *Shabbat* observance affirms the essence of Judaism, while its desecration constitutes an act of public rebellion. Thus, *mechallel Shabbat* is not only a sinner but a public, defiant heretic who is, therefore, outside of the Judaic pale.

All of this obtains, however, only when the act of *c'hillul Shabbat* is an act of rebellion. However, if the act of *Shabbat* desecration is done not out of defiance, but rather out of convenience (*letei'avon*) or out of ignorance (even as to the severity of such behavior), then while certainly wrong the perpetrator is, according to many *achronim*, not to be deemed as a non-Jew.[22] This line of reasoning is expanded upon by Rabbi David Zvi Hoffman,[23] who points out that the rule of *mechallel Shabbat b'farhesiah* ought to apply only in an environment where the overwhelming majority of Jews observe *Shabbat*. In such a situation, the act of desecration is a direct form of public rebellion against God and Jewish Life. In an era, however, wherein the majority of Jews violate *Shabbat*, an individual who desecrates it is not necessarily rebelling. He or she may be just conforming to peer pressure or reacting to personal exigencies. Such a violation of *Shabbat*, concludes Rabbi Hoffman, can hardly be deemed to place the transgressor in the category of a non-Jew! In a similar vein, Rabbi Ya'akov Ettlinger in *Resp. Binyan Tziyyon*[24] asserts that someone who desecrates *Shabbat*, yet prays in a synagogue and recites *Kiddush* on Friday night, may not be categorized as a Gentile, for he is a believer in God. Thus even though the individual has a concept of *Shabbat* (and is therefore not fully innocent), nevertheless his transgression does not render him a Gentile because it is not done out of rebellion against God![25]

In our own day, Rav Isaac Hutner adopted this approach in his collection of essays, *Pachad Yitzhak*.[26] In the context of an interpretation of the "Wicked Son" in the Passover Aggadah, Rav Hutner discusses the definition of a *mumar*. He asserts that an *apikoros* who is read out of the Jewish People is only one whose heresy was the result of rebellion or "wickedness" (*rishut*). Anyone who lacks this element of vindictive evil is not excluded from *k'lal Yisrael* totally but is likened to a "child taken captive" (*tinok she'nishba*) or a "child of Karaites."[27]

In light of the new statistics concerning intermarriage, the same line of argument may be applied to this transgression as well. Intermarriage is wrong. It is a grievous violation of Jewish Law and Tradition. Yet, the very fact that most Jews presently marrying do so out of the faith, and yet may seek to maintain or assert their identities as Jews, suggests that the act of intermarriage is itself no longer to be viewed as one of unmitigated rebellion.[28]

Logically, one might object that there is a definite distinction to be made between the sin of violating *Shabbat* and that of intermarriage, on the grounds that the former is a personal transgression while the latter is an assault upon the integrity of the Jewish People as a whole. At the same time, however, the harsh reaction that halachah has to both clearly seems to emanate from the motivation of the sinner and not from the seriousness or extent of the transgression. Thus, just as a *mechallel Shabbat* whose disqualification as a Jew is explicit in the *poskim* need not be so deemed today, so an intermarried person who previously might have been excommunicated (if not de jure, then de facto) ought to have his case similarly reevaluated.

IV. It is important to emphasize what this line of argument should achieve and what it should not. It is not proposed that intermarried Jews ought to be fully enfranchised, for intermarriage is wrong.

There is no intent, moreover, to inveigh against those who do, and have, advocated the traditional hard line against intermarriage. In the past such a procedure was most appropriate, and is still so in many instances.

Rather what is proposed is that changed circumstances, and the nature of the relevant *halachot* themselves, offer a wider field of action to the rabbi in dealing with intermarried Jews than had hitherto been granted (or assumed). When such individuals come to the synagogues, depending upon the judgment of the rabbi, they need not be summarily rejected as "not our problem" but may be considered as part of *k'lal Yisrael.* The rabbi has leeway to count them as part of the minyan or merely to have them pray with the minyan. All rests not with a priori judgments but *l'fi re'ot eynei HaMoreh,* i.e., it is within the purview of each rabbi's judgment.[29] It may be argued, though, given the rampant nature of the problem and the relative innocence (Jewishly) of most of the offenders, that every Rav's calculations should take seriously into account the possibility of rescuing souls and preserving *k'lal Yisrael.*[30]

Addendum

Reference must be made to a collection of responsa that were written/reviewed and authorized by HaGaon HaRav Shaul Yisraeli and bear the written approbation of both Chief Rabbis of Israel, HaGaon HaRav Avraham Cahana Shapiro and HaRav Mordechai Eliyahu. Rav Yisraeli was the senior member of the Supreme Rabbinical Court of Israel, the *posek* for much of the religious Zionist world, a *Rosh Yeshivah* at Yeshivat Merkaz Harav and the *Rosh HaKollel* of Kollel Eretz Hemda, which trains outstanding *talmidei chachamim* to be *dayanim.*

In a collection of responsa entitled *She'elot U'Teshuvot B'Mareh Habezek* (Jerusalem 1991, p. 8), there is a question received from a rabbi in Santiago, Chile that (in part) concerned the feasibility of including an intermarried man in a minyan or of calling him up for an *aliyah.*

HaRav Yisraeli rules (Response 5, *Responsa B'Mareh HaBezek,* HaRav Shaul Yisraeli): A Jew who lives with a Gentile woman—regardless of whether or not he married her in a civil court—is not deemed married according to halachah. Indeed, living with her is consider a great sin. Nevertheless, great halachic authorities have ruled that one should not delegitimize such a person from inclusion in a minyan or from his being called to the Torah, unless he was specifically put in excommunication, which is not done in our day. Some (moreover) are stringent and do not permit such a Jew to receive an *aliyah* to the Torah.

Therefore, such a person may be called to the Torah after the seven obligatory people are called up to the Torah. (Free Translation)

Note a responsum of HaGaon HaRav Shlomo Kluger (*z"l*), which is found in *Responsa Tuv Ta'am V'Daat* (I, no. 229). The case involved a Jew who married a non-Jewish woman who subsequently gave birth to a daughter. The father came to the synagogue, was given an *aliyah*, and expressed his desire to bestow a Jewish name on his newborn daughter. The local Rav refused his request because the child was not Jewish. Evidently, a communal dispute regarding the Rav's ruling ensued. The case was submitted to Reb Shlomo Kluger for final adjudication. He, in turn, fully supported the Rav's ruling. He noted that since the child was not halachically Jewish, it was wrong to "name" her in the synagogue, since such action might generate the false impression that the child was Jewish. Furthermore, he asserts that the custom of giving the father an *aliyah* on the occasion of the birth of a child derives from the (now inoperative) need to bring a sacrifice in the *Bet HaMikdash* (*sh'yibaneh bimhaira b'yameinu, Amen.*). Yet such a custom is only relevant when the child is Jewish, hence, the *chiyuv aliyah* would be out of place in this context. In other contexts it might be appropriate, since a Jew who intermarries, concludes Reb Shlomo Kluger, is narcissistically wicked (*mumar letei'avon*) and not necessarily deemed a rebel against Judaism.

From this case we see that a person who was known to be intermarried was given an *aliyah* as a matter of course. The point at issue was the propriety of that *aliyah* being given on the unique occasion of his daughter's birth solely for naming purposes. There was no concern as to whether such a person could receive an *aliyah* at all. Thus, each Rav and/or synagogue may generate their own halachic policy on this matter.

Kabbalat Mitzvot At Conversion

QUESTION: What form of commitment must take place at a conversion?

RESPONSE: Halachic scholars have ruled that *kabbalat mitzvot*—the requirement for a potential convert to commit himself (or herself) to observe commandments—is a vital element of conversion. Indeed, should this aspect be lacking, then the entire conversion process is deemed invalid. Of concern, however, is a need for a definition of the particulars of *kabbalat mitzvot*. Namely, what specifically must transpire at a conversion? The actual requirement of *kabbalat mitzvot* also needs analysis.

I. Basic to the problem is that the Rambam rules that should *bet din* "neglect to inform" (the convert) of mitzvot and their punishments (should they be violated) the conversion is still valid (*Halachot I'surai B'ia*, ch. 13, Law 17). The Magid Mishna remarks that such a law for informing (the convert about) mitzvot is simply not essential (ibid.)

This suggests that, perhaps, the entire process of *kabbalat mitzvot* may not be important to conversion.

Rabbi Dovid Hoffman cites scholars (Beit Yitzchok, et al.) who distinguish between a commitment to observe mitzvot and knowledge of rewards and punishments of mitzvot. The latter is immaterial, while the former is vital to conversion. Yet, based upon the Magid Mishna's note that knowledge of mitzvot is nonessential to conversion, Rabbi Hoffman poses the question, "How can one commit himself to observe mitzvot if he does not know (anything) about commandments?" (*M'lamid L'Hoel, Yoreh Deah*, Responsum 87).

Rabbi Yechiel Yaakov Weinberg (the final successor to Rabbi Hoffman as Dean of the Hildesheimer Rabbinical Seminary in Berlin) notes the problem but makes no reference to the qualms expressed by Rabbi Hoffman. Citing the *Shulchan*

Aruch, he articulates the principle that *kabbalat mitzvot* is a commitment to assume the responsibility for observance: a commitment to observe commandments incumbent upon a Jew. This is vital to conversion. What is nonessential is the discussion of rewards and punishments of *mitzvot* (*Seridei Esh*, vol. 2, *Yoreh Deah*, Responsum 105). The assumption is that a commitment is invalid without a prior knowledge of mitzvot.

What is of interest is that Rabbi Hoffman is not willing to assume that it is only knowledge of rewards and punishments that is immaterial to a conversion. Indeed, a careful reading of the text of the Rambam and the *Shulchan Aruch* discloses a major distinction in law.

The Rambam rules a conversion valid even if "mitzvot and their punishments" were not noted by *bet din* (op cit.). The *Shulchan Aruch* states that should *bet din* neglect to inform the convert of the rewards of *mitzvot* and their punishments then the conversion is valid (*Yoreh Deah* 268:12).

In other words, both are dealing with completely distinct issues. Rabbi Weinberg relates to the wording of the *Shulchan Aruch*, while Rabbi Hoffman is concerned about the terminology of the Rambam. Indeed, Rabbi Weinberg cites his proof from the Codes.

What is the rationale behind the debate?

HaGaon R. Yosef Dov Solovietchik cites his father who noted that according to the Rambam, *kabbalat mitzvot* differs from *milah* and *tevilah* in that it need not be a specific ritual overtly performed during the conversion process. This does not mean it is immaterial to a proper conversion or that a conversion is valid even with its absence. No, *kabbalat mitzvot* is essential to halachicly legitimatize a conversion, yet it need not be manifested through ceremonial oral statements of commitment by a proselyte in the presence of *bet din*. Should *bet din* believe that the *ger* truly will observe Torah and commandments, such an assumption of *kabbalat mitzvot* for the *ger* is as valid as a ceremonial oral commitment. Yet, *tosafot* contend that such a presumption is not sufficient and that a specific ritual commitment must take place in the presence of *bet din* (see R. Yosef

Dov Soloveitchik, *B'Sod HaYachid V'HaYachad*, notes on page 389). Thus Rabbi Hoffman's question may be easily diffused. *Bet din* need not observe the ceremony of *kabbalat mitzvot*, yet, as long as *bet din* has the presumption that *kabbalat mitzvot* will, indeed take place—that is, the convert will, because of his nature, background, personality, etc., assume the responsibility to observe mitzvot—such is sufficient to validate the conversion. Such a presumption may be even if the convert is ignorant of Jewish law and mitzvot. As such, the convert need not make a commitment based upon ignorance. It is *bet din* that makes a judgment that the conversion will entail observance. *Kabbalat mitzvot* may, therefore, be either a formal commitment by the convert or a presumed future commitment judged by *bet din*.

It is apparent that the *Shulchan Aruch* disagrees with this position for it rules that lack of *kabbalat mitzvot* before a *bet din* of three (judges) and (the process transpiring) by day invalidates a conversion (*Yoreh Deah* 268:3). Now, if a conversion is invalid because the *bet din* lacked three judges at *kabbalat mitzvot*, it certainly would be invalid if *kabbalat mitzvot* was totally missing. The implication is that a presumption of *kabbalat mitzvot* is not sufficient. An actual ceremonial oral commitment must take place in the presence of *bet din*. This requirement for an oral commitment suggests a precondition of knowledge of basic commandments. As such, it is vital for a convert to be informed of mitzvot and customs prior to the conversion. Its absence definitely questions the validity of the commitment. For this reason the *Shulchan Aruch* delineates that a lack of knowledge of the rewards and punishments does not invalidate the conversion. For as long as there is a basic knowledge of mitzvot, commitment is valid even without a proper appreciation of specific rewards and punishments.

IIA. An alternate orientation may be developed from the notation of the Lubavitcher Rebbe who suggests that the Rambam delineates in his discussion of a *ger tzedek* (a righteous convert) a distinction between *kabbalat ol malchut shemayim*—the acceptance of the Yoke of Heaven—and *kabbalat mitzvot*—the commitment to observe commandments. The rationale is that a conversion procedure should simulate the original conversion of *k'lal Yisrael* at the revelation (see H'Admur of Lubavitch, "Sheva Mitzvot B'nai Noach," *Hapardes* [*Sivan* 5745, page 9]).

The Rambam's terminology manifests three distinct aspects of Judaism that must be conveyed to a potential convert.

1. "He is [to be] informed of the fundamental [principles] of the religion, namely, the [belief in] the unity of God and the prohibition of *avodah zarah*" (Rambam, *Isurei B'ia*, chap. 14, Law 2).

2. He is [to be] informed of some lenient and stringent mitzvot (ibid.).

3. He is [to be] informed of the punishments for violations of mitzvot (ibid.) as well as the reward for observance (Law 3).

(See also *Shulchan Aruch, Yoreh Deah* 268:2, which records the same three principles.)

The Magid Mishna notes that the first principle is not noted in the Talmud. Yet the Rambam included it, for such is basic to being a Jew. As such it appears that a potential convert must receive three tiers of information for commitment.

1. *Kabbalat ol malchut shemayim*—the acceptance of the Yoke of Heaven: the belief in God.

2. *Kabbalat mitzvot*—the commitment to observe mitzvot.

3. Reward and punishment—the need to know punishment and reward of mitzvot.

Accordingly, the Rambam may rule that *kabbalat mitzvot* and reward and punishment need not be orally discussed at a conversion, but, perhaps, *kabbalot ol malchut shemayim* cannot be presumed but must be orally committed. Indeed, the Rambam makes no reference to a conversion that lacks the first principle. This suggests an alternate theory for the Rambam. Namely, once *kabbalat ol malchut shemayim* is orally committed to *bet din*, then, and perhaps only then, may the other items be presumed by the *bet din*.

The *Shulchan Aruch*, however, may concede that a discussion of reward and punishment are not necessary, yet mandate *kabbalat mitzvot*, which of necessity must include *kabbalat ol malchut shemayim*. Thus, even the Rambam may require of the convert an oral commitment in the presence of *bet din* to believe in the unity of God.

IIB. The Talmud (*Yevamot* 4b) derives the rituals required by conversion from items noted at the conversion of *k'lal Yisrael* at revelation.

It is important to note that at revelation the Jewish people made the following commitments:

They said, *Na'aseh v'nishma*—"We will do and hear" (Exodus 24:7). This verse is traditionally interpreted to mean first a commitment to observe *mitzvot* and subsequently a commitment to learn Torah (see *Bet Halevi, Parshat Mishpatim*).

As such, two major laws regarding conversion may be derived from this verse.

1. The original commitment of *k'lal Yisrael* was to obey the commandments of God even prior to knowledge of the details of such commandments. (This diffuses the question of Rabbi Hoffman previously noted.) It suggests that commitment prior to knowledge simulates the conversion at Mount Sinai. Accordingly, such a commitment is valid for conversion purposes.

2. *K'lal Yisrael* made an oral commitment to observe mitzvot. A presumption of commitment did not occur. To the extent that general conversions must simulate Sinai, so too must an oral commitment transpire. While the Rambam may require such oral commitment only for *ol malchut shemayim*, the *Shulchan Aruch* obligates this commitment even for *mitzvot*.

Converts: Halachic Orphans

QUESTION: What is the source for the talmudic axiom "When a convert immerses in a *mikvah*, he is comparable to a newborn child" (*Yevamot* 48b)?

RESPONSE: Of concern is whether this rule is derived from Scripture, or is it an ancient tradition transmitted through the Oral Torah? Chatam Sofer noted that though he toiled to seek an explicit source for this ruling, his research was inconclusive (Commentary Chatam Sofer, *Avodah Zarah* 64).

HaGaon Rav Meir Simcha contends that *chumash* itself clearly establishes the rule. Subsequent to the revelation on Mount Sinai, the Torah says: "Return ye to your tents" (Deut. 5:27). This was a declaration that all men should return to their wives, for biblical terminology utilizes the word "tent" as a synonym for "wife" (see *Shabbat* 87a, which contends that Moshe decreed, prior to the revelation, that the men should separate themselves from their wives—thus this verse was his biblical decree permitting each man to return to his wife). Yet such a process poses halachic problems. Indeed, it is known that prior to the revelation many men married women who would not be permitted to them according to biblical law. For example, Amram, Moshe's father, married Yocheved, his aunt. Such a marriage is prohibited according to Scripture. Logic presumes that numerous such marriages must have transpired. Yet the Torah states, "Return ye to your tents." This is a general permission for all men to return to their wives. No group was eliminated from this general declaration, yet numerous problematic marriages must have existed. The rationale must be that at Mount Sinai all Israel underwent conversion and were classified as newborn children. Consequently, even past incestuous relations were annulled due to this newborn status (*Meshech Chachmah*, *Parshat Vaetchanan*).

Of interest, is that the Baal HaTurim presents an overt source for the concept that a convert is deemed "newborn." The Torah says: *Lo ta'teh mishpat ger yatom* ("Do not twist the rights of a *ger yatom*") (Deut. 24:17). The Hebrew word *ger* means either "stranger" or a "convert." The word *yatom* means "orphan." Commenting on this phrase the Baal HaTurim notes that there is no connecting letter (no vowel meaning "and") signifying that the *ger* is someone distinct from the orphan. Indeed the Torah is not saying that one should prevent injustice to both a *ger* and a second person who is an orphan. Rather, the Torah is emphasizing that the *ger* is an orphan. Yet such is not necessarily always the case. A convert may have one or more parents. Since, however, the Torah does describe the convert as an orphan, it must be because of the principle that every convert has the status of a newborn child. Accordingly, every convert is a halachic orphan and must receive special attention.

Delegitimatizing a Dayan *to Serve on a* Bet Din *for Conversion*

QUESTION: May a rabbi known for piety and observance of *mitzvot*, who also is a Torah scholar, yet serves as the spiritual leader of a nonhalachic synagogue (namely, a Conservative or Liberal Temple) serve on a *bet din* for conversion purposes?

RESPONSE: The issue relates to a halachic concern as to whether the nonhalachic synagogue affiliation taints an otherwise suitable rabbi even when he performs rituals according to halachic standards. The following is not a polemic but, rather, a halachic discourse.

Sanhedrin 26a

> Rabbi Chiya ben Zarmuki and Rabbi Shimon ben Yehozadak once went to Asia to intercalate the year. They were met by Resh Lakish, who joined them, saying, "I will come and see their procedure." On the way, he (Resh Lakish) saw a man ploughing and remarked to them, "A *kohen* is ploughing?" [I.e., to the extent that it was a sabbatical year (*shevi'it*) such action was prohibited.] But they replied, "Can he not say: I am an imperial servant on the estate?" [I.e., he was merely

working on a Gentile estate. To the extent that the land belonged to non-Jews, its ploughing would be permitted (see Rashi).] Further on he saw a man pruning a tree and again observed, (why) is a *kohen* pruning? [I.e., such action is also prohibited.] But, they demured, "he might say: I need [the twigs] to make a bale (*akkel*) for the wine press [a legitimate purpose]." "The heart knows whether it is for *akkel* (the bale) or *akalalot* (perverseness)," he retorted. . . . They said: "He is a troublesome person." [I.e., Resh Lakish is ready to find fault with everything.] . . . and so on reaching their destination, they ascended to the upper chamber [the roof] and removed the ladder [to prevent Resh Lakish from following them]. He [Resh Lakish] went before Rav Yochanan and asked: "Are people suspected of trespassing sabbatical laws qualified to intercalate the year?" [I.e., anyone who serves as an advocate for the wicked should be classified as wicked. See Rashi.] But on second thought, he said: "This presents no difficulty for there is a similar case of three cowherds upon whose calculations the Rabbis relied."

Subsequently, however, he said: "There is no comparison between the two cases; there [by the cowherds] it was the Rabbis who eventually decided and declared the year intercalated, whereas here it is a confederacy of the wicked (*kesher resha'im*) and such may not be counted." [I.e., a *bet din* must have a specific number of judges. Wherever a *bet din* is classified as a *kesher resha'im* they are not counted towards the minimum number. See Rashi.]

Rav Yochanan replied: "That is a misfortune [that you called them wicked; see Rashi]".

When they [Rabbi Chiyya and Rabbi Shimon] came before Rav Yochanan, they complained: "He described us as cowherds and you made no objection whatever." Rabbi Yochanan answered: "Even had he called you shepherds, what could I have said?"

What is [the reference to] a confederacy of wicked men? It is as follows: Shavna expounded [the law before thirteen myriads (Great Men)] . . . When Sennacherib [King of Assyria 705–681 B.C.E.] besieged Jerusalem, Shavna wrote

> a note, which he shot on an arrow [into the enemy's camp declaring] "Shavna and his followers are willing to conclude peace; Hezekiah and his followers are not." . . . So Hezekiah was afraid and said: "Perhaps, Heaven forbid, the mind of the Holy One Blessed Be He, is with the majority [who were with Shavna] and since they wish to surrender, we must do likewise." Thereupon, the Prophet came and reassured him . . . that it is a confederacy of the wicked, and as such cannot be counted [for the purpose of a decision; i.e., the multitudes were with Shavna and not to be calculated so as to provide a majority opinion].)

HaRav Aharon Soloveitchik derives from this text the ruling that once a person is part of a *kesher resha'im*, he loses legal standing and cannot subsequently be included in a *bet din*. Shavna, for example, was considered one of the great scholars of his generation (a *gadol hador*) (see *Sanhedrin* 36a). Yet, since Shavna associated with a *kesher resha'im*, even he could not sit on a *bet din*. Resh Lakish wished to classify the two sages as belonging to a *kesher resha'im* in that they sought (excessively) to defend sinners. The Talmud rules that Resh Lakish was wrong: the rabbinic sages were not to be classified as *kesher resha'im*. But, anyone who would indeed be validly classified as a member of *kesher resha'im* would definitely have no halachic standing as part of a *bet din*. As such, reasons Rav Soloveitchik, even a rabbi who is learned in all aspects of Torah and observant of all mitzvot, but who is a member of the Conservative Rabbinic and Synagogue movement, is definitely to be deemed a member of *kesher resha'im* and unfit to serve as a member of a *bet din*. This unsuitability is not because of lack of scholarship or inability to observe halachic procedures. The legal classification of *kesher resha'im* is one that simply delegalizes standing to serve as a member of a rabbinic court. Consequently, any conversion emanating from a *bet din* on which such a person serves as a member is totally invalid. The conversion rituals must be redone, even the *berachot* must be rechanted (Rav Aharon Soloveitchik, *Hepardes*, *Choveret* 2, *Shana* 61, p. 18).

Analysis of Rav Soloveitchik's position, however, demonstrates that it is not necessarily supported by logical inference nor by talmudic citation.

According to Rav Soloveitchik, a Torah-observant rabbi, well-versed in all aspects of talmudic and halachic scholarship, who is also a card-carrying member of the Conservative Movement, becomes—because of such membership—*pasul* (unfit) to subsequently sit upon any *bet din*, even should the *bet din* rule on the basis of halachic principles.

Rav Soloveitchik cites two supportive citations. First, Shavna was definitely a great Torah sage (*Sanhedrin* 36a); his problem was that he was associated with *kesher resha'im* (*Sanhedrin* 26a). The implication of such logic is that Shavna's sole sin was his association with *kesher resha'im*. But that is simply not the case. *Tosafot* suggests that the talmudic citation listing Shavna as a great Torah sage should be deleted from the text. Why? Shavna was deemed a *rasha* (a wicked person) and was not to be granted legal standing (see *Tosafot, Sanhedrin* 36a). In other words, Shavna's sin was not that he was a member of *kesher resha'im*—an association with a wicked person (a *rasha*)—but that he was a *rasha* himself. Accordingly, his presence disqualified the other members associated with him. It's a sort of domino effect of delegitimatization. The *rasha*'s presence invalidates the entire proceedings even should Torah principles and halachah rules guide the process. But, should the non-*rasha* members of such a federation actively involve themselves in a Torah proceeding apart, distinct, and separate from any presence of a *rasha*, it appears illogical to presume that the previous association with the *rasha* would subsequently taint the members for life. *Kesher resha'im* is a principle that requires the *rasha*'s presence to be operational. To extend its application, even without the *rasha*'s presence, to subsequently disqualify non-*rasha* members from all Torah proceedings, is a theory not supported by the Talmud. The concept is derived from Shavna's incident. Accordingly, it must relate to Shavna's circumstance, which definitely manifests the presence of the *rasha*.

The so-called second proof of Rav Soloveitchik is also

flawed. Resh Lakish charged that the *bet din* set up by the two sages was a *kesher resha'im.* Why? What sin did Resh Lakish allege that they committed? Rashi says that the sages were suspected of violating sabbatical laws, for they served as defense advocates for the wicked (*Sanhedrin* 26a). Thus, Resh Lakish castigated the rabbis for being actual sinners. That is, Resh Lakish assumed that those who excessively defend sinners were to be categorized as sinners themselves. Moreover, once the rabbis were so classified, Resh Lakish presumed that their presence in a *bet din* would invalidate the entire process because of the principle of *kesher resha'im.* In other words, the castigation occurred prior to their formal convening of a *bet din.* Yet Resh Lakish was ruled to be wrong; a defense of "so-called sinners" does not merit being castigated as a *rasha.*

Thus, there is no talmudic textual support for Rav Soloveitchik's extreme position. Namely, there is simply no precedence for his ruling that a person involved in a *kesher resha'im* association, who is a Torah scholar and scrupulous in observance, is deemed invalid to sit in a subsequent *bet din* that is set up according to halachah.

It is important to yet further hone the rule of *kesher resha'im.* Does it pertain, for example, only to matters of a *bet din*? Or is it applicable to any membership association with *resha'im*? To the extent that Shavna's case is the classic example of *kesher resha'im,* logic dictates that the parameters of this principle must be manifested in Shavna's situation. The Talmud rules that Hezekiah was disturbed over the fact that Shavna had a greater number of followers than he. Thus, he worried that the Almighty would join forces with the majority position and seek peace with Sennacherib, which was contrary to Hezekiah's position. To this the Talmud decides that Shavna's multitude was a *kesher resha'im* and consequently his numbers had no legal standing (*Sanhedrin* 26a). A simple reading of the case suggests that *kesher resha'im* applies to any association with *resha'im.*

Of interest is that Rashi notes that Shavna's yeshivah was greater than Hezekiah's yeshivah (*Sanhedrin* 36a). Yet, why is it necessary to designate Shavna's followers as part of his Yeshivah? What is wrong with merely stating that Shavna had more people subscribing to his political position than did Hezekiah? Rashi may be pinpointing an integral element of the concept of *kesher resha'im.* Perhaps it applies only to a *bet din* situation. A general rule is that one *bet din* cannot annul the ruling of another (*bet din*) unless it is greater in wisdom and *numbers* (*Megillah* 2a). From this we see that numbers play a significant role in establishing the rule of a *bet din.* Hezekiah's concern was not of a plebiscite that placed him in the minority. It was that the decision of Shavna's *bet din* to seek peace had greater strength of numbers than did his personal *bet din*, and thus Shavna's *bet din* might have greater validity. As such *kesher resha'im* may simply not be applicable to a non-*bet din* condition. In a non-*bet din* sphere of concern, dealing with nonhalachic issues, perhaps *kesher resha'im* may not be operational at all. In other words, in an association wherein numbers of a majority view have no bearing on halachah, then the fact that such an association lacks halachic legal standing is superfluous. *Kesher resha'im* is not an issue in any condition wherein numbers are not germane.

Thus three rules may be derived from the citation in *Sanhedrin* 26a:

1. *Kesher resha'im* requires the presence of a *rasha* to be operational.
2. *Kesher resha'im* may be a principle only operational in a rabbinic court system.
3. Defense of sinners does not automatically merit the stigma of being classified as a *rasha.*

Caveat

The above presentation relates solely to the issue of whether a synagogue affiliation automatically halachically taints a Rav from rendering halachic *Din Torah* decisions. It does not render judgment concerning the propriety or desirability of imposing precautionary safeguards (*gezeirot*) to sustain Orthodox viability.

The Jewish Attitude Toward Converts: A Critique of the Historical Theory

QUESTION: Did adverse historical conditions alter rabbinic legal orientations to conversion?

RESPONSE: In recent years, numerous studies have been recorded concerning the high rate of Jews marrying outside their faith. To the extent that in such instances the Jew frequently abandons his faith and adopts the religion or non-religion of his spouse, these studies have alarmed the Jewish community and provoked debate concerning the future of American Jewish communal life.

An interesting and unique means of securing vitality to Jewish communal life has been envisioned by Morris Adler. He believed that many people will find in Judaism the form of spiritual satisfaction that will meet their religious needs and, as a result, converts to Judaism will increase in future years.[31] Using conversion as a vehicle to offset losses through intermarriage is a theory that requires much analysis and investigation in order to bring it out of the aura of vision into the reality of an active program.

Basic to the problem is the attitude of the rabbinate. Conversion lies within the scope of religious law and the rabbinate generally has a formal negative orientation toward aggressive and even non-aggressive conversion.

Milton Himmelfarb maintained that most rabbis are unenthusiastic toward converts for three reasons:

1. Conversion is not traditional.
2. A would-be convert is probably disturbed.
3. Jews should seek to care for their own before involving themselves with others.

He answers each by contending:

1. Oppressors of Judaism made proselytizing a capital crime and, therefore, not traditional.

2. Our imports are better than our exports.

3. Success with conversion would stimulate the morale of many Jews.

His final plea is that any effort to seek converts must be prompted by a forceful initiative from the rabbinate.[32]

To the extent that the act of conversion is a religious ritual prescribed by Jewish law and custom, it appears that a study of the origins and development of the rituals and attitudes toward converts would be necessary in assessing a proper understanding of the Jewish attitude toward this matter. At present, no definitive study of the subject has been made. All information is scattered in fragmentary sources. Indeed, while it is the prevalent opinion that Jews frown upon conversion, it is not clear how this attitude has developed nor whether it is at all accurate. Since, moreover, popular debate seeks in part to determine a means of offsetting demographic losses to Jews, it is necessary to trace and analyze the Jewish view toward conversion.

Disregarding the utilitarian and functional concerns, the material itself requires scholarly research. This essay will serve as an introduction to the subject matter by providing sources of information, discussion, and problems for research concerning the overt conflicting accounts recorded in rabbinic literature relating to converts and conversion. The following sources will serve to illustrate the basic problem.

In ancient, traditional, legal rabbinic accounts one may find numerous positive statements relating to converts.

1. A person who converts is considered (as pure) as a newborn child.[33]

2. The conversion of a person who converts for other than religious reasons is considered valid.[34]

3. A proselyte may serve as a judge to decide monetary matters.[35]

4. One is legally prohibited from vexing a convert by reminding him of his past.[36]

In the Midrash[37] and Aggadah[38] the high reward for converts is also quite noticeably recorded.

1. A proselyte who studies the Torah is comparable to the High Priest.[39]

2. Because of the expectation for proselytes, Abraham was not circumcised till the age of ninety-nine. Had Abraham been circumcised at the age of twenty, no convert would have subjected himself to this ordeal at an advanced age. The Lord therefore purposely waited with His command so that the door to proselytes would always be open.[40]

3. In Paradise, there are several thrones of gold, silver, and precious stones. The throne of silver is reserved for the righteous proselytes.[41]

4. Hezekiah prayed to the Lord to add years to his life for the sake of his ancestors who built the Temple and brought many proselytes into the Jewish fold.[42]

These rabbinic references concerning proselytes may be traced back to prophetic and biblical[43] sources. Prophetic and biblical literature is replete with high praise and consideration for converts. Speaking in the name of the Lord, reproach, punishment, and consternation is continually preached to those who vex or oppress the *ger* (interpreted to mean "proselyte") by such prophets as Jeremiah,[44] Zechariah,[45] Malachi,[46] and Ezekiel.[47]

These prophets' social utterances are basically extensions and reiterations of the numerous formal laws set forth in the Pentateuch to protect the religious legal rights and personal emotional feelings of proselytes.

The Bible in numerous areas directs itself to the problem of the stranger who joins the Jewish community.

1. One law shall be to him that is homeborn and unto the stranger that sojourneth among you.[48]

2. And a stranger shalt thou not wrong, neither shalt thou oppress him; for ye were strangers in the land of Egypt.[49]

3. And a stranger shalt thou not oppress; for ye know the heart of the stranger, seeing ye were strangers in the land of Egypt.[50]

4. And whatsoever man shall there be of the house of Israel, or of the strangers that sojourn among them, that eateth any manner of blood, I will set My Face against that soul that eateth blood and will cut him off from among his people.[51]

5. And thou shalt not glean thy vineyard, neither shalt thou gather the fallen fruit of thy vineyard; thou shalt leave them for the poor and for the stranger.[52]

6. The stranger that sojourneth with you shall be unto you as the homeborn among you, and thou shalt love him as thyself; for ye were strangers in the land of Egypt.[53]

So concerned is the Bible for the care of the *ger*[54] that its prohibition against harsh treatment and wrong attitudes is repeated constantly.[55]

Yet, despite these biblical statutes, prophetic messages, and rabbinic utterances of praise, protection, and interest in both converts and proselytizing, a strong case may be developed to show a most negative and limited legal and moral rabbinic attitude toward proselytes.

The following limited view toward proselytes may be noted in rabbinic law.

1. The daughter of a proselyte man and woman is prohibited from marrying a *kohen*.[56]

2. One is not permitted to appoint a leader over a community unless his mother was a born Jewess.[57]

3. Proselytes never received a share in the land of Israel.[58]

4. The one hundred shekels of silver given to the father of a woman who was falsely slandered is not required unless the woman was both conceived and born a Jewess. A woman whose mother converted after becoming pregnant is excluded.[59]

In the nonlegal midrashic and aggadic accounts a negative viewpoint toward converts may also be noted.

1. Proselytes . . . withhold the coming of the Messiah.[60]

2. Proselytes who followed the Jews out of the land of Egypt were responsible for the golden calf.[61]

3. Evil will befall he who accepts converts.[62]

4. Do not believe a proselyte till twenty-four generations have lapsed since his conversion.[63]

Comment

Commenting upon the apparent contradictory statements relating to proselytes, some scholars view the matter in terms of an historical perspective. The negative orientations are a result of disenchantment with proselytes due to many forsaking the Jewish fold and attempting to slander Jewish beliefs and followers.[64] References in praise of proselytes are considered to be early sources while those with negative attitudes are maintained to be later statements. The negative accounts, moreover, are believed to have been made in times of oppression. Should the status of the Jewish nation not have been so disgraced and disdained, it is felt that a harmonious and peaceful relationship between born Jews and proselytes would have developed.[65]

It is believed that an analysis that maintains that the historicity of certain adverse conditions, namely, disenchantment with proselytes and adverse political decrees, influenced Jewish traditional thought to such a degree that law and legend were changed from a positive to a negative viewpoint is not entirely accurate in dealing with the subject matter nor in answering the overt contradictions. Though it is quite plausible that this historical viewpoint has some validity in one area, it is highly questionable in another. In terms of the homiletic and aggadic statements of the rabbis, a favorable case may be developed maintaining that the negative remarks concerning proselytes were a result of political and social conditions. The negative attitudes were but expressions that gave vent to particular common practices of the day. They were means of safeguarding the fold from actions and attitudes that might have jeopardized the Jewish nation. Yet, in the sphere of Jewish law it is extremely questionable that historical conditions brought about prejudicial, limited laws concerning proselytes. It is highly unlikely that the total outlook of the rabbis was adversely influenced to change Jewish law as a result of political or social conditions. This assumption is based upon the following premises.

I. If negative orientations toward converts are a result of

historical developments, it appears problematic that both positive and negative accounts are formally harmonized side by side into law.

According to the historical view, should not limited constricting laws have an early account of a liberal approach to the *same law*? Should not early law be completely positive and favorable to proselytes and later laws be of a negative nature?

It may be shown that early legal prescriptions are of a most limited nature: (1) The offspring of male and female proselytes is forbidden from marrying a *kohen*.[66] The opposite is not stated. (2) It is recorded that proselytes never received a share in the land of Israel.[67] Nowhere is a more liberal interpretation of this aspect mentioned. (3) When the daughter of proselytes is falsely slandered, the accusor is not obligated to pay one hundred shekels.[68] No positive statement giving consideration to the child of proselytes in such a matter is recorded. (4) In questions relating to whom shall be saved in periods of danger, a bastard has precedence over a proselyte.[69]

In none of the above-quoted laws does one find a more liberal viewpoint. Thus we find early law of a limited nature, without corresponding laws presenting a liberal viewpoint. These statutes are recorded into a body of laws that contain liberal attitudes towards proselytes. According to the historical view, it is difficult to explain the early so-called discriminatory laws.

The fact, moreover, that both humane and constricted laws pertaining to proselytes are found side by side in talmudic codes suggests that at least in the minds of the rabbis both were compatible. Some rationale needs to be presented as to how the rabbis who presented harsh decrees understood the liberal biblical and prophetic injunctions.

It should be noted, moreover, that there are instances of overt contradiction embodied in ancient law. In the Hammurabi code, for example, one may note primitive barbaric statutes[70] retained side by side with more humane decrees.[71] Commenting upon this matter, Morris Jastrow maintained that in ancient times a law was considered a divine decree—an oracular decision of a deity. Since all decisions in a dispute were rendered by the deity, they were, therefore, binding for all times. While these laws could not be annulled, various modifications were introduced that practically changed their intent. Moreover, since these modifications were in the form of emendations superimposed upon the original law, the old was formally retained by the side of the new.[72]

Edward Chiera views the contradictions in a different fashion. He believes that one must look to the early history of the Babylonians for a proper understanding of the laws. His contention is that Hammurabi's immediate Semitic ancestors were only slightly civilized when they came to Babylon and entrenched themselves in a civilization radically different from their own. Hammurabi, in his endeavor to establish his statutes as the law of the land, had either to sanction or reject the differing practices that had arisen between these different cultures. On the one hand were his Semitic followers, whose laws were primitive and extremely stringent, and on the other were the interests of the civilized group mainly of a non-Semitic culture. The statutes, therefore, are an attempt to conciliate opposing groups without causing too much hostility from either side.[73]

From a cursory point of view, one might suggest that both Jastrow's and Chiera's theories may be applicable to an understanding of the halachic attitude toward proselytes, namely, that harsh and humane laws are retained side by side because biblical law could not be nullified. Thus, later modifications were superimposed upon original laws and retained together with the early declarations. In addition, the retention of both forms of law was a conciliatory effort to assimilate various cultural orientations toward proselytes. While both theories are certainly plausible pertaining to an understanding of Hammurabi's code, it is felt that they may not be easily transferred to the arena of talmudic law.

Talmudic or traditional Jewish law differs from Hammurabi's code in that it seeks to interpret biblical law. The Bible serves as the guide or standard for all legal discussions, and all rabbinical decrees or interpretations must be compatible with biblical law or traditional practices. Whenever a law is discussed that appears to contradict a biblical passage, some means of harmonizing the biblical quote with the law discussed is presented.

An example of this is the talmudic debate concerning the proper statement to be made before a bride. The school of Hillel maintains that one must be full of praise for the bride's charm and beauty. Immediately the problem is posed concerning a bride not noted for her beauty. If one praises her beauty, is one not violating the biblical injunction against telling a lie? The implication is that a falsehood or "white lie" is always wrong, regardless of the circumstances. The Talmud answers this question by maintaining that the biblical injunction against telling a lie does not apply when the withholding of the complete truth would create family harmony and peace.[74] Thus, the original biblical intent is qualified and limited.

Yet, in discussions and interpretations of limited or so-called harsh laws relating to proselytes, the Talmud never questions the obvious contradiction of the biblical statement "One law shall be to him that is homeborn and unto the *ger* (stranger) that sojourneth among you."[75] Indeed, whenever the rabbis limit the rights of proselytes no question is directed to the numerous biblical quotes demanding love to strangers, which the rabbis themselves interpret to refer to proselytes. This implies that all so-called discriminatory laws were thought, by the rabbis, to be in accordance with biblical law, suggesting that the apparent contradictions were not viewed by the rabbis as such. To the extent that they did not view the matter as replete with contradictions, it appears plausible that the rabbinic attitude combined both harsh and liberal laws in a unified system. Thus, to say that laws could not be nullified and, therefore, later emendations stood together with outdated statutes or that the views display conciliatory attitudes toward proselytes does not fit into the system of talmudic law.

In talmudic law, the question must be posed as to how seemingly conflicting statements harmonize with each other, ancient traditions, or biblical phrases. To state that the different viewpoints recorded concerning proselytes are results of historical conditions fails to explain how the talmudic rabbis, according to their own ways of thinking, harmonized both views into a holistic body of law.

II. Another objection to the historical point of view is that Jewish law never completely nullified a general religious law or enacted decrees against it as a result of oppression or political conditions. Indeed, instead of nullifying the law, Jews have always strengthened their position in the face of a frontal attack by demanding full devotion and strict observances.

The Talmud relates and states as law that if there is any royal decree forbidding the practice of Judaism, one is obligated to suffer martyrdom rather than transgress even a minor precept.[76] Moreover, the rabbis maintain that if Jews wore a distinctive shoe strap and heathens did not so dress, it was obligatory to incur martyrdom rather than change one's shoe strap and give up a distinctive Jewish custom under force.[77] With such a law, whose purpose was to prevent heathens from weakening Jewish observance and morale by political decrees,[78] it appears quite improbable that the talmudic rabbis reversed their positive position concerning proselytes as a result of harsh decrees.

It should be noted that the Talmud does relate instances wherein Jews forsook the observance of certain commandments as a result of political decrees forbidding such observance. It is recorded that the Romans made it a capital crime to observe the commandment of phylacteries and that the Jews did not incur martyrdom for this commandment.[79] This case is said not to conflict with the law requiring martyrdom when decrees demand even a change of the lace of shoes because in the latter case, Jews were identifiable by a specific color of shoelace and, to change the Jewish attire and adopt the heathen one would make the Jew lose apparent observable Jewish identity and, therefore martyrdom was required instead. In the case of phylacteries, the Jew not publicly wearing them could not be pointed out as one who bowed to heathen decrees, but rather as a person who, in the privacy of his home, had already observed the commandment.[80]

Whatever the reason for not incurring martyrdom under the decree making it a capital crime to wear phylacteries, nowhere do the rabbis of the Talmud praise the Jews for not wearing phylacteries and saving their lives from a penalty of death. Indeed, just the opposite position is taken. It is stated that as a result of Jews not submitting their lives for the observance of phylacteries, the commandment will always be feebly observed.[81] Nowhere is it recorded that as a result of harsh oppressive acts the rabbis permanently eliminated the observance of any commandment or religious custom. In no record is found rabbinical statements speaking against the entire concept of phylacteries because of negative decrees. At no time do we find the rabbis denouncing the concept of phylacteries because the people did not observe correctly the commandment.

Assuming that Jewish involvement with rites of conversion would be considered a capital crime, it appears logical that this case would be more similar to the case of phylacteries than to the one involving the change of a shoe strap. The Jew not involving himself with missionary practices may be one who has not the opportunity to do so, and not one admitting to heathen laws. As a result, it would be logical to assume that martyrdom would not be obligatory. But why would it be necessary to give in to heathens by limiting the entire concept of conversion? Would this not be alien to the talmudic mind?

On the other hand, if missionary work is a cardinal aspect of Judaism, would not martyrdom be considered obligatory in such a case? If the Jews considered the spread of the belief in the religion one of their basic roles, would not the rabbis show devotion to their mission in times of oppression, rather than submission? Does it not seem more logical to assume that the spread of Judaism and missionary work among heathens would be more important than a meaningless change of a shoe strap?

In addition, it may be shown that political pressures had no effect upon religious interpretations of scriptures. It is recorded that Rabbi Simon Bar Yohai, a student of Rabbi Akiva,[82] spoke harshly against the Romans. A converted Jew heard the lecture and made Bar Yohai's words public. As a result, the Romans heard of the rabbi's statement[83] and Bar Yohai had to flee to a cave to protect his life.[84] This rabbi, who certainly felt the brunt of Roman oppression as a result of a proselyte, speaks of proselytes in a most glowing and positive fashion. He says, "Proselytes are beloved by the Lord."[85] Nowhere is it recorded that he changed his opinions of proselytes as a result of personal experiences.

The rejection of the historical viewpoint suggests that research is yet necessary to develop a viable theory for the numerous contradictions noted in rabbinic literature concerning converts. The major concern should be the realization that scholars should enter into the mind of the talmudist and view the issues from such a perspective. This means that an attempt should be made to discern the inner structure of talmudic social and religious orientations and to construct a viable holistic theory within such a frame of reference. The biases of modern values should not be utilized nor presumed to have existed in the past. The vehicle for research should be the constant probing of the following question: "How would a talmudist living in his own age have viewed the problem?"

Basically, this mode of research utilizes the insights of the discipline called the Sociology of Knowledge. It contends that the realm of ideas and substructure of society are closely intertwined and interrelated with each other. Each culture has its own perspective on truth. Each culture has within it some means of answering its own inner contradictions and problems. Thus, any modern theory and criticism concerning the Jewish attitude toward converts must await a prior understanding of how the talmudic scholars themselves viewed the issue.

Part III

Shabbat, *Holidays*, *and* Kiddush

Invitations that May Generate Shabbat *Violations*

QUESTION: Is it proper to invite Jews to a synagogue service or private event on *Shabbat* if they will probably violate the *Shabbat* in order to attend?

RESPONSE: At issue is whether the person extending the invitation violates Torah standards by inducing another to, for example, ride on *Shabbat* because of the invitation.

Mai'sit U'Maidiach

Mai'sit u'maidiach is the term used to describe the sin of inciting another to commit idol worship (namely, *avodah zarah*—apostasy). The sin is classified as a capital crime. Of interest is that the Talmud says that in a capital case, the judges of Sanhedrin (themselves) put forward the best defense for the defendant even should the defendant himself not offer a viable defense. In other words, the Sanhedrin always presents arguments to in some way demonstrate that the defendant was not guilty or culpable of the sin committed. This general rule, says the Gemorah, does not apply to the sin of *mai'sit u'maidiach*, however. In a case of incitement to *avodah zarah*, the judges do not help with the defense of the defendant. Accordingly, should the judges be aware of a rational defense that could exonerate the defendant yet the defendant does not himself advance such an argument, the judges do not intervene by suggesting the best defense.

This rule is noted as being derived from the case of the original serpent (*machash hakadmoni*) who incited Eve to eat the forbidden fruit from the tree of knowledge. The Talmud contends that there was available a plea that could have exonerated the serpent, namely, when one is commanded by a master or Rebbe and then this is contravened by a directive presented by a student, logically one should follow the dictates of the master and not those of the disciple. Accordingly, the serpent should have advanced this argument. He should have noted that Adam and Eve were commanded by God not to eat the forbidden fruit. The fact that he, the serpent, intimated otherwise should not have had any impact upon Eve. She should have harkened to the command of God and not obeyed the words of the serpent. Yet the Bible notes that the serpent was punished. This means the serpent did not advance the above-noted defense, nor did anyone else. Why did no one present this defense? This teaches us that when a person is on trial for the sin of *mai'sit u'maidiach*, they are on their own. Should they fail to provide a good defense, it is not brought forth to help their case (*Sanhedrin* 29a).

Of concern to HaGaon Reb Moshe Feinstein (*z"l*) was that the sin of the serpent in the Garden of Eden was not a sin of apostasy or *avodah zarah*. It was, rather, the sin of eating of fruit prohibited by God. Accordingly, it appears difficult to derive from the biblical incident support for any law relating to *mai'sit*, which exclusively is the sin of incitement to commit *avodah zarah*.

Because of this question, HaGaon HaRav Moshe (*z"l*) developed the position that the prohibition against *mai'sit* is a general sin not limited to cases of *avodah zarah*. Any incitement of another to commit a sin is a violation of Jewish law, regardless of the type of sin transgressed. The distinction is that the sin of "incitement" is punishable by a *bet din* only in cases of *avodah zarah*. However, from a heavenly account (*min hashamayim*) all incitement to sin (even to violate *Shabbat*) is a transgression. For this reason the Talmud derives the general rule that a *bet din* does not advance a defense for a person accused of the sin of incitement from the biblical story of the Garden of Eden. Any case in which one incites others to commit a sin is a violation of the biblical command.

Based upon the above analysis HaGaon HaRav Moshe (*z"l*) rules that an invitation to *daven* in a synagogue on *Shabbat* made to a person who can only attend (due to the distance of his residence) by violating *Shabbat* (namely, driving to *shul*), is a classic case of *mai'sit,* which is forbidden by Jewish law. In the event, says Rav Moshe (*z"l*) the person has an opportunity to attend without driving, then the above prohibition is not operational[86] (see Iggrot Moshe, *Orech Chayyim,* vol. 1, *Siman* 99, pp. 159–160).

The basis for this novel halachic approach appears to be the propriety of considering the sin of eating from the forbidden fruit as an example of *mai'sit.* Should this concern be defused, then there would be no sources to substantiate the position that any act that incites another to commit any sin is a violation of the biblical prohibition against *mai'sit.*

Of interest is that the Margolit HaYam (*Sanhedrin* 29a) poses the same question as that of HaGaon Rav Moshe (*z"l*), namely, that the sin in the Garden of Eden should not be classified as a form of *mai'sit.* The incident had nothing to do with apostasy. His answer was that in the Garden of Eden only one Heavenly command was operational. As such, the violation of that singular mitzvah was akin to apostasy. When there is only one mitzvah and that is transgressed, it is a form of *avodah zarah.* The sin, therefore, had overtones of renunciation and was classified as a grievous violation of the word of God.

Accordingly, acts that incite others to commit the sin of violating *Shabbat,* for example, would never be comparable to the sin in the Garden of Eden and would therefore not violate the principle of *mai'sit.* According to the theory of Margolit HaYam, *mai'sit* has no relevance to the propriety of inviting a Jew to a synagogue in a case wherein the Jew lives too far away to attend without driving a car and violating *Shabbat.*

***Lifnai Iver*—Biblical**

The Torah specifically prohibits inducing, inciting, or contributing to the sin of another. It is written: "One should not put a stumbling block before a blind man"—*Lifnai iver lo titain michshol* (Leviticus 19:14). Tradition has it that the Torah here deals not only with one who is physically blind—indeed, anyone who even simply prepares the way, or enables another to sin, is also guilty of the sin of *lifnai iver*. Accordingly, the Talmud rules that giving a cup of wine to a *nazir* (a person prohibited to drink wine) is a violation of *lifnai iver* (*Pesachim* 22b). Thus an invitation to a Jew who would drive his car (which is a definite transgression of the *Shabbat*) to attend an event, should be prohibited as an overt violation of the biblical law of *lifnai iver*. It should be deemed as if the Jew drove his car and violated the *Shabbat* at the instigation of the person who extended the invitation.

This prohibition, however, may not be operational in the case at hand. The Talmud notes that it is forbidden to extend wine to a *nazir* only in a situation wherein the *nazir* is separated from the person extending the wine by a body of water (*Avodah Zarah* 6b). In other words, the *nazir* simply could not acquire the wine by himself. Thus, the prohibition of *lifnai iver* is not operational unless one serves as a *causal* factor, not as merely a *contributing* factor. A person who will violate the *Shabbat* on a regular basis (with or without any invitation to attend a synagogue) is not transgressing *Shabbat* solely because of the invitation. This person constantly drives on *Shabbat*. As such, the invitation is not the cause of the transgression. It is comparable to the case of the *nazir* who had the ability to acquire wine by himself.

Lifnei Iver—Rabbinic

At issue is the concern whether a rabbinic injunction against aiding a sinner is applicable in the event that the biblical prohibition is not operational. The Talmudic citation (*Avodah Zarah* 6b) notes that where the *nazir* may acquire the wine without the help of another Jew, it is not only not a violation of the biblical law of *lifnei iver* but it is also permissible to provide him with wine. This overtly indicates that in the absence of the biblical prohibition, no rabbinic injunction is operational. Yet

Tosafot (Shabbat 3a) and Rabbenu Asher (*Shabbat,* ch. 1) explicitly rule that there is definitely a rabbinic ban against aiding sinners even when the violation of a Jewish law may transpire without the input of another Jew.

In *Shulchan Aruch* (*Yoreh Deah* 151:11) the Rema presents two views:

1. It is prohibited to sell to Gentiles items used for *avodah zarah* only when without the services of a Jew the Gentile would not be able to acquire such items. Should the Gentile be able to acquire such items without the help of the Jew, then it is permissible (Mordechai, *Avodah Zarah* ch. 1).

2. Some (sages) stringently prohibit the sale of such items even if the Gentile may acquire them without utilizing a Jew.

The Rema notes that common practice is to be lenient (like the first position) but one who assumes for himself higher standards should be stringent for himself.

The Shach (*Yoreh Deah* 151:6) suggests that the two positions do not conflict with each other, for each relates to a different circumstance. The permissible view related to a Gentile and Jewish *mumar* (a Jew who repeatedly violates Jewish law). The stringent position relates to an observant Jew. Just as one must refrain from permitting a minor to violate halachah, certainly this is applicable to an observant person.

The Dagul Mervava (ibid.) finely hones the Shach's position. Why, he asks, should one not be obliged to save a Jewish *mumar* from committing a sin? He is yet a Jew. To this he contends that the entire concept of requiring one Jew to prevent another from violating halachah relates only when the Jew committing the sin is a *shogaig*—a person who is unaware of the culpability of his action. He knows not that his action is a sin, comparable to a minor who has not full knowledge of his actions. Yet, for one who is a *maizid*—a person who willingly and knowingly violates Jewish law—a Jew has no obligation to withhold such a person from a sin.

Another position is that of the Turei Even. He contends that the rabbinic prohibition is applicable only when a Jew has a reasonable option of preventing the occurrence of the sin. In the event the sinner will violate halachah regardless of the efforts of another, then no rabbinic injunction is operational (*Avnei Meeluim, Hagigah* 13).

HaRav Shlomo Kliger suggests that a rabbinic ban was imposed when the object by which to commit the sin is in the control of another Jew. When, however, the control of the object is within the hands of the sinner, then the Rabbis did not impose a rabbinic ban (*Avodat Avodah, Avodah Zarah* 6b).

A further consideration is the fact that at the moment when the violation of *Shabbat* takes place the Jew who extended the invitation is not involved. The Binyan Tziyyon rules that a rabbinic prohibition against serving as a contributory factor to a sin (*mesai'a*) is imposed only when the person who enabled, induced, or contributed to the sin is somehow simultaneously involved with the actual violation itself—for example, he gives the *nazir* the wine to drink. In the event, however, where the action (or words) of the person who contributes to the violation ceases long before the actual sin takes place itself, the Rabbis did not impose a rabbinic prohibition (Responsa Binyon Tziyyon, no. 15).

Based upon the above analysis, an invitation to a Jew who will most probably drive on *Shabbat* to attend an event may not be prohibited as either a biblical or rabbinic violation of *lifnai iver*.

Goal of an Invitation

An invitation to a non-observant Jewish man or woman to attend a synagogue service or a *Shabbat* meal may, even, be defended as a praiseworthy concern. The synagogue service and/or the *Shabbat* meal may be viewed as a means of generating a love for Judaism and step one in the process of becoming a *Baal Teshuvah*. In such a case, perhaps the Rabbis did not deem the invitation as prohibited.

A source for this position may be noted in the following

interpretation of the biblical dialogue between Yaakov and Rivkah. Rivkah wanted Yaakov to masquerade as Esau in order to acquire Yitzchak's blessing. Yaakov, however, was apprehensive about misrepresenting himself as Esau to his father. The Torah cites his fear: "Perhaps my father will touch me, and I will be in his eyes as a deceiver and I shall bring a curse upon me, not a blessing" (Genesis 27:12). To this Rivkah responded, "Upon me be thy curse, only obey my voice" (Genesis 27:13). The Rebbe, Reb Heshel of Krakaw, posed this question: Why was Yaakov so certain that Yitzchak would curse him in the event that he ascertained that Yaakov was attempting to fool him? Maybe in such a circumstance Yitzchak would simply not grant him his parental blessings. But why does Yaakov fear a parental curse? To this Reb Heshel says that the Torah informs us that prior to entering the land of Israel, *k'lal Yisrael*, in unison, made the vow "Cursed be he that makes a blind man wander out of his path" (Deut. 27:18). In other words, the process of misrepresenting oneself to a blind person (Yitzchak) is assumed to be deserving of a curse. This was Yaakov's apprehension. To this Rivkah demurred. She believed that the curse applied only when the misrepresentation was for the purpose of hindering or harming the blind person. When, however, the goal was for beneficial values and "goodness" for the blind man, no "curse" was operational (see *Chanukat HaTorah, Parshat Toldot*). Indeed, history condoned Rivkah and Yaakov.

The same argument may be extended to validate an invitation to a person to attend on *Shabbat* a synagogue service or a *Shabbat* meal—namely, perhaps, the sages never imposed a rabbinic ban of *lifnai iver* when the purpose of the inducement was for the bolstering of *mitzvot.*

In addition, perhaps the host or person extending the invitation should make available a place for the guest to stay wherein it is not necessary to violate the *Shabbat.* Though such an invitation does not ensure that the guest will utilize the option, it may remove from the host the onus of serving as a contributing agent to a violation of *Shabbat.*

Conclusion

It is apparent from the above analysis that a Jew who seeks to satisfy the dictates of all rabbinic sages pertaining to *Shabbat* should refrain from any invitation that may induce even a semblance of a *Shabbat* violation. However, those who altruistically wish to spread Judaism and hope to influence Jews to be favourable toward observance of *mitzvot* should be aware that an invitation to engender such positive goals may be sanctioned by halachah.

Note: The ruling is based on the halachic orientation that the ultimate goal is not the *Shabbat* meal nor the synagogue service but the observance of *Shabbat* itself. As such the act of driving a car on *Shabbat* even to attend a synagogue service is still prohibited. This was never permitted. Accordingly, the above discourse was to analyze whether the person who gives an invitation violates halachah, not to in any way condone the violation itself. The sanction for the invitation is merely step one in developing a *Baal Teshuvah.* The difficulty is the concern with a regular pattern of *Shabbat* violations. Rabbis have been known to be lenient in individual cases yet stringent when the violation became a regular pattern. This (stringent) approach is not necessarily the halachah. The Rema (*Orech Chayyim* 307:2) noted that many had the custom of requesting Gentiles to light candles for *Shabbat* meals. Though the Rema and the overwhelming majority of authorities objected to this practice for a variety of halachic reasons, no reference is made to the issues of infrequent occurrence or regular usage. Accordingly, such a distinction is a personal consideration that some may apply and others may with equally good judgement reject. A rabbinic judgement must therefore be assessed to permit a regular *Shabbat* violation even for purposes of becoming a *Baal Teshuvah.*

Services of a Gentile on Shabbat

QUESTION: Does halachah provide any acceptable formula for requesting a non-Jew to provide service to a Jew on *Shabbat*?

RESPONSE: The *Shulchan Aruch* unequivocally rules that if a Jew is prohibited to do a certain action on *Shabbat*, he is also precluded from requesting a Gentile to do it in his behalf, even if the request is made prior to *Shabbat* (*Orech Chayyim* 307:2).

The Rema adds the principle that it is even prohibited to hint or suggest to a Gentile that he perform any action on behalf of a Jew on *Shabbat* (*Orech Chayyim* 307:2).

This prohibition is termed *amira l'akum* and is generally considered to be rabbinic in nature (*Shabbat* 150a). Though the Yerai'im (113) rules that the prohibition is biblical, Rav Yosef Engel contends that the Yerai'im limits the biblical statute to cases wherein the prohibited action involves items owned by a Jew. In a case, however, where the Jew requests a Gentile to perform, for example, an action with the Gentile's own fire to benefit a Jew, then even the Yerai'im would agree that it is deemed only a rabbinic law (Gilyonei HaShas, *Shabbat* 150a).

Three major reasons are presented for the prohibition:

1. *V'dabar davar.* On *Shabbat* a Jew should withhold himself not only from certain actions but also from speech that creates a violation of *Shabbat* (Rashi, *Avodah Zarah* 15a).

2. *Shlichut.* A Gentile requested to perform an action becomes the agent of the Jew. Just as a Jew cannot violate *Shabbat*, neither may his agent (Rashi, *Shabbat* 153a).

3. *Sacredness of Shabbat.* A Jew may not ask a Gentile to perform actions on *Shabbat* as a safeguard against Jews performing such actions themselves (Rambam, *Laws of Shabbat* 6:1).

The Avnei Nezer notes that according to the first reason alone, it would be permitted to make a request of a Gentile prior to *Shabbat* (Responsa, *Orech Chayyim* 43:6). Because of the other reasons, however, even this is prohibited.

The Rema notes that some authorities maintain that *amira l'akum* is permissible for the performance of a mitzvah (Baal HaItur). Based on this concept, "many practiced the leniency of telling Gentiles to light candles for purposes of a [*Shabbat*] meal, [or] specifically for a wedding party or circumcision, and no one would protest [such practice]." The Rema, however, concludes that since most halachic authorities dispute this premise, one should be stringent except in cases of great need (*Orech Chayyim* 276:2). Thus, common custom was to utilize the services of Gentiles on *Shabbat* to perform *mitzvot*. Though the Rema disagrees with the basis for this practice, he notes that authorities did not protest its use.

It is difficult to rely on such a theory in modern times for several reasons. The Magen Avraham notes that the reason for the nonprotest was the principle that it is better for Jews to sin unintentionally (*shogaig*) than to do so purposely (*Orech Chayyim* 276:9). The implication is that should such Jews be warned that the practice was forbidden, they would still continue its use. Therefore, it is better for them not to hear from rabbis that it is wrong. This certainly cannot and should not be the guiding principle of pious Jews. Indeed, should Jews be of a heart to harken to the decisions of the rabbis, the *Aruch HaShulchan* rules that one is obliged to protest such practice. The *Aruch HaShulchan* adds that the overwhelming majority of all authorities maintain that *amira l'akum* is simply prohibited for purposes of a mitzvah. In addition, he says, "In our times we have not heard [anyone] being lenient on this" (*Orech Chayyim* 276:14). Accordingly, this law cannot be the basis for its use.

There are, however, legal loopholes relating to *amira l'akum* that do have pragmatic application. The Mishneh Berurah specifically rules that on Friday it is permitted merely to hint or suggest to a Gentile that some service is required on *Shabbat* (*Orech Chayyim* 307:10). This means that only a formal, outright request on Friday or a hint on *Shabbat* to perform some action is prohibited.

Of interest is a case where a Jew asks Gentile A to request Gentile B to perform a task on behalf of a Jew. To the extent that the Jew never directly requested Gentile B to perform any task on *Shabbat*, such an instance may not be automatically prohibited. Indeed, the Beir Haitiv (*Orech Chayyim* 307:3) cites a rabbinic debate on this issue. Rabbenu Gershon (*Avodat Gershuni*) prohibits such an action, whereas the Chav'at Yair contends that it is permissible (see Responsa Chav'at Yair, nos. 49 and 53). The Shaarei Teshuvah notes the leniency of the Chav'at Yair and cites the Shevut Yaakov (vol. 3, no. 22), who agrees with this ruling (*Orech Chayyim* 321:6).

My grandfather, the Minchat Shabbat (90:25), and the Mishneh Berurah (*Orech Chayyim* 307:24) rule that one may rely on the lenient view of the Chav'at Yair when there is a great loss (*hefsid merubah*).

Though the Mishneh Berurah contends that whenever the lenient view is observed the Jew should not personally enjoy the *melachah* (307:11), the Pri Magedim disagrees and makes no such limitation. He does contend, however, that the second Gentile is not to be aware that the original request was made by a Jew (*Mishptzot Zahav* 276:5).

The Shmirat Shabbat K'halachah suggests that perhaps one may rely on the Chav'at Yair if the action of the Gentile is for the performance of a mitzvah (ch. 30, n. 48). Yet, the Minchat Shabbat cautions that any matter that is questionable, whether it is a mitzvah or not, may not be relied upon to offset *amira l'akum* (*Orech Chayyim* 90:29).

The Chatam Sofer rules that the debate concerning the propriety of asking one Gentile to request a second Gentile to perform an action on *Shabbat* relates only to an instance where the Jew made his request to the first Gentile on *Shabbat* itself. In a case where the Jew requested Gentile A on Friday to ask Gentile B to perform an action on *Shabbat*, then it is permitted according to all authorities (Responsa, *Orech Chayyim* 60).

The Biur Halachah (of the Mishneh Berurah) cites this view of the Chatam Sofer, yet contends that it is a *chiddush* (an innovative theory) and is disputed by the Rashbah (*Orech Chayyim* 307:2).

Based on the above citations, it would appear that to request the services of a Gentile to perform a *melachah* on *Shabbat* would be permitted according to the majority of halachic authorities on the following conditions: the Jew *alludes* on Friday to Gentile A to inform Gentile B of the need to perform an action on *Shabbat.* (Assume that a person wishes to attend synagogue services and to return to eat a *Shabbat* meal. It is a form of *safek safaikah.)*

1. According to the Baal HaItur, it is permitted to direct a Gentile, even on *Shabbat,* to facilitate the performance of a mitzvah, even to the majority who disagree;

2. According to the Chav'at Yair, it is permitted to direct Gentile A to tell Gentile B on *Shabbat* to perform an action, even to those who disagree;

3. According to the Chatam Sofer, all permit directing Gentile A to inform Gentile B if the first directive occurred prior to *Shabbat,* even according to Mishneh Berurah, who implies he disagrees;

4. According to the Mishneh Berurah, it is permitted to hint on Friday to do an action on *Shabbat.*

5. According to the Shmirat Shabbat K'halachah, one may rely on the Chav'at Yair (and tell Gentile A even on *Shabbat* to tell Gentile B) for the performance of a mitzvah. Thus one certainly may rely on this process when the direction occurred on Friday (Chatam Sofer) and such direction was merely in the form of a hint and the purpose was to perform a mitzvah.

A word of caution. In a recent conversation with a contemporary hasidic sage relating to the pragmatic implementation of many of the principles discussed (i.e., theories of Chav'at Yair and Chatam Sofer, etc.), the following objection was raised. The previously cited authorities provide legal lenient rulings for using the services of a Gentile only when the need occurs on an *infrequent basis.* At such times the *poskim* decreed that under certain limited guidelines, the action did not constitute a violation of *Shabbat.* This, however, should not be construed as a blanket permission to utilize such principles frequently and regularly to circumvent the prohibition of *amira l'akum*. Regular, weekly use of such theories would definitely be prohibited, as that would be viewed as a contrived method to vitiate the prohibition altogether.

Yet, this novel (stringent) approach is not necessarily in consonance with general procedures. The Rema (*Orech Chayyim* 307:2) noted that many had the custom of requesting Gentiles to light candles for *Shabbat* meals. Though the Rema and the overwhelming majority of authorities objected to this practice for a variety of halachic reasons, no reference is made to the issues of infrequent occurrence or regular usage. Accordingly, such a distinction is a personal consideration that some may apply and others may, with equally good judgment, reject.

Playing Ball on Shabbat *and* Yom Tov

QUESTION: Is ball playing permitted on *Shabbat* and *Yom Tov*?

RESPONSE: The proliferation of *eruvin* has granted observant Jews the freedom to carry in "public" areas on *Shabbat*, an activity that had hitherto been off-limits. This license has, however, generated the impression that within the perimeters of the *eruv*, any activity that involves "carrying" is permitted, including ball playing. Concomitantly, as Jews frequent an ever-expanding number of kosher resorts, it is assumed that there are no limits on usage of hotel facilities on *Shabbat* and *Yom Tov*, including tennis courts. Our concern here will be the halachic propriety of ball playing on *Shabbat* and/or *Yom Tov*.

I

The *Shulchan Aruch* rules that "it is prohibited to play ball on *Shabbat* and *Yom Tov*." Rema notes, "Some permit it and the common custom is to be lenient."[87] Since Rema does not qualify his permissive ruling, it appears applicable to all, regardless of gender, age, or location. It thus appears that ball playing, while perhaps not a spiritual means of observing *Shabbat* or *Yom Tov*, is a halachically acceptable activity for those who enjoy it. It is a means of physically expressing *oneg* on *Shabbat* and *Yom Tov*. Indeed, *Tosafot* explicitly ruled that ball playing on *Yom Tov* is permissible.[88] A review of halachic authorities, however, indicates that the issue is not so clear cut and that a more restrictive approach may be in order.

Rabbi Shlomo Luria (Rashal) openly criticizes the blanket allowance for ball playing on *Yom Tov*. He notes that ball playing has no normal function or purpose on *Yom Tov*. It is tolerable "only for young children who do not fall within the age of obligation (*chiyuv*)." As for "adults, it is a bad practice (*minhag ra*), a form of *kalut rosh*." Had he the authority, he suggests, he would have "abolished ball playing altogether on *Yom Tov*."[89] According to this line of reasoning, ball playing should also be prohibited on *Shabbat*, even within a private building or the perimeters of an *eruv*.

Later *Achronim* relied upon Rashal to modify Rema's ruling. Magen Avraham[90] and Taz[91] both cite Rashal's opinion and rule that ball playing is permitted only to minors. Mishneh Berurah also cites Rashal. He adds that ball playing on *Yom Tov* is not as licit an act as commonly conceived, since *Shulchan Aruch* clearly prohibits it.[92] Thus, Mishneh Berurah appears to imply that since the status of ball playing on *Shabbat* and *Yom Tov* is a matter of contention between *Shulchan Aruch* and Rema, those who accept the lenient view should at the very least follow Rashal's mediating ruling that leniency is appropriate for minors only.[93]

Aruch HaShulchan responded to Rashal's argument by noting that as long as ball playing is dear to some, even if it is to a "lowly spirit" (*da'ato hashfaila*), it should not be withheld from them.[94] Still, the practical upshot of his words is unclear. On the one hand, one might deduce therefrom that ball playing is allowed. On the other hand, there are those who see in *Aruch HaShulchan*'s words only a justification for extant practice, which under other circumstances would be prohibited.[95] In any event, we should elevate the expression of the sanctity of *Shabbat* and *Yom Tov*, and not cater to "lowly spirits."

There are special reasons for not permitting ball playing on *Shabbat* or *Yom Tov*. Bet Yosef notes a tradition[96] that the city of Tur Shimon was destroyed because its residents played ball.[97] HaRav Avraham Chaim Na'eh writes that the city may have been destroyed in order to teach *k'lal Yisrael* that *Shabbat* is meant to be devoted to *kedushah* (holiness), and the exertion and behavior associated with ball playing are totally inappropriate for that day.[98] The Vilna Gaon cites this passage from the *Yerushalmi* as the central source of the ruling of the *Shulchan Aruch* banning ball playing.[99] Evidently, the destruction of this city so affected *Chazal* that they were moved to ban ball playing entirely on *Shabbat*.

In discussing the restrictive position of Bet Yosef on this question, *Shulchan Aruch HaRav* points out that Bet Yosef prohibits ball playing because the ball itself is not a *keli* and therefore *muktzah*.[100] Based upon the remarks of Mishneh Berurah[101] and *Shulchan Aruch HaRav*, it appears that Bet Yosef's debate with Rema revolves around the issue of whether the ball itself is *muktzah* or not. Furthermore, the fact that Rashal allows limited ball playing, i.e., to minors, means that the ball cannot be characterized as being *muktzah*. Hence, the concern for Rema and Rashal is with ball playing and not with the ball itself. The result is that when ball playing *is* allowed, as when young children play, the ball may not be considered *muktzah* even for an adult.[102]

A careful reading of Rashal's formulation shows that he did not allow all minors to play ball on *Yom Tov* either. It should be recalled that Rashal tolerated the activity "only for young children who did not fall within the age of obligation *(chiyuv)*."

It is reasonable to interpret the "age of obligation" as being the age of *chinuch.* The exact age of *chinuch* a matter of some disagreement among *rishonim.*[103] What is clear, however, is that a child after his/her Bar/Bat Mitzvah is certainly no longer a minor. This means that rabbis and yeshivah educators should make it clear to young people that ball playing after Bar/Bat Mitzvah is not acceptable on *Shabbat* or *Yom Tov.* A fortiori adult ball playing on such occasions is definitely improper. In fact, even minors who play ball on *Shabbat* or *Yom Tov* must be taught to do so discreetly (e.g., in back yards) and not to make of it a public event.[104]

II

An examination of some of the sources of Rashal's position provides insight into his rationale. Bet Yosef reports:

> Agur writes in the name of Shibbolei HaLeket that it is prohibited to play ball on *Shabbat* and *Yom Tov.* Such balls are not fit to cover jars. They are disgusting since they are filthy with tar and dirt. A wooden ball may also not be handled and played with. Yet *Tosafot* in the first chapter of *Betza* . . . writes that . . . it is not only permitted to take out a child for purposes of circumcision but even just for recreation (*tiyol*). In fact, we find that people do play with a *filuta* ball on *Yom Tov* in a public domain (*rishut harabbim*), which certainly qualifies as recreation. From this practice, therefore, it appears that it is permitted to handle (*l'taltel*) the ball on *Yom Tov* as well as on *Shabbat* for in these matters *Yom Tov* and *Shabbat* are equal. However, I found in *Yerushalmi, Ta'anit* that Tur Shimon was destroyed for two reasons. One was due to sexual promiscuity (*z'nut*). The second was because they played ball [emphasis added].[105]

Commenting upon this passage, Rema notes:[106]

> It is evident that even those who permit (ball playing) on *Shabbat* would prohibit playing in a public domain on *Shab-*

> *bat,* or even in a *karmelit,* for in such a situation the ball could easily fall outside of four cubits . . . but on *Yom Tov* it is permitted to play even in a public domain.

The actual text of the Shibbolei HaLeket provides a conceptual framework for an appreciation of the halachic issues raised by ball playing on *Shabbat* and *Yom Tov.* Shibbolei HaLeket cites his brother, Rabbi Judah da Piatelli, to the effect that:

> our balls are not even considered "useful vessels" (*keli*), and the intention to play with them does not make them so. What is more, whether it is considered a *keli* or not, handling or playing with a ball is still prohibited on *Shabbat* and *Yom Tov* for there is no constructive purpose served by its handling. Neither could it be used to cover another vessel, since it is disgusting by virtue of its being soiled with mud and dust. In a similar fashion a wooden ball may not be handled or played with. And we find in *Midrash Eicha,* "The people of Tur Shimon would distribute three hundred barrels of cake to the poor every *Erev Shabbat.* If so, why was it destroyed? One cannot say that it was due to licentiousness, for there was only one prostitute there and she was sent away from there. Rav Huna said: It was because they played ball on *Shabbat.*

Shibbolei HaLeket thus states the following:

1. Balls are filthy items and hence unfit to serve as a *keli.*
2. Balls are *muktzah* because they serve no constructive purpose.
3. Wooden balls are also prohibited.

The Shibbolei HaLeket, however, does not explain why wooden balls are *muktzah.* They were certainly not as grimy as other balls, so why was it prohibited to handle or play with them?

Our attention must first be focused on a prior difficulty in the formulation of Shibbolei HaLeket. Why is the issue of whether the ball is *muktzah* predicated on its ability to serve as the cover for another vessel? It is a *keli* on its own terms through its use in playing ball. The conclusion must be that ball playing on *Shabbat* and *Yom Tov* is not a legitimate activity.[107] Yet why is this the case?

It seems that Shibbolei HaLeket's reasoning is as follows: It is prohibited to use either a regular or a wooden ball on *Shabbat* or *Yom Tov*. This is because ball playing has no halachically proper place on holy days. Most likely, this resulted from an edict issued by *Chazal* after the destruction of Tur Shimon.[108]

Upon closer examination, the reaction of Shibbolei HaLeket to the destruction of Tur Shimon is only one side of a debate over the nature of that reaction.

Mateh Moshe, for example, adopts a very different position. He contends that the inhabitants of Tur Shimon sinned in that they played ball at a time earmarked for Torah study. Ball playing was thus a cause of *bittul Torah* on *Shabbat* and *Yom Tov*. Accordingly, he writes, it is obvious "that ball playing when no *shi'ur* occurred would be permitted. So too is the reported position of *Tosafot*, *Betza*, viz., that it is permitted to play ball on *Shabbat* and *Yom Tov*.[109] In other words, even *Tosafot* would have prohibited ball playing during public Torah lectures and classes. Thus, ball playing was prohibited not because it detracted from the sanctity of *Shabbat* but due to its attracting Jews away from Torah learning. This indicates that even *Tosafot* never granted ball playing a blanket license.

Mateh Moshe's theory requires further thought. Was Tur Shimon destroyed just because it so happened that ball playing took place at the same time as actual *shi'urim*? If so, the entire debate could be resolved by revising schedules. It is suggested, however, that Mateh Moshe's position is that ball playing is prohibited on *Shabbat* and *Yom Tov* whenever public *shi'urim* could be held.

Mateh Moshe notes that after *mincha* on *Shabbat*, common custom was not to publicly study the Oral Law, for tradition had it that Moshe Rabbenu passed away at that time, and the rule is that when a great scholar dies, all *Batei Midrash* are closed in his honor.[110] Thus, ball playing would be allowed after *mincha* on *Shabbat* according to Mateh Moshe.

This interpretation of Mateh Moshe is not accepted by all authorities. According to another midrash, cited by Rosh, Moshe Rabbenu wrote thirteen Torah scrolls on the day of his death. One was given to each tribe and the last placed in the Arc of the Covenant.[111] Rosh argues that this tradition refutes the contention that Moshe died on *Shabbat*, for if so how could he have written these Torah scrolls?! Therefore, he concludes, there is no basis to the custom of abstaining from study between *mincha* and *ma'ariv* on *Shabbat* afternoon.[112] Should one accept this view of Rosh, that Torah study is permitted all during *Shabbat*, then ball playing would consequently be prohibited the entire day.[113]

Rashal may have been disturbed by this conflict between the tradition regarding Tur Shimon and the common custom of playing ball on holidays. Rashal may be seen to have harmonized the two by noting that ball playing serves no purpose on *Yom Tov*. It is an activity for children, not adults. In addition, Rashal states that ball playing is not "comparable to carrying a minor child; for in the latter instance the father is happy and derives pleasure from his child, such that this is termed *simchat Yom Tov*." In other words, an activity with a minor child is permitted, while ball playing is forbidden. Yet why should the joy of ball playing with adults be less than doing so with children? In addition, Rashal rules that in the event that an *eruv* was established one may carry from one courtyard to another even items that may have no purpose on *Yom Tov*. This lies in contradiction to Rashal's ruling about balls and ball playing. Why could Rashal have not extended permission to the latter within the confines of an *eruv*?

The answer appears to be that the basis for the prohibition of ball playing was the traumatic reaction to the destruction of Tur Shimon, which caused the Sages to ban all adult ball playing on *Shabbat* and *Yom Tov*. They did not wish holy days to be given over to ball games rather than to matters spiritual. This is Rashal's unique position, which is derived from Shibbolei HaLeket. Apart from the above reactions to the destruction of Tur Shimon, a number of interpretations may be offered. One might even contend that the rabbis prohibited only ball playing that took place throughout most of *Yom Tov* and *Shabbat*. The rabbis did not wish such holy days to be devoted to ball games rather than spiritual events. Accordingly, should a person go to the synagogue for communal prayer and even attend public Torah sessions, then, perhaps ball playing would also be permitted. Yet, such a position is not even noted by the sages. In addition, insofar as Rashal's opinion was accepted by the majority of decisors, it appears that his interpretation of the reaction to Tur Shimon is normative.

Taz,[114] and Magen Avraham,[115] and Mishneh Berurah[116] all cite Rashal as prohibiting adult ball playing and make no exception when an *eruv* is present.[117] The obvious implication is that Rashal's prohibition of adult ball playing on *Shabbat* and *Yom Tov* is operational even within the confines of an *eruv*.

III

The organization of and participation in a ball game for children above the age of *chinuch* may be a violation of the Torah's injunction that *Shabbat* and *Yom Tov* be "sacred assemblies" (*mikra'ai kodesh*). As expressed by Ramban in his commentary on the Torah, this mitzvah teaches that *Shabbat* and *Yom Tov* must be distinguished from the rest of the week by the modes of dress, eating, and general deportment of each individual. In this way, one's total ambience will be conducive to the creation of a day that is declared by God to be holy.[118] Sforno notes that the meaning of *mikra'ai kodesh* is that *Shabbat* should be devoted to assemblages for purposes of *kedushah*.[119]

Another area of *Shabbat* halachah that is germane here is the Torah's command that "On the Seventh day you shall rest."[120] Organized ball games may be a violation of this mitzvah.[121]

Finally, it is apparent that ball playing and the like constitute a violation (*bittul aseh*) of the Torah's command that we

"Remember *Shabbat* to *make it holy*."[122] Ramban explains that the Torah's intent here is to teach us to refrain from preoccupation with worldly things and to give ourselves spiritual pleasure in the ways of God, through the active cultivation of activities that are conducive thereto.[123]

The conclusion to be derived from the above is clear. The halachah stated by most major codifiers, including Mishneh Berurah, should be implemented in our communities. Rabbis, as the authorities responsible for the spiritual welfare of their communities, should unite with parents and educators to assume responsibility and ensure that our children learn to respect the special spirit of *Shabbat* and *Yom Tov*. Specifically, the following recommendations ought to be made:

1. Organized ball games (or other athletic activities) involving anyone over the age of Bar/Bat Mitzvah appear to be in violation of *uvda d'chol* and contravene the injunctions of *mikra'ei kodesh* and *ba'yom hashevi'i tishbot*. Thus they should be discouraged in the strongest terms.[124]

2. Under the age of 5, ball playing is permitted according to Ashkenazic authorities, but prohibited by Sephardic Halachists who accept the view that a ball is a *muktzah*.[125] The Ashkenazic approach implies that an adult may play along with the child. Of course, this is only applicable as long as attendant *Shabbat* prohibitions are not violated (e.g., *hashva'at gumot*).

3. Between the ages of 5[126] and Bar/Bat Mitzvah, the propriety of ball playing may be a matter of dispute among *poskim* due to a difference of opinion regarding the age of *chinuch*. Therefore, its appropriateness will depend upon the evaluation by the rabbi of the individual children involved and the requirements of the community.

4. Alternate forms of activity should be designed to occupy, educate, and entertain children in keeping with the atmosphere of *Shabbat*.

The sanctity of *Shabbat* warrants special extra precautions and considerations. The Modern Orthodox Community must rise to the occasion to protect it.

Riding a Tricycle on Shabbat

QUESTION: Is a minor permitted to ride a tricycle on *Shabbat* (in an area encircled by an *eruv*)?

RESPONSE: The Debritziner Rav, Rabbi Moshe Shtern, ruled that a minor is permitted to ride a tricycle on *Shabbat*, but not a bicycle. He contended that a child below the age of *chinuch* may ride his/her tricycle and no one should be negative about such usage. Above the age of *chinuch*, it is preferable not to ride a tricycle, but (*al pi din*) a parent need not restrain a child from such enjoyment. (The bell of the tricycle should either be removed or made to be unworkable on *Shabbat*.) Bicycles, however, may not be ridden at all on *Shabbat* (or *Yom Tov*) for the following reasons: (1) They may break down and one may violate *Shabbat* by fixing them. (2) *Uvda d'chol*—it certainly is not a *Shabbosdik* activity (see Responsa *Bai'er Moshe*, vol. VI, resp. 16).

Carrying Car Keys on Shabbat

QUESTION: On *Shabbat* in an area circled by an *eruv* or on *Yom Tov*, is it permissible to carry a key ring containing keys for the home as well as for one's car?

RESPONSE: HaRav HaGaon Rav Moshe Feinstein (*z"l*) ruled that a person who generally smokes ten cigarettes in a period of time that he is away from his home was permitted carry on *Yom Tov* a full pack containing twenty cigarettes (Iggrot Moshe, *Orech Chayyim*, part II, *siman* 103). Based upon this ruling the

Shmirat *Shabbat* K'Hilchata contended that one may also carry a ring of keys that may include those not utilized on *Shabbat.* The rationale is that the case of the key ring should be comparable to the packet of cigarettes. Just as HaGaon Rav Moshe (*z"l*) ruled that one may carry the entire pack of cigarettes and need not remove the amount of cigarettes that the person will not smoke, so too may one carry a key ring with keys containing certain keys not used at all on *Shabbat* or *Yom Tov* (Shmirat *Shabbat* K'Hilchata, ch. 19, *s'if* 6; see Ot 17).

Of major interest, however, is that HaGaon Rav Moshe (*z"l*) explicitly reviewed this issue and ruled that it is prohibited to carry (in area of an *eruv* or on *Yom Tov*) a key ring containing keys that will not be used during such period of time. Moreover, he noted that the case of the key ring is distinctly different from the case of the cigarettes. In the latter situation, each individual cigarette has a potential usage. As such, the entire packet may therefore be carried. The case of the key ring deals with keys that simply cannot and will not be used at all. Accordingly, the keys that have no potential usage—for example, the car keys—should be removed prior to *Shabbat* or *Yom Tov* (Iggrot Moshe, vol. VIII, *Orech Chayyim*, part V, *siman* 35). The implication is that the car keys acquire the status of *muktzah.*

Carrying by Mistake on Shabbat

QUESTION: A person leaves his home and while walking in the street becomes aware that he is carrying something in the pocket of his suit. What should he do?

RESPONSE: The assumption is that the area is not enclosed by an *eruv*. This incident may involve two violations of *Shabbat*: (1) It is prohibited to transfer any item from a private domain (a house, for example) to a public thoroughfare (a sidewalk or street). (2) In addition, one is not permitted to carry anything in a public domain a distance of over four *amot*. Accordingly, a method must be devised to avert or mute both prohibitions. The first Mishneh of *Shabbat* delineates the prohibition against transferring items from a private to a public thoroughfare. It notes that the process of transferring items (*hotza'ah* or *hachnasah*) entails two distinct actions: (1) *akirah*—the item was picked up from a stationary position; (2) *hanachah*—the item was put down or placed in a stationary position. Should both take place, then the action is deemed to have violated biblical law. Should one of these actions be performed it would be prohibited only from a rabbinic view. Should, moreover, none of these conditions apply, then no violation transpires. In addition, to violate *Shabbat* it is necessary to be aware of what one is doing at the time the activity commences.

The Talmud reports: "If one is laden with food and drink and goes in and out all day (from private to public ground), he is liable only when he stands still. Said Abaye: Providing that he stands still to rest" (*Shabbat* 5b). Rashi provides the following rationale: The person laden with food had no intention to transfer items from a private to a public domain. He simply wanted to carry items from one area in a home to another. Later on he decided to go out, but he never stopped and stood still. He was constantly moving. To violate *Shabbat* it is necessary to emulate the service at the tabernacle in the wilderness (*mishkan*), which was an intentional conscious process. Indeed, whenever one does not intend to violate *Shabbat*, one is not liable. Accordingly, an item that was never originally picked up to be carried out of the house would also not be a violation of *Shabbat*. Moreover, as long as the person never stopped, the action lacked both the *akirah* and *hanachah* (see also *Tosafot* 3b).

Based upon the above one may resolve the dilemma of a person who while in a public area noted that he or she was by accident carrying on *Shabbat*. First, the item was never consciously picked up to be transferred. Indeed, when the person left his home he was even unaware that he was carrying anything. As such, the issue lacks an *akirah*. The moment the person stood still or stopped, he would have a *hanachah* without an *akirah*. This is not a biblical violation, but it is still a prohibited rabbinic action. An *akirah* without a *hanachah* or a *hanachah* without an *akirah* is still not to be performed on *Shabbat* (*Shabbat* 3a). Yet, the Talmud (5b) specifically notes that when *akirah* does not take place one may return home. Why? For as long as the person did not stop, there would be no *hanachah*. By returning home without stopping, no violation would emanate at all, for any carrying of an object without an *akirah* (it was never originally picked up to be carried) or *hanachah* (the item was never transported to a stationary position) is permitted even from a rabbinic viewpoint. So the most viable suggestion to a person who accidentally became aware of carrying an object is to not stop but to return to his original place of departure, his home. In other words, just go back home without stopping.

Carrying a Tallit *Home from* Shul *on* Shabbat

QUESTION: A person resides in an area enclosed by an *eruv*. In the event he carried his *tallit* to *shul* for usage during *tefilot*, may he carry his *tallit* home after *davening*? The issue is that he has no further need whatsoever for the *tallit* on *Shabbat*. As such, it should be prohibited to carry his *tallit* home after *davening*.

RESPONSE: The *Shulchan Aruch* rules that an item that is permissible to use on *Shabbat* or *Yom Tov* (namely, it is not *muktzah*) requires a purposeful usage on *Shabbat* itself for movement. Should one have no purposeful need on *Shabbat*, then the item may not be moved. It may, however, be handled and moved to prevent its being lost or stolen (*Shulchan Aruch, Orech Chayyim* 308:4).

From the above halachah, it is evidently clear that should a person be apprehensive that unless he took his *tallit* home on *Shabbat* it may be lost or stolen, then it is permissible to carry his *tallit* home.

The *Aruch HaShulchan* provides the rationale for this leniency. Something that one may utilize on *Shabbat* is not *muktzah*. Some rabbinic scholars, however, are stringent even for these items and require a purposeful need on *Shabbat*. Yet, since the items are not essentially *muktzah*, any form of *ta'anug* (personal pleasure or emotional need) is sufficient to permit usage (*Aruch HaShulchan* 308:15). The Minchat *Shabbat* (my grandfather) concurs with this reasoning. He cites the Shla Hakodesh who notes that every item moved or carried on *Shabbat* should have a *tzorech ma* for *Shabbat* itself. The latter phrase is interpreted by the Minchat *Shabbat* to mean any form of a need, even if it is of a minor nature. Indeed, this is the general rule to be observed. The Minchat *Shabbat*, moreover, notes that in his era many had the custom to move and carry items even without any need whatsoever. This leniency, he contends, is based on those sages who hold that once an item is permissible to be moved, it may be moved and carried without any purpose at all on *Shabbat* itself. Though such is common practice, it is not the preferable *minhag* and one should be scrupulous to at least have some form of a *Shabbat* need (Minchat *Shabbat* 88:53).

Leather Sneakers

QUESTION: On Yom Kippur and Tishah b'Av, when it is prohibited to wear leather shoes, is it permissable to wear leather sneakers, namely, shoes wherein the soles are rubber but otherwise made out of leather?

RESPONSE: Dealing with Tishah b'Av the Mishneh Berurah rules that leather shoes are prohibited even if the leather is only on the top of the shoe and not the bottom (Mishneh Berurah 554:31).

To the extent that sneakers even without leather are extremely comfortable, this suggests that the prohibition of leather shoes has nothing to do with comfort or pain. A homiletical reason may be as follows: The world is composed of the following stages of creation: (1) stone, (2) vegetable, (3) animal, and (4) human beings. Each subsequent item is an advance over the previous item. Man is the highest level of creation. The wearing of leather shoes manifests that man is above all creations. All forms of creation, even animals, are subordinate to man. On Yom Kippur and Tishah b'Av, man is to manifest a humble and modest demeanor. The refraining from wearing leather shoes is a symbolic manifestation that man is in a lowly status during this period and therefore does not demonstrate superiority and control over the animal kingdom.

Music in the Privacy of One's Home (or Car) on Sefirah

QUESTION: Is it prohibited for a person in his home or car to listen to music during Sefirah?

RESPONSE: HaGaon HaRav Rav Moshe Feinstein (*z"l*) rules that even in the privacy of one's home one should not listen to music. His argument is as follows: As a result of the destruction of the Holy Temple, our sages enacted a number of ordinances to manifest a degree of sadness and mourning. One such decree was the prohibition from listening to music.

The Rema contends that this general (year-round) prohibition applied only to people who awoke in the morning and retired at night to the accompaniment of music (i.e., kings). In addition, the Rema notes that those in attendance at a *bet mishteh* (banquet party) were also included in the ban against music. The Mishneh Berurah adds that this latter rule would extend the music ban even to those who are not generally accustomed to listen to music. The prohibition was applied because of the presence of wine at the *mishteh* (meal) (*Orech Chayyim* 560:3; see Mishneh Berurah, ibid., 560:12). This suggests that a person who did not regularly listen to music throughout his daily activities and did not attend a banquet (*bet mishteh*) would be permitted to hear music.

To this HaGaon Rav Moshe demurs. He states that even the Rema would prohibit Jews from attending a public musical event throughout the year because it is a form of excessive *simcha*. To the extent that the rabbis imposed a ban against music during Sefirah (or the nine days), one must logically conclude that such a ban would be above and beyond that which is normally prohibited because of the *churban*. Since a public musical event is not permitted a whole year, the extra stringency of Sefirah must relate to music even within the confines and privacy of one's home (Iggrot Moshe, *Yoreh Deah* vol. II:137).

This ruling is difficult to comprehend. It is based on the principle that it is prohibited throughout the year to attend a public musical event. Yet except, perhaps, for *gedolai hador* and *tzaddikim*, hardly anyone refrains from listening to music because of the *churban*. It also is not proper to contend that *k'lal Yisrael* simply is in violation of halachah.

This suggests a need to review the actual laws prohibiting music a whole year. The Mishneh Berurah rules that those who daily eat their meals to the accompaniment of music are committing a sin (*Orech Chayyim* 560:12). Commenting upon this law the Mishneh Berurah himself, in his notes entitled *Shaar HaTzion*, says that some scholars have ruled that music is prohibited at a banquet in circumstances wherein only drinking takes place, not eating, for the Gentile custom was to drink to the accompaniment of music. In a setting wherein food is also served then there is no prohibition against listening to music. As such, one should not protest against the practice of having music regularly accompany a meal (see *Orech Chayyim* 560, *Shaar HaTzion* 23). This indicates that the general prohibition against music throughout the year was limited to drinking parties. Indeed, music without drink may never have been prohibited even at large gatherings.

Using HaGaon Rav Moshe's argument, one must assume that the prohibition against hearing music during Sefirah (or the nine days) was more extreme than that throughout the year. The Rabbis, therefore, may have extended the prohibition from having music to meals with food as well as drink. Indeed, they may also during Sefirah have prohibited all public musical events even without food or drink. Accordingly, they may never have prohibited music heard in the privacy of one's home. There are sufficient areas of concern to prohibit music without restricting or eliminating listening to music in one's home.

Filling the Kiddush *Cup*

QUESTION: Must the cup of wine used for *Kiddush* be filled to the brim?

RESPONSE: The Talmud rules: "Rabbi Yochanan said: Whoever says the blessing over a full cup is given an inheritance without bounds" (*Berachot* 51a). Thus a blessing cup (*kos shel berachah*) should be filled. The implication is that in the event the cup is not filled to the top one simply loses out on the bountiful reward, but it is not sinful. As such, should a person make *kiddush* on a very large goblet, containing more than a *revi'it* but not filled to the top, he still observes the mitzvah.

This rule may be derived from the following case. The Talmud notes that should a person taste wine with his finger or with a spoon, the goblet may yet be used for *kos shel berachah.* The Talmud then asks: "The cup must have a certain quantity and he diminishes it?" The implication is that with the skimming of some wine, the goblet lacks the minimum dimension of a *revi'it.* To this the Talmud responds that the cup has more than absolutely needed (*revi'it*) but not enough for two cups (*Berachot* 52a).

At issue is a question not even asked. Namely, once some wine is skimmed off, the cup is no longer full. As such, it is not a proper *kos shel berachah* and one should be prohibited from reciting a *berachah* over it. The fact that such a concern is not even a problem must be because ex post facto it is not necessary to fill the cup to its maximum capacity. One may simply state that a goblet lacking such a small amount is still considered full.

Indeed, the Bach presents a lenient rule that in general it is not necessary to ever fill the *kos shel berachah* to its brim. The principle that a majority is comparable to an entirety (*rubo kekulo*) justifies this procedure (*Tur, Orech Chayyim* 472).

The Bach's position may be challenged by the view that *rubo kekulo* is operative only when one actually has the full amount. That is, a majority is proper providing one had a total amount to begin with. For this reason a *bet din* of two cannot be validated on the principle of *rubo kekulo.* Indeed, based on this concept one must start out with a *revi'it* or *a kezayit,* or a minyan, and not merely the greater proportion of such items (*Chatan Sofer, Rubo Kekulo,* p. 14).

The Bach's response may be that the Torah did not mandate a full cup. It required a *revi'it.* Hence a *revi'it* must be present, not a majority of a *revi'it.* The full cup of wine is not a biblical or rabbinic ordinance. It is a *siman berachah.* As such, even if most of the cup is filled it still may be classified as a full cup.

Should the Havdalah *Cup Overflow?*

QUESTION: Should the goblet used for *Havdalah* be so filled that wine overflows?

RESPONSE: The Rema records an ancient custom of actually pouring some of the wine from the *Havdalah* goblet onto the ground. The rationale presented by the Rema is that "any home where wine is not poured like water lacks a sign of a blessing (*siman berachah*)" (see *Eruvin* 65a). The custom, says the Rema, takes place on Saturday night as a sign of a blessing for the coming week (*Orech Chayyim* 296:1).

The Magen Avraham rules that the above-noted custom of pouring wine onto the ground is not a halachic practice and should not be observed, for it would be a form of repudiating and disgracing the *Havdalah* blessing. He suggests that the proper custom is to fill the goblet to the brim so that it overflows onto the ground. Indeed, the Magen Avraham even contends that the entire custom noted by the Rema is an ex post facto reaction rather than a mandate for an *ab initio* procedure. Nowhere does it state that (*lechat'chila*) one should pour wine on the ground. It states, rather, ex post facto (*b'dieved*), should wine be spilled, it is a *siman berachah.*

Says the Magen Avraham, this custom was basically set up so that people should not get angry in the event wine did spill. People generally get very perturbed when someone spills wine. In such an event, the halachah states that getting angry is a terrible sin, for any house wherein wine is spilled like water is a sign of a *berachah.* Indeed, he notes that pouring a lot of wine over the brim is a form of wasteful destruction of food. Accordingly, even the amount spilled over the rim should be minimal so as not to waste food and drink (*Orech Chayyim* 296:11).

Mishneh Berurah cites the above practice of overflowing

the goblet with a minimal amount of wine so as not to waste drink (*Orech Chayyim* 206:5). My grandfather, the Minchat *Shabbat*, cites scholars who note that the common custom is not to pour (or spill on the ground) but to overflow the cup so that it spills on the table (or in a saucer) (*Minchat Shabbat* 96:19).

The *Aruch HaShulchan* further modifies the Rema's position. He contends that even the Rema would negate any active pouring of wine on the ground (or even on the table). Indeed, even to consciously fill the goblet to such an extent that wine overflows is wrong for it is a form of shaming a mitzvah (*b'zui mitzvah*). He suggests the following interpretation of the custom. The cup should be filled as are all goblets used for a blessing (*Berachot* 57a). Yet while reciting the blessing and holding the wine goblet there is a tendency for one's hand to shake. This natural hand movement generates some wine to spill. The halachah directs that should this take place, one should not spill too much. Yet it should be noted that if a small amount did spill, it is still considered a full cup. After *Havdalah*, then we intentionally pour wine in a vessel to extinguish the lights and to place on one's eyes (*Aruch HaShulchan* 296:11).

From the above it is obvious that the halachic authorities looked with disfavor upon those who simply wasted good wine by a major overflow (Magen Avraham and Mishneh Berurah) or to none at all (*Aruch HaShulchan*).

Of interest is that though the Rema noted the "wine pouring custom" to be specifically a Saturday night procedure as a good sign for the coming week, many follow the same custom even for Friday night or *Yom Tov Kiddush.*

The Mateh Moshe, a compilation of customs by a disciple of the Maharshal, cites sources for pouring wine that indicate that the custom is limited to Saturday night. Some examples: "From Esau and Yishmael emanate 70 powers who are dormant on *Shabbat* but on Saturday night seek to castigate Israel. The Hebrew word for wine is *yayin*, which has a numerical value of 70. The wine (symbolizing the 70 troublemakers) is thrown to the ground right after *Shabbat* to weaken their powers." "At *Havdalah* we must formally separate ourselves from the children of Korach by pouring wine on the ground . . ." (Mateh Moshe 504). Accordingly, such mystic (or kabbalistic) reasons are simply not operational on *Shabbat* or *Yom Tov.*

Holding the Kos Shel Berachah

QUESTION: Should the goblet of wine used for *Kiddush, Havdalah,* or any other mitzvah be held in a special way?

RESPONSE: Yes. Most people simply wrap their hand around the side of the goblet. In such a fashion the goblet is held by the fingers and the bottom of the goblet generally has no hand contact at all. They simply hold the goblet in the same manner that they hold any glass or cup for drinking purposes.

Of interest is that such a procedure is not an accepted halachic practice.

The Magen Avraham cites the Shelah who contends that one should place the goblet on the palm of one's hand and hold it in place by one's fingers (*Orech Chayyim* 186:6). The *Shulchan Aruch HaRav,* however, notes a preference to place the bottom of the goblet not on one's palm, but rather on one's four extended fingers (*Orech Chayyim* 183:7). Accordingly, both practices are contrary to common usage. The Mishneh Berurah, moreover, cites only the custom of holding the goblet (*becher*) in one's palm (*Orech Chayyim* 183:15), while the *Aruch HaShulchan* cites both practices (*Orech Chayyim* 183:5).

The *Shulchan Aruch* also notes that a left-handed person should hold the goblet in his left hand, contrary to the practice of right-handed people, who hold the goblet in their right hand (*Orech Chayyim* 183:5). The Taz, however, demurs. He contends that for rabbinic mitzvot one should not make any distinction between right-handed and left-handed people. All should follow the prevalent mode, which is to use the right hand (*Orech Chayyim* 183:9). Both the Mishneh Berurah and *Aruch HaShulchan* do not cite this position of the Taz. The Taz bases his view on the halachic position that even a left-handed person should hold the *lulav* and *etrog* in his right hand, for the actual requirement of using the right hand for *lulav* is not a biblical requirement. Since, however, the Rema explicitly rules that a left-handed person should hold the *lulav* in his left hand (*Orech Chayyim* 651:3), the same should hold true as the correct procedure for holding a goblet of wine used for a mitzvah.

Of interest is that the Vilna Gaon notes that the above concerns are but forms of enhancing the mitzvah (*hiddur mitzvah*) but certainly issues that would not require repetition of the *berachah* (Mishneh Berurah 183:20).

As such, even should the goblet be held in a manner not preferred by halachah, ex post facto it is still a valid *berachah.*

Holding the Havdalah *Cup*

QUESTION: During *Havdalah* on Saturday night, upon conclusion of the wine *berachah* should the wine goblet yet be held while other *berachot* are chanted?

RESPONSE: The *Shulchan Aruch* records the following proper procedure for the recitation of *Havdalah*: "The wine is held in the right (hand) and the *myrtle* in the left (hand); [after] the blessing for the wine, one then takes the *myrtle* in the right (hand) and the wine in the left (hand); one makes a *berachah* on the *myrtle* and then returns the wine to the right (hand)" (*Orech Chayyim* 296:6).

This halachah is reported without any dissenting view. It delineates four important procedures: (1) Whenever one recites a *berachah* for a mitzvah upon an item that may be held, the specific item (i.e., wine, spice, *lulav*, etc.) should be held in the right hand while the *berachah* is actually chanted (see Taz, *Orech Chayyim* 296:6). (2) The second item to be used (spice) should be held in the left hand while the first *berachah* is chanted. (3) When the second *berachah* (spice) is recited, the wine must yet still be held in the left hand. The rationale for not putting down the wine, suggests the Mishneh Berurah, is that it is a mitzvah for all blessings of *Havdalah* to be [somehow] related to the cup of wine (Mishneh Berurah 296:30). (4) The spice may be left on a table and not held subsequent to its *berachah* (Mishneh Berurah 296:31).

The *Aruch HaShulchan* remarks that the procedure to hold items in the left hand is not mandatory. Accordingly, his common custom was not to hold the spice in the left hand while the *berachah* was recited for the wine. In addition, the wine was not held but, rather, placed on the table when the spice *berachah* was recited. He concludes that it is a fine custom to hold the second item to have a blessing pronounced over it in the left hand while the first is chanted, but such is simply not obligatory (*Orech Chayyim* 296:17).

The Aishel Avraham reflected on his personal custom to hold the goblet of wine in his right hand at *Havdalah* but not to hold any items in his left hand. To the extent that he could not recall the rationale for not following the procedure detailed in the *Shulchan Aruch*, he suggested that any personal qualms (lacking substantiation) should not merit discontinuance of the *Shulchan Aruch*'s mode of *Havdalah.*

In addition, holding the items before and after the *berachah*, he notes, may be a form of displaying affection and enhancement for the mitzvah (*chibuv mitzvah*). As such, it would appear that the preferential mode would be to follow the *Shulchan Aruch*'s set procedure (*Aishel Avraham, Mahadura Batra, Siman* 296:6). Indeed, the concept of displaying affection for mitzvot (*chibuv mitzvot*) is not an unpopular principle. The Rema contends that the custom of kissing *tzitzit* and placing them over the eyes is a means of demonstrating love for the mitzvah (*Darchai Moshe*,

Orech Chayyim 24). Accordingly, the principle delineated by the *Shulchan Aruch* should be the preferential mode with the recognition that ex post facto (*b'dieved*) it is only necessary to hold the item in one's hand while the *berachah* for that item is chanted.

The Challah Cover

QUESTION: Why must the *challot* be covered during *Kiddush*? Is it permissible to utilize a mesh or "see-through" challah covering? Is there any tradition of using only a white covering?

RESPONSE: The Taz cites two reasons presented by the Tur for covering the *challot*: (1) To the extent *Kiddush* is recited over wine, the *challot* are covered to symbolically shield them from the embarrassment of being present yet not used for the *berachah*. (2) The two *challot* symbolize the manna that came from heaven on the eve of *Shabbat* when the Jews were in the wilderness. Such manna had a covering of dew both under and above it. According to the first reason it would not be necessary to cover the *challot* when *Kiddush* is recited over challah. Yet the general custom, says the Taz, is to cover the *challot* even under such circumstances, due to the second reason (*Orech Chayyim* 271:9). The Magen Avraham additionally notes that based upon the first reason it would be proper to remove the cover directly after the *berachah* for wine. But the custom is not to remove the cover until after the entire *Kiddush* is recited in order to afford proper dignity (*Orech Chayyim* 271:20). The Mishneh Berurah cites the Pri Megadim who rules that the cover should be on the *challot* until after *Kiddush*. Yet the Chayai Adam notes that according to the second reason it should be covered until after the *berachah* of *hamotzi* (Mishneh Berurah, *Orech Chayyim* 271:41).

What is apparent is that the stringencies of both explanations presented for covering the *challot* are operational at all times. As such, the following additional concerns should be noted: (1) My grandfather, the Minchat *Shabbat*, suggests that according to the first reason it is necessary to totally cover up the *challot* to shield their (symbolic) embarrassment due to the *Kiddush* over wine. This would exclude from usage any cover that is "see-through," for such would not "hide" the *challot* (see Shiurai Mincha, *Minchat Shabbat* 77:8). (2) According to the second reason, the covering of the *challot* is not related to any issue over wine or *Kiddush*. Thus it would appear that during the third *Shabbat* meal in the afternoon the *challot* should also be covered; for indeed, *lechem mishneh* is obligated at this meal (see Baier Yaakov, *Orech Chayyim* 271:18). (3) In addition, according to the second reason a tablecloth under the *challot* is always necessary to sustain the symbolism of the manna.

A side issue relates to the color of the *challot* cover. Some scholars (Eliyahu Rabba) contend such covers must be white. The Tehila L'David suggests that, perhaps, the concern is that the cover be clean and not previously used to be eaten upon; for the color of the *challot* cover does not seem to be an issue of concern (*Tehila L'David* 271:13).

Part IV

Prayers and Synagogue Rules

Prayers

Gates of Tears

QUESTION: The Talmud contends that "from the day that the *Bet HaMikdash* was destroyed, the gates of prayer were locked . . . but the gates of tears were never sealed" (*Bava Metzia* 59a, *Berachot* 32b). The implication is that tears have an impact upon prayers—or better yet, tearful prayers are always in order. Wherein are tearful prayers more significant or potent than simple prayers without tears?

RESPONSE: The Talmud states (*Soteh* 11a) that prior to the enactment of the evil decrees that enslaved the Jews in Egypt, Pharaoh sought the counsel of three sages. Job was silent at this meeting and subsequently was punished by the Almighty for his silence by the affliction of pain. Yet punishment in the Bible generally relates in some form to the nature of the crime. In this situation the punishment of pain in no way relates to the sin of Job. Also, it is necessary to determine the nature of Job's immoral behavior. What sin did he commit by being silent? His silence may be construed as a form of acquiescence to the slavery of the Jews promulgated by Pharaoh, but is it not possible that Job firmly believed that any action or statement on his part would be to no avail? What impact would his demurral have upon Pharaoh? How could one individual go against the powerful Egyptian military machine? Sensing, therefore, the futility of any contrary position, Job merely was silent. Was this silence such a grievous crime that Job was subsequently punished by the agony of constant physical pain and sickness?

Our sages contend that the punishment of pain was a divine lesson to Job, and through him to all mankind, that the argument of futility is not morally adequate to sustain silence in times of danger. Job was afflicted with such severe ailments that he cried out constantly because of the unbearable agony of the pain. Why did he cry? Why did he publicly bemoan his physical pain? Did he not know that screaming and moaning would not help the condition? Is it not futile to moan when one is in pain? The answer is that it is the nature of man to cry out when he hurts. *Crying does not stop the pain, but, rather, gives evidence that the pain exists.* It is the manifestation that something is wrong. The silent person is basically one who does not poignantly feel pain: All is well, there is no reason to cry. Job's reaction to his own plight, and his silence in the face of impending danger to Jews, proved that Job felt no internal pain when Jews were killed. Job cried over his personal problems, not over pogroms of Jews. The enslavement and the possible ultimate destruction of the Jewish people did not disturb Job's emotional tranquility. Had Job been a friend to the Jewish people, then silence would have been impossible. The natural human strands of emotions would have evoked a verbal crescendo of pain. Silence was, therefore, evidence of no concern and no personal involvement. For this reason, Job's silence was marked as a message of immorality (*Sichot Musar*; HaRav Chayyim Shmuelevitz, Rosh HaYeshivah, Mir, Jerusalem, 5733, *Ma'amar* 5).

Thus, tears or crying are merely outward manifestations that something hurts. It is an indication that one wishes the pain to be removed. A change of status is desired; the status quo must be eliminated. This is what prayers with tears represents. God is recognized as having the power to take away the pain. The penitent is aware that unless a change takes place, the pain is unbearable. This type of prayer is always acceptable to God. It is reflective, meaningful, and relates to man's need to extricate himself from an unbearable situation.

Slow Daveners in a Minyan

QUESTION: How is a person who *davens* very slowly to participate in the communal responses of a minyan?

RESPONSE: A Baal Teshuvah complained to me as follows: He takes an inordinately long time to recite the *Amidah.* As such, he rarely ever has an opportunity to recite *Kedushah* or to hear the *Kaddish* at the end of *Minchah.* Perhaps, he suggested, it would be preferable to start his personal *Shemoneh Esrai* much before others commence to *daven* so that he could conclude in sufficient time to respond to *Kedushah* and *Kaddish* together with the minyan.

Of interest is that this question was posed by the Mishneh Berurah in his commentary, *Bai'ur Halachah.* The halachah states that in the event a person comes late to synagogue services and has yet to *daven* the *Amidah,* he must make a judgment as to his future actions. Should his assessment be that he could start and conclude the recitation of the *Amidah* prior to the *shliach tzibur*'s commencement of *Kedushah,* then so should he do. If, however, his judgment is that the *shliach tzibur* will start the *Kedushah* while he was in the middle of the *Shemoneh Esrai,* then he is not to *daven* the *Amidah* at that time, but rather listen to the *shliach tzibur* and recite the *Kedushah* and the subsequent *Kaddish* together with others in the minyan (*Orech Chayyim* 109:1).

This halachah suggests that it is more important to respond to *Kedushah* and *Kaddish* than to say the *Amidah* with the minyan. Accordingly, perhaps it is proper to inform slow *daven*-ers to start their *Shemoneh Esrai* prayers prior to the entire minyon so that they would have an opportunity to at least respond to *Kedushah* and *Kaddish.*

The Mishneh Berurah discounts this proof. He contends that the above-noted halachah deals specifically with a person who comes late to *shul.* This means that the latecomer is not present when the community starts to *daven* the silent *Amidah.* As such, he lacks the true mitzvah of *daven*ing with a minyan (*tefila b'tzibur*), which takes place when all start *daven*ing together. That is why the halachah mandates a preference for reciting *Kedushah* or *Kaddish* over saying the *Amidah.* But, having a choice to observe the mitzvah of communal prayer by starting to *daven* with everyone or to *daven* early to respond to other matters such as *Kedushah* and *Kaddish,* it may be preferable simply to *daven* with all. Two reasons are presented:

1. The mitzvah of *telifa b'tzibur daven*ing with a minyan precedes the mitzvah of responding to *Kedushah* and *Kaddish.* It therefore takes priority over the subsequent mitzvot.

2. By starting to *daven* with the minyan, one may be absolved from responding to other prayers for he is deemed comparable to one who is unable to *daven* through no personal fault (an *a'nus*). This person was instructed to acquire his mitzvah of *tefila b'tzibur* and therefore is freed of other responses during this period of time (see *Bai'ur Halachah, Orech Chayyim* 109).

Relying on the Services of a Hazzan

QUESTION: May one rely on the services of a *hazzan* throughout the year?

RESPONSE: The general rule is that a person who knows how to pray may not use the services of a cantor (or *shliach tzibur*) to fulfill personal obligations (Magen Avraham, *Orech Chayyim* 124:1). Mishneh Berurah contends that this rule is applicable not only *ab initio* but also ex post facto (*b'dieved*) (*Orech Chayyim* 124:1). Thus, anyone who purposely relies on the prayers of the cantor would be obliged to repeat the entire *Amidah.*

Yet there is an exception to this rule. The *Shulchan Aruch* notes that in the event a person recited the *Shemoneh Esrai* but neglected to say *Ya'aleh V'Yavo,* he may pay attention to the *shliach tzibur*'s prayer and be included in that prayer (*Orech Chayyim* 124:10). The reason, says the Bet Yosef (*Orech

Chayyim 124), that a person who knows how to *daven* may rely on the *shliach tzibur*, is that he at least did, in fact, pray. All he did was forget a special prayer such as *Ya'aleh V'Yavo* (or *Mashiv HaRuach*) (Mishneh Berurah, *Orech Chayyim* 124:39).

The procedure for relying on the *shliach tzibur* is to listen attentively to every *berachah* he recites (*Orech Chayyim* 124:10). To the extent that most people simply cannot listen so carefully, the preferred mode is to just *daven* again oneself (*Mishneh Berurah* 124:40).

The *Bai'ur Halachah* cites Rav Akiva Eiger, who provides an interesting nuance to the aforementioned concept. There are times when, due to an error, it is not necessary to repeat the entire *Amidah*, just to return to the last section, which begins with *Retzah*. Should this occur, one should not conclude the *Amidah*, but wait silently for the *shliach tzibur* to recite the *Amidah*. It is, moreover, not necessary to have *kavana* during the entire *Amidah*, but only from *Retzah* onward. Accordingly, it may not be so difficult to be attentive for such a short period of time.

Coupled to this is the recognition that the *shliach tzibur* definitely includes in his prayers those who are not proficient. Some say that should the *shliach tzibur* be a *hasid* who knows and actually has proper *kavana* for all *berachot*, perhaps such a person can include others who, compared to him and his level of spiritual *kavana*, are classified as "those who know not how to pray" (see *Be'er Mosheh, Orech Chayyim* 124:17, cited in the name of the Aishel Avraham).

Quivering While Praying

QUESTION: Is it necessary to shake and quiver (*shokel*) during prayer?

RESPONSE: The Rema notes that those who are scrupulous have a custom to quiver while praying, to symbolize the concept that "all my sinews speak (of God)" (*Orech Chayyim* 48). Both the Mishneh Berurah (*Orech Chayyim* 48:5) and the *Aruch HaShulchan* (*Orech Chayyim* 48:3) rule that quivering during prayer is a matter of personal preference. If it stimulates *kavana* (intentions of prayer), then it is desirable. If, on the other hand, it distracts one from serious prayer, then *it should not be practiced.*

As such, each person may decide upon the mode of prayer most beneficial to crystallize the proper aura for serious contemplation. In addition, one who cannot concentrate while quivering should not presume that it is a mitzvah to quiver even though it distracts from personal serious prayer.

Making Two Minyanim *Rather than One*

QUESTION: Is it permissible to divide up one large minyan into two or more smaller *minyanim* so that more than one person may have the honor of leading services?

RESPONSE: Many congregations are confronted with this problem when more than one person commemorates a *yahrzeit* and both wish to lead the services. A simple solution is to divide up the assemblage and have each lead a separate minyan. At issue, of course, is whether such a procedure has halachic propriety.

Initial reaction is that one large minyan is better than two smaller groups. This is based upon the following: The Talmud records that in the event people were (learning Torah) in a *Bet*

Midrash at the conclusion of *Shabbat* and light was brought in (so that the *Havdalah* ceremony could be recited), Bet Shammai said that each should make a blessing over the light for himself while Bet Hillel said that one person should say a *berachah* on behalf of all because it is written (Proverbs 14:28), "In the multitude of people is the king's glory (*berov am*)" (*Berachot* 53a). Halachic tradition follows the ruling of Bet Hillel. Namely, halachic propriety mandates all to do a mitzvah together rather than for each to observe the mitzvah independently. Accordingly, it would appear that it would also be preferable for one large minyan to pray, as opposed to two smaller *minyanim*. Indeed, the actual division of the large minyan would be an overt action violating the principle of *berov am*. Just as the individual's desire to recite the *Havdalah* light blessing by himself is deemed secondary to the overriding benefit of participation in a large assemblage, so too should the will to lead services be subordinate to the advantage of *daven*ing in one large minyan.

HaRav HaGaon Rav Shlomo of Vilna, however, deduces from yet another talmudic citation halachic permission to divide up the large minyan into smaller components.

It is known that the *kohen gadol* performed a number of tasks on Yom Kippur. He read from the Torah and also brought a number of sacrifices. The Mishnah reports that "He who sees the high priest when he reads (the Torah) does not see the (sacrifices of) the bullock and he-goat that were being burnt. . . . (Why?) Not that he (the observer) was not permitted, but because the distance apart was great, and both rites were performed at the same time" (*Yoma* 68b). Commenting upon this mishnah the Gemorah was concerned with the necessity to detail that it was permissible for a person to observe both the ritual of the burning of the *korban* (sacrifice) as well as the *kohen gadol*'s reading of the Torah. Was it not self-evident that both acts were permissible for observers to watch as well as to go from one to another? To this the Talmud notes that there is a precept that might appear to be violated. It is the rule that one does not leave one mitzvah to attend to another. To this the Talmud questions, "And what mitzvah is here?" That is, spectators are not performing any mitzvah. The Talmud responds that there is the mitzvah of "in the multitude of people there is the king's glory (*berov am*)." Rashi notes that, generally, it is prohibited to leave one mitzvah to perform another. The reason why it is permitted to leave observing the mitzvah of burning the sacrifices or watching the *kohen gadol* is that the spectators were not actually involved in the performance of the mitzvah itself (*Yoma* 70a).

Rav Shlomo of Vilna notes that this talmudic citation overtly suggests that a violation of the principle of *berov am* takes place only after one has commenced the mitzvah or been actively involved in the mitzvah itself. Prior to personal involvement in the mitzvah there is no violation of *berov am*, should one depart from the assemblage. Accordingly, before a group begins actually *daven*ing, there would be no violation of *berov am* to divide up into smaller *minyanim* (see *Responsa Binyan Shlomo*, vol. II, *Siman* 13).

Blessings Over the Birth of a Grandchild

QUESTION: May a grandparent recite the *berachah* of *She'hecheyanu* upon the birth of a grandchild?

RESPONSE: At issue is whether a person truly overjoyed at being able to personally witness a particular event has the halachic right to express such happiness by reciting the complete *berachah* of *She'hecheyanu*.

The halachic key to resolving this question is an understanding of the following: The Talmud cites Raba's concern as to whether the *berachah* of *She'hecheyanu* should be recited on

Rosh Hashanah and Yom Kippur. Rav Yehuda remarked that he personally chanted this *berachah* whenever he viewed a new crop of pumpkins. To this the Talmud responds that Rav Yehuda's custom has no bearing on the issue at hand and does not, in any way, resolve Raba's question. Why? The rationale expressed was that Raba was not concerned with whether a person could voluntarily recite the *berachah* of *She'hecheyanu*. Raba's issue was whether one was obligated to recite the *berachah* on Rosh Hashanah and Yom Kippur (*Eruvin* 40b).

From this citation HaGaon HaRav Yechezkel Landau (the Noda B'Yehuda) derives the principle that there is nothing wrong halachically with a person reciting the *She'hecheyanu berachah* on a voluntary basis to express joy and/or appreciation to God. Such a voluntary recitation of the *berachah* does not even verge upon the prohibition against taking God's Name in vain. Raba was concerned only with whether an obligation to say this *berachah* at certain times was operational. But should someone for personal reasons of happiness decide to recite the *berachah*, it appears to be permissible (*Tzlach*, *Berachot* 60a).

Of interest is that numerous distinctions could have been delineated limiting the recitation of *She'hecheyanu* to specific cases (i.e., annual events). The fact that the above scholar makes no such qualifications indicates that the voluntary recitation expressing joy is a personal judgment call and is permitted. As such, should a grandparent be overjoyed at being alive to be privileged with a grandchild, the *berachah* of *She'hecheyanu* may be chanted.

The Mishneh Berurah may not necessarily agree with the above position. He rules that a person who has many sons and truly looks forward to the birth of a daughter still does not make a blessing (*Hatov U'maitiv*) upon the daughter's birth (see *Orech Chayyim* 223:2). The implication is that the Mishneh Berurah rules that the father in this case ought not to recite any *berachah*.

Another reading may be that such blessing is not to be automatically recited or deemed obligatory, but a voluntary recitation is permissible. The latter theory seems viable, for the

Mishneh Berurah makes the following concluding remarks. He rules that a person who has a daughter born to him may recite the *She'hecheyanu berachah* when first he sees his daughter. The rationale presented is that a new father should be deemed to be in the same category as one who has not seen a friend for over thirty days. Such a person is permitted to recite the *berachah* to express the joy at seeing his friend once again. A new child is no less a happy event than meeting an old friend. Accordingly, experiencing the joy of a new grandchild should certainly be comparable, and a *berachah* should be permissible.

Of interest is that the Talmud notes—and it is so recorded in the Codes—that a personal, private pleasure mandates the *berachah* of *She'hecheyanu*, while a shared or communal joy requires the *berachah* of *Hatov U'maitiv* (see *Berachot* 59b; also *Orech Chayyim* 221:2). As such, perhaps, the proper *berachah* to be recited over the birth of a grandchild should be *Hatov U'maitiv* rather than *She'hecheyanu*. Harav Yitzchak Arielli, however, cites scholars who rule that the blessing of *Hatov U'mativ* is reserved for physical and material benefits, not spiritual or emotional joys (see *Einayim LaMishpat*, *Berachot* 59b). A grandchild is definitely an emotional and spiritual joy.

Tzitzit *and Ball Playing*

QUESTION: Must *tzitzit* be worn while playing ball games?

RESPONSE: The *Aruch HaShulchan* discusses the issue of wearing *tzitzit* in the *bet hakisai* (lavatory) and the *bet hamerchatz* (bath house). He notes the practice of removing a *tallit gadol* in a *bet hakisai* but not that of taking off the *tallit katan* worn under garments. His basic theory is that one should never defame or desecrate the *tzitzit*. Thus, *tzitzit* should not be brought to an inappropriate or unclean place. Yet the Sages did not wish to generate undue difficulties for people. As such a *tallit gadol* was removed prior to entering these places for there was no great difficulty (*tirchah*) in the removal. Since it was more of an effort to take off a *tallit katan* each time one went to the bathroom, the Sages did not impose an obligation of removal (*Aruch HaShulchan, Orech Chayyim* 21:6).

The implication of this halachah is that should a person be scrupulous over the sanctity of the *tzitzit* and wish to take off his *tallit katan* prior to entering a bathroom, he would certainly be permitted to do so. The halachah did not obligate him to take off such *tzitzit*, but he may certainly volunteer such activity.

In addition, clarification is needed to explain why *tzitzit* may be a problem altogether in a *bet hamerchatz* (bath house). The simple response is that the garment may become filthy or dirty with perspiration. Accordingly, to preserve the cleanliness and sanctity of the *tzitzit*, halachic standards would not be violated should *tzitzit* be removed prior to playing ball. Just as one does not wear *tzitzit* with a bathing suit at a beach, one also does not wear *tzitzit* over or under a uniform while playing basketball. This means that *tzitzit* may be removed to keep them clean so that they do not become full of perspiration during a ball game. The rationale for the removal of the *tallit katan* at ball playing thus becomes a means of preserving and enhancing its sanctity and not an irreligious gesture. Of course one is not required to remove a *tallit katan* during ball playing. The removal, however, may be granted to preserve its cleanliness.

Blessing a Jewish Scientist

QUESTION: Is it proper to recite a blessing (*berachah*) upon meeting a renowned Jewish scientist?

RESPONSE: The Talmud reports: "On seeing the Sages of Israel (*chachmei Yisrael*), one should say: Blessed be He Who has shared His wisdom (*Baruch she'chalak*). On seeing the sages of other nations, one says: Blessed be He Who has given of His wisdom (*Baruch she'natan*)" (*Berachot* 58a).

The implication appears to be that Jewish wise men (*chachmei Yisrael*) mandate a *berachah* regardless of the type or quality of knowledge they possess. Accordingly, it would be proper to recite a *berachah* upon meeting a brilliant Jewish scientist. Yet a careful reading of the codes suggest that the above is not operational. HaGaon HaRav Yitzchok Hutner (*z"l*) points out that the codes state: "Should one see wise Gentiles who are scholars in secular knowledge, one says blessed be He . . . Who has given from His wisdom to human beings" (*Orech Chayyim* 224:7). Note the specific terminology of the codes. The blessing is reserved for Gentiles who are knowledgeable in secular wisdom. Apparently, Jews who are masters of secular wisdom are not to receive a *berachah*. By the same token, Gentiles who excel in Talmud also would not be granted a *berachah*. Why?

In dealing with *berachot* (blessings) there is a guiding principle of primary and secondary purpose: *ikar* and *tafel*. For example, a blessing for spice is only made when the spice is originally set up solely for the purpose of providing fragrance. Should the spice, however, have other purposes, then even if it gives a pleasant fragrance, one does not recite a *berachah* upon enjoying its fragrance. The pleasing fragrance that commands a *berachah* must emanate from its essential purpose (see *Orech Chayyim* 217:2). So too, concludes HaGaon HaRav Hutner (*z"l*), does it relate to blessings over people. The prime purpose of the Jew is to learn Torah. This is the goal of his existence. Everything else, including secular scholarship or scientific knowledge, is of a secondary value to the Jewish soul. They are important—they may even be vital to life, but they are still secondary to Torah. As such, a *berachah* on a person is recited only when a Jew excels in his primary role—the study of Torah. So too with the Gentile. A blessing does not take place even when he excels in Torah, for that is not his primary role (see *Pachad Yitzchok, V'zot Chanukak, Ma'Amar* 9:2 and 9:6).

The Last Z'man *for* Minchah

QUESTION: Must the entire *Minchah* service be concluded prior to the time given to recite this *tefilah*? Or is it merely necessary to start *daven*ing in the proper time frame even though the conclusion takes place at a time after it is too late to start *daven*ing *Minchah*?

RESPONSE: The *Aruch HaShulchan* suggests that the halachic limits established for the conclusion of the *Minchah* service relate only to the last moment that one may start the *Minchah Amidah*, not to when it should be concluded. His substantiation is as follows: The Talmud notes that *k'lal Yisrael* is privileged in that even though they may have deserved God's anger, which lasts but a second, God did not express His anger to them. Commenting upon this, *Tosafot* asked, "What could be said in a second?" In other words, the time of a second is so minute that even had God, *chas v'shalom*, manifested anger to Jews, nothing could have been heard. To this *Tosafot* responded that once the anger (or curse) started in the proper time it would have continued subsequent to the formal moment of anger (see *Tosafot, Berachot* 7a).

From this, says the *Aruch HaShulchan*, one may derive the rule that once a prayer is started within the proper time frame, then even should the conclusion be after the prescribed time, it is permissible. The rationale is that if the starting time is the crucial period for a Divine Curse (or anger), it certainly should be the same for blessings (see *Orech Chayyim* 110:5).

Based upon this ruling, the *Aruch HaShulchan* provides a

unique twist to yet another halachah. The rule is that should there be not sufficient time to *daven Minchah,* then it is permissible to have the *hazzan* immediately commence the public, audible *Amidah.* That is, in such a case it is not necessary to first have all say the silent *Amidah* and then to have the *hazzan* repeat the process. At issue to the *Aruch HaShulchan* was the specific prayer that could not be concluded in a proper time. According to the above-mentioned rule the concern must be that should everyone *daven* in the normal mode, then there would not be sufficient time for the *hazzan* to even start the public *Amidah* in time. For should there be time for the *hazzan* to start in the proper time, then there should be no qualms when he concludes (*Orech Chayyim* 124:6).

A Siddur *on a* Chumash

QUESTION: Is it permitted to place a *siddur* or Gemorah on top of a *Chumash*?

RESPONSE: Common custom considers such a practice as a form of disrespect to the sanctity of the Bible. The source may be the following: "One may lay one Torah scroll upon another Torah scroll—and a Torah upon *Chumashim* (namely, one of the five books of Moses entirely written as a *sefer Torah* on parchment and then rolled together)—and *Chumashim* may be placed on (books) of the prophets or (sacred) writings, but one may not place books of the prophets or (sacred) writings on *Chumashim,* nor *Chumashim* upon Torah scrolls (*sifrai Torah*)" (*Megillah* 27a). From the above it is evident that there are various levels of sanctity, with the Torah being on the highest rung of *kedushah.* As such, neither a *siddur* nor a Gemorah should be placed on top of a *Chumash.*

Of pragmatic interest is the observation of the codes on this talmudic dictum. The Rema notes that the rule prohibiting placing a book of the prophets on a *Chumash* relates only to a *Chumash* that was written on a scroll like a *sefer Torah*. In the event the *Chumash* was not so written, then there is no distinction (as to comparative levels of *kedushah*) between a *Chumash* and a book of the prophets (*Yoreh Deah* 283:1). The *Aruch HaShulchan* makes the following clarification: Every holy book of the Bible (*Torah*, *Nevi'im*, and *Ketuvim*) has *kedushah*, but this is a general sense of sanctity that relates to the nature of its essence, to its contents. Apart from this, there is another distinct degree of *kedushah* that is granted to specific forms of texts. In other words, in addition to the contents, the format of how the text is written and reproduced adds another level of *kedushah*. In this regard, a *sefer Torah* is afforded the highest level of respect and sanctity. Yet when the contents are not in the form of a (Torah) scroll but, for example, printed in book form, as is so in our times, one book does not have any more sanctity than another. Indeed, the written Torah does not have (in book form) any more sanctity than the oral Torah. As such, there should be no halachic qualms over placing a Gemorah on top of a printed *Chumash*. Once the format for reproducing Torah texts was altered from handwritten scrolls on parchment to printed books, rules the *Aruch HaShulchan*, all these books, regardless of contents, have a comparable level of *kedushah* (*Aruch HaShulchan*, *Yoreh Deah* 283:6). One may, therefore, even place a *siddur* over a *Chumash*.

Preserving Sifrai Torah

QUESTION: Are there any special means of insuring that *sifrai Torah* are properly preserved?

RESPONSE: Apart from the requirement to protect the *kedushah* of a *sefer Torah* and to store it properly, there may be an added requirement for a certain type of usage that insures the *sefer Torah* is well preserved.

The Mishnah rules that "if one found *sefarim* [books in the form of scrolls] . . . he should roll them [from beginning to end to air them out to prevent their decay (see Rashi)]." Dealing specifically with Torah scrolls used as a deposit, the Talmud notes that it should be "rolled once every thirty days . . . Sumchos says, a new scroll [should be rolled] every thirty days, with an old scroll [once every twelve months], Rabbi Eliezer ben Yaakov [ruled] in either case [both new and old] it is required to be rolled once every twelve months" (*Baba Metzia* 29b).

Of interest is that the Codes maintain that one who finds a *sefer Torah* should roll it once in thirty days, while storing a *sefer Torah* as a deposit requires rolling once in twelve months (see *Choshen Mishpat* 267 and 292). The P'nai Yehoshua cites the Shach, who distinguishes between a deposit and a lost item. His theory is that a lost item requires special added care, for the owners are unaware as to the location of the *sefer Torah.*

From the above it is evident that scrolls, especially *sifrai Torah,* should be aired at least once a year to prevent them from becoming dusty or spoiled. As such, there are numerous *sifrai Torah* deposited in the Arks of synagogues in almost every Jewish community throughout the world. To preserve their integrity, perhaps, all should make certain that they are "rolled" from beginning to end at least once a year. Do we not have that obligation to care for the *sifrai Torah* in our possession? My feeling is that leaders of synagogues are at least comparable to those who are caring for scrolls put in their possession for safekeeping. The rolling of *sifrai Torah* scrolls located in synagogues may not be a mandated obligation, but it certainly should be an assumed responsibility of care and concern.

Brich Hu *of* Kaddish

QUESTION: What is the proper communal response when hearing the word *kudshah* recited in the *Kaddish*?

RESPONSE: There are three general responses: (1) Some call out *Brich Hu*, "Blessed be He." (2) Others await hearing the words *Brich Hu* and then respond "Amen." (3) The position of the Vilna Gaon is to be silent, to not respond at all. His rationale is that the phrase *Kudshah Brich Hu* is basically one word. It is the Aramaic form of *Hakadosh Baruch Hu* (the Holy One, Blessed Be He). As such it should not be subdivided into sections.

Of interest is that during the *Yamim Nora'im*, the word *leayla* is doubled. As a result, the next word, *min* (meaning "from"), is eliminated and in its place a *mem* (also signifying "from") is prefaced to the next word. The reason for this exchange is that according to kabbalah there is to be only twenty-eight words in the paragraph commencing with the phrase *Y'hai Shmai*. To the extent that between Rosh Hashanah and Yom Kippur an extra word is added to the *Kaddish*—namely, *leayla*—one word had to be eliminated to preserve the numerical count of twenty-eight (see *Mateh Ephraim Siman* 582:1).

Should one actually count the words of the paragraph commencing with *Y'hai Shmai Raba*, the number twenty-eight will be reached prior to the last two words, *V'imru amen*. Thus the last two words are not part of the kabbalistic formula. Yet, should one follow the ruling of the Vilna Gaon that *Kudsha Brich Hu* is one word, not three, then the phrase *V'imru amen* is an integral part of the twenty-eight words of this section. This adds a measure of credence to the Vilna Gaon's theory.

Praying with Bare Feet

QUESTION: Is it permitted to *daven* with bare feet?

RESPONSE: Rema rules that "one should not walk barefooted" (*Orech Chayyim* 2:6). Magen Avraham (2:7) and Vilna Gaon (2:6) contend that this is an imperative to wear shoes and is based on the talmudic precept mandating "selling even the beams of one's house in order to purchase shoes" (*Shabbat* 129a). Rashi contends that nothing is more shameful (or embarrassing) than a person walking in the street without shoes. Maharsha suggests an alternate theory. He contends that walking without shoes makes a person more susceptible to catching colds. As such, the mandate to wear shoes is a health remedy to prevent sickness.

According to Rashi, it would appear that within the confines or privacy of a home, there is no reason to wear shoes. Maharsha would also admit that where concern for "catching a cold" is not applicable then the mandate for shoes is also not operational. It should be noted that the above concern for wearing shoes is a general orientation, not one specifically related to prayer. Mishneh Berurah, moreover, reports that the entire halachah is not applicable to societies wherein the general custom is to not wear shoes at all. In addition, the Shela reports that should a person not wear shoes as a mark of penance, then it is permissible (*Orech Chayyim* 2:14).

This position, which in some way equates religious fervor with not wearing shoes, seems to be in harmony with biblical sources. Moshe Rabbenu, for example, is directed to "put off thy shoes from thy feet, for the place whereon thou standest is holy ground" (Exodus 3:5). Rav Samson Raphael Hirsch notes that "taking off" shoes expresses giving oneself entirely to the meaning of a place, "to take . . . a position without any intermediary." Another meaning may be that without shoes a person poignantly feels every minute stone or change in the contour of the land. It generates the sensitivity that is necessary for true religious feelings.

At issue is whether it is proper to pray with bare feet, for the above discussion relates only to the necessity of wearing shoes in general.

Shulchan Aruch rules that one should not pray with bare feet "if common custom is only to stand before people of stature wearing shoes" (*Orech Chayyim* 91:5). The Mishneh Berurah adds that should clothes cover the bare feet or should one reside in an area wherein it is dignified to be barefooted, it is proper to so *daven* (*Orech Chayyim* 91:13). *Aruch HaShulchan* suggests that those sages who permit *daven*ing without shoes do so only if socks are worn. In the event one's feet are truly bare, then even wherein it is dignified to not wear shoes prayer would not be permitted (*Orech Chayyim* 91:5).

This latter position appears to be contradicted by the common practice of *kohanim* in the *Bet HaMikdash*. In the *Bet HaMikdash* the *kohanim* did not wear shoes. The Talmud overtly notes that there was not to be any substance of any kind (no *hefsik*) between the feet of the *kohanim* and the floor of the *Bet HaMikdash*. Just as no item was permitted to interfere between the hands of *Kohanim* and the holy vessels (when used) so too was no substance to be between the *kohanim*'s feet and the floor of the *Bet HaMikdash*. Since the *korbanot* could only take place in the *Bet HaMikdash*, the floor itself assumed a holy status (see *Talmud Zevachim* 24a, *Rambam Hilchot Bi'at HaMikdash* 5:17). Accordingly, proper procedure for *kohanim* was to be barefooted. Rambam suggests that the long coats (*ketonet*) they wore extended to a length "above the heel" (*Kelai HaMikdash* 8:17). Accordingly, they also prayed with bare feet. Indeed, no injunction or directive is made to the *kohanim* to cover their bare feet during any of their services in the *Bet HaMikdash*.

Magdil *and* Migdol Yeshuot Malko

QUESTION: In the concluding portion of *Birkat HaMazon*, two practices are noted in *siddurim* relating to the recitation of either *Magdil yeshuot malko* or *Migdol yeshuot malko*. The former, *Magdil*, is a verse in *Tehillim* (18:51) and is translated to mean "Great deliverance he gives to his king." The latter, *Migdol*, is also a verse in Samuel II (22:51) and is interpreted as "He is the tower of salvation for his king." Both verses conclude with the exact following phrase: "and shows kindness to his anointed, to David and his seed, forever." Common custom is to recite *Migdol* on *Shabbat* and *Yom Tov*, as well as on Rosh Chodesh. What difference is there between the two verses? Why is one more appropriate for *Shabbat* and holidays than the other? Also, what should be recited at a wedding or *brit milah*?

RESPONSE: Ancient sources indicate that the word *migdol* with a *cholam* ("o" sound) is a higher, greater level of power and kingly prestige than *magdil*, whose *chi'rik* ("e" sound) symbolizes a low level of royalty. In addition, the verse with the phrase *Magdil* is located in *Tehillim*, which represented the phase of David's life prior to his being anointed king. However, *Migdol* is located in the Book of Samuel and represents the period after David had become king (see Abudram; also *Likutai Ma'harich*).

The implication is that *Shabbat*, *Yom Tov*, and Rosh Chodesh warrant enthroning God with the highest level of royal power and influence. Also, when referring to King David at such important periods of time, it is proper to utilize only verses that extoll him at the height of his power and reign.

Tradition has it that a bridegroom is deemed a symbolic king. As such, it would appear most appropriate to dramatically make him aware that no matter how great or powerful or royal he may believe he is, God's kingdom is greater. HaShem is the true king of the Jews. This suggests that just as *Shabbat* deserves the mentioning of God's greater royalty, so too does a wedding celebration. Every bridegroom must be reminded that God's reign is above us all. This lesson is certainly proper during *Birkat HaMazon,* which is a formal ritual for the expression of appreciation. Though it is not common custom, there is precedent in that the Kaf HaChayyim rules that *Migdol* should be recited at a wedding as well as at a *brit milah* (see *Siddur Tz'luta D'Avraham,* Commentary, *Shi'ruta D'Tz'luta*). Just as *Shir Ha'maalot* is recited at a wedding even on weekdays, so too should *Migdol* be chanted. A wedding is a *Yom Tov* for the bride and groom. A *Yom Tov* demands a higher level of royalty.

Lights in a Synagogue

QUESTION: Is there a preference for synagogues to be bright with light even when religious services are not held? In other words, is there a custom to manifest lights in a synagogue as a means of homage to the synagogue itself regardless of functional or utilitarian purposes?

RESPONSE: The *Havdalah* ceremony includes a special *berachah* for light. This *berachah* may be recited only over light that has a functional purpose. Of concern to the Talmud was the nature of lights in a synagogue. The issue was whether such light had a functional basis or was merely an aesthetic gesture. Two contradictory traditions were noted: In one a *berachah* was permitted, while in another such a *berachah* was disallowed. To resolve the difficulty, the Talmud noted that each tradition related to a different circumstance. "One is where an eminent guest is present; the other is where no such guest is present" (*Berachot* 53a). What is not clear is which case mandates a *berachah* and which case prohibits the recitation of a *berachah.*

Rashi suggests that when an eminent guest was present, the synagogue lights were kindled as an expression of honor to such a person. To the extent that the lights were not for functional purposes, no *berachah* was recited. If, however, no such guest was in attendance then the synagogue lights were kindled to enable worshippers to read their prayers. Thus, even if communal prayers were concluded, the lights lit in synagogue may be utilized for the blessing of the *Havdalah* ceremony.

Tosafot cite Rabbenu Hananel, who contends that should an eminent person be in attendance, then the synagogue candles were kindled for purposes of light and the *berachah* may be chanted. If, however, no guest was available, then the synagogue candles were lit as a form of *kavod Bet HaKnesset* (homage to the synagogue). This suggests a special tradition of maintaining lights in a synagogue to manifest its unique religious importance.

Rabbenu Asher rules that since in his day lights were lit in synagogues even by day for purposes of *kavod*, no *berachah* should be chanted. This must be based on the talmudic dictum that light used by day and by night does not mandate a *berachah* (*Berachot* 53a).

The *Shulchan Aruch* cites Rabbenu Hananel's position and also notes Rashi's view in the form "some say." The fact that Rav Hananel's view is reported without the preface of "some say" (*yeish omrim*) suggests that the mainstream tradition was for synagogues to have light for purposes of *kavod* (*Orech Chayyim* 298:11).

The *Shulchan Aruch HaRav* notes that the general custom was to have light in synagogues even by day for *kavod HaShechinah* (homage to the Holy Presence). As a result, even if such illumination was also utilized in the evening for purposes of light, no *berachah* may be recited. Why? Because such light was used by day. However, if additional candles were lit in the evening so that there would be more light, than a *berachah* may be recited (*Orech Chayyim* 298:17).

The Mishneh Berurah cites the custom noted by Rabbenu

Asher and contends that the synagogue light kindled by day for *kavod* refers to the illumination by the *amud* (in front of the synagogue). However, those candles held by each person in the synagogue were definitely for light, and upon them a *berachah* may be recited (*Orech Chayyim* 298:30).

Of interest is that the *Aruch HaShulchan* contends that the general custom was to kindle synagogue lights only for pragmatic purposes of light and, therefore, a *berachah* may be recited over such light (*Orech Chayyim* 298:15). This, of course, would not refer to the *ner tamid* or *yahrzeit* lamps, which definitely are only for *kavod*.

Thus, a variety of synagogue customs developed:

1. By day and night, lights were kindled for *kavod* of the synagogue (*Shulchan Aruch HaRav*).

2. Light in the synagogue was only for pragmatic reasons (*Aruch HaShulchan*).

3. Light wherein the leader of the services stood was kindled for purposes of *kavod*, while other illumination was only set up for purposes of light (Mishneh Berurah).

As a result, no halachic guideline is presented. It is conjectured that the variety of customs may have been dependent upon the affluence of the community. Perhaps the more affluent the community, the greater the tendency to sustain light in the synagogue for purposes of *kavod*. Common custom is to have a *ner tamid* (Eternal Light, always lit directly near the *Aron HaKodesh*). The above discussion suggests that this light be sustained even when no one is in the synagogue. Since such light is symbolic of the ancient menorah in the Holy Temple, it should never be extinguished. Also, to the extent that such light is for the purposes of *kavod*, this implies that the illumination should be of such a degree that it be noticeable even by day. In addition, the tradition of the Mishneh Berurah should be considered. That is, some light should be placed at the lectern wherein the *hazzan* prays for purposes of *kavod HaShechinah*.

Not all synagogues have such a custom. Of interest is that this practice generally persists today at services in the home of a mourner, wherein candles are lit prior to prayer. To the extent that its function is not pragmatic but symbolic, it would appear that indirect lighting would not meet this requirement.

Finally, if financial concerns are not a major problem, preference would be for synagogues to be lighted and bright.

To Stand or Sit and Direction of Prayers

Yishtabach

QUESTION: What is the reason for the custom to stand while reciting *Yishtabach*?

RESPONSE: The *Shulchan Aruch* rules that the *hazzan* for *Shacharit* (morning) services should stand and commence his role at the recitation of *Yishtabach* (*Orech Chayyim* 53:1). The Bach poses a number of concerns:

1. The *Yishtabach* prayer is the conclusion of the *berachah* for *P'sukai d'zimra*, which began with the prayer *Baruch she'amar*. As such, it seems strange that the *hazzan* for *Shacharit* should commence with the concluding *berachah* of a preceding section. Would it not be more suitable to begin his role with either *Kaddish* or *Barchu*?

2. The fact that the *hazzan* is mandated to stand for the recitation of *Yishtabach* implies that the congregation may be seated. Why is there such a distinction between the posture of the *hazzan* and that of the congregation?

3. The basic halachic guideline is that those prayers that require the *kedushah* of a *minyan* mandate all to stand (i.e., *Kaddish, Barchu, Kedushah*). It is a form of emulating angels, who stand while sanctifying God. Since *Yishtabach* does not require a *minyan* for its recitation, no one should be required to stand.

4. If for some reason *Yishtabach* does intrinsically require one to stand, why then is it that the Bet Yosef neglected to comment on the proper posture for chanting *Baruch she'amar?* Should not both the beginning and the end of the *P'sukai d'zimra berachah* require a similar posture? (Note: The *Shulchan Aruch* does not mandate standing for *Baruch she'amar*. This custom is stated by the Rema, *Orech Chayyim* 51:7.)

The Bach, therefore, suggests that the rationale for mandating the *hazzan* to stand for *Yishtabach* has no relationship to the general rule requiring standing for prayers that require a *minyan*. The reason why the *hazzan* stands also has nothing to do with the integral importance of the *Yishtabach* prayer. It is a secondary concern that imposes the *hazzan* to stand. In general, it is not deemed proper to have any interruption between *Yishtabach* and *Kaddish*. One prayer should flow directly into the other. Accordingly, it was not deemed suitable to await the arrival of the *hazzan* on the *bimah* after *Yishtabach* concluded. To ease the flow of continuity, the *hazzan* started his role with *Yishtabach* so that he might recite the *Kaddish* immediately without any interruption. This custom generated the communal response. The congregation also stood up during the chanting of *Yishtabach* so that they, too, could respond to *Kaddish* without any movement or interruption.[127]

On *Shabbat*, however, many were of the custom to sit. Why? Since the *hazzan* would spend considerable time singing, there was no reason for the congregation to stand idly. At such times they would rise at the beginning of the *Kaddish*. This rationale suggests that when a person does not pray with a *minyan*, it is not necessary to stand while saying *Yishtabach*.

Of concern to the Bach was the motivation for the custom to stand for *Baruch she'amar*. None of the reasons presented applies to this prayer. The Bach cites an ancient source (*Sefer Tola'at Yaakov*), which contends that the *Baruch she'amar* prayer was inaugurated by the men of the Great Assembly based upon an epistle that fell from heaven and contained eighty-seven words. This prayer is recited while standing (to emulate the role of angels) to signify its Divine status (Tur, *Orech Chayyim* 53).

The Mishneh Berurah notes that the Rema appears to indicate that one should always stand for *Yishtabach*, even when one prays without a *minyan* (see *Orech Chayyim* 51:6). He makes a distinction between a case in which one is mandated to stand according to *din* and one where standing is merely a custom (*minhag*) (*Orech Chayyim* 53:1). The implication is that standing for *Yishtabach* has a halachic mandate (*din*) when praying with a *minyan* and is simply custom when praying alone. The Vilna Gaon (*Orech Chayyim* 51:12) is cited as a corroborating source for the distinction. The actual phrase used by the Vilna Gaon should be noted. On the Rema's glosses that custom mandates standing while reciting *Baruch She'amar*, *VaYevaraich David*, and *Yishtabach*, the Gaon remarks: "for purposes of stringency" (*l'chumra b'alma*). In other words, all these prayers require standing only as a custom of stringency. Yet, when relating to standing for *Yishtabach* prior to *Kaddish*, the Vilna Gaon presents the Bach's rationale (*Orech Chayyim* 53:1).

The Blessing for the New Month

QUESTION: Why does the congregation stand for *Birkat HaChodesh* (the blessing for the new month)?

RESPONSE: The Magen Avraham suggests that the common custom to stand during *Birkat HaChodesh* is derived from the custom in ancient times to stand for *Kiddush HaChodesh*, the actual sanctification of the new moon (month) (Magen Avraham, *Orech Chayyim* 417:1).

HaRav Akiva Eiger was perturbed over the above rationale. His concern was that the Talmud does not clearly state that *Kiddush HaChodesh* was performed while standing. Indeed, just the opposite: The Talmud suggests that sitting was the proper mode.

An analysis of the talmudic citation relating to *Kiddush HaChodesh* provides insight into HaRav Akiva Eiger's dilemma. The Talmud notes that *Kiddush HaChodesh* required witnesses to testify before a *bet din*. The procedure was that the witnesses were required to testify while standing and the members of the *bet din* were mandated to sit while sanctifying the new month

(*Rosh Hashana* 25b). Rav Akiva Eiger's problem was that he was unsure as to the role of the congregation in modern times during the prayers for the new month. Is the assemblage comparable to witnesses giving testimony? In such a case then all should stand. On the other hand perhaps, the congregation is in lieu of *bet din* sanctifying the new month. Accordingly, all should sit. Rav Akiva Eiger seems to suggest that the latter view is the normative position.

A number of scholars have attempted to resolve Rav Akiva Eiger's quandary. HaRav Moshe Yakobzon (Hamburg) cites a *pesikta* (*Parshat Emor* 29) and a *semak* who note that any mitzvah that contains the phrase *Lachem* ("To you [plural]") must be performed while standing. As such, a *brit milah* and the mitzvah of wearing *tzitzit* are performed while standing (see Bet Yosef, *Orech Chayyim* 417). Since the term *Lachem* is an integral part of the scriptural mandate for Rosh Chodesh, it too must be observed while standing. Though the Talmud notes that the *bet din* sat during the sanctification of the new month, perhaps they sat while they heard the testimony but subsequently stood up together with all assembled to sanctify the new moon.

The above position was submitted to HaRav Marcus Mordechai Horovitz, Rav Frankfort-on-Main. HaRav Horovitz contended that the implication of the Talmud was that the *bet din* actually remained seated when they sanctified the month. He also rejected the relevance of the *pesikta*'s rule. He agreed that one must stand during the performance of mitzvot, but in a matter that requires an action of a *bet din* performing its function, it should take place while sitting. Of interest is that at *Kiddush HaChodesh* not only witnesses but assembled guests apart from *bet din* stood (see *Tosafot Shavuot* 30). Rav Horovitz contended that therefore the entire congregation may, perhaps, be comparable to an assemblage of witnesses and guests. Hence all stand (see Responsa *Matteh Levi*, part II, *Orech Chayyim*, no. 24).

An analysis of yet another talmudic citation appears to shed light upon a unique role performed by a congregation at

Kiddush HaChodesh that was apart and distinct from either *bet din* or witnesses. The Mishnah rules that the *Rosh Bet Din* concludes the sanctification process by chanting *Mekudash* ("It [the month] is sanctified") and the people present respond after him, *Mekudash, mekudash* ("It is sanctified, it is sanctified"). The Gemorah derives the mandated role of the assemblage from scriptural verses (see *Rosh Hashana* 24a).

Commenting on this procedure the Turai Even says that the *pesak* of *bet din* concludes with the *Rosh Bet Din*'s utterance of the phrase "It is sanctified." That statement of the head of the *bet din* is necessary to actually conclude the judicial process. Indeed, the utterance of the congregation is separate from the role of *bet din*, for the congregation's obligation is a special biblical mandate to respond to the decision of *bet din* (see Commentary, ch. III). Accordingly, the role of the congregation to sanctify the month is a mitzvah, apart from the judicial role of *bet din*. As such, it is to be observed while standing, as are all other mitzvot. It is not an integral part of *bet din*. For this reason all stand while *Birkat HaChodesh* is recited to commemorate the role of the assemblage to publicly voice affirmation of the new month. This role is not comparable to either *bet din* or the process of testimony. The community has a mitzvah to orally proclaim the new month. This mitzvah is what we re-enact during *Birkat HaChodesh*.

The Hazzan's Amidah

QUESTION: When the *Amidah* is repeated aloud by the *shliach tzibur*, should the congregation stand or sit?

RESPONSE: An halachic argument may be presented for either standing or sitting during the repetition of the *Amidah*.

The Rema rules that all should stand when the *hazzan* repeats the *Amidah* (*Orech Chayyim* 124:4). The Mishneh Berurah notes that all stand and pay attention to the prayers of the *hazzan*, and it is then deemed as if they are actually praying themselves (*Orech Chayyim* 124:20). The Vilna Gaon notes that all stand because the *hazzan*'s role is to include, through his prayers, those who do not know how to pray (*Orech Chayyim* 124:8). Accordingly, suggests HaRav Yosef Hakohen Schwartz (Grosswardein), perhaps those who do know how to pray need not stand. In fact, the custom of sitting during the *Amidah* repetition may be to demonstrate that they are proficient in prayers and need not be included in the prayers of the *hazzan* (Responsa, *VaYitzbar Yosef, Orech Chayyim* 39). The *Aruch HaShulchan* suggests that those who have difficulty standing for reasons of health may certainly be seated (*Orech Chayyim* 124:9).

Mizmor Shir Leyom HaSabbat

QUESTION: Why is it that during the Friday evening *Shabbat* prayers some people stand during the recitation of the *Mizmor Shir Leyom HaShabbat* prayers?

RESPONSE: The rationale is rooted in another custom. On Friday night some *siddurim* record that the *Bameh Madlikim* section (namely, the second chapter of the Mishnah, tractate *Shabbat*) should be recited directly before *Barchu*, while others note that it should be said after *Ma'ariv*. *Aruch HaShulchan* provides the following rationale for both customs. (It is well known that when a woman lights candles on Friday night she ipso facto assumes the sanctity of *Shabbat* by the recitation of the Friday evening *Shabbat* prayers.) At issue, says the *Aruch*

HaShulchan, is the specific Friday evening *tefilah* which for men is tantamount to *Kabbalat Shabbat.* In olden times, men assumed the *kedushah* of *Shabbat* (they were *mekabel Shabbat*) at the moment they recited the *Barchu* on Friday night. As such, the *Bameh Madlikin* was placed in the *siddur* directly before *Barchu* as an introductory preparation prior to the onset of *Shabbat.* The basic reason is that the *Bameh Madlikin* contains a number of admonitions and advice in order to properly usher in the *Shabbat.* For example, one is explicitly directed to make certain that lights were kindled for *Shabbat.* Consequently, it was deemed important to say the *Bameh Madlikim* right before *Barchu.* However, says the *Aruch HaShulchan,* in his day it was common practice to assume the onset of *Shabbat* by the recitation of the *Mizmor Shir Leyom HaShabbat* prayer. Accordingly, it was no longer necessary to say the *Bameh Madlikin* prayer before *Barchu* for people had already assumed the onset of *Shabbat* by previous prayers (*Orech Chayyim* 270:2). This, therefore, was the motivation for saying the prayer after *Ma'ariv.*

My grandfather, the Minchat *Shabbat*, cites the Beur Haitiv, who rules that whenever one is *Mekabel Shabbat* one should stand to express awe and reverence as if in the presence of royalty or grandeur (*Minchat Shabbat* 76:14, *Beur Haitiv* 262:5). Indeed, the Chida remarks that he took it upon himself to stand whenever he recited *Mizmor Shir Leyom HaShabbat* on Friday night (*Minchat Shabbat* 75:5).

Thus this *tefilah* symbolizes *Kabbalat Shabbat* and therefore mandates the reverent posture of standing. Since, moreover, this prayer represents the essential acceptance of *Shabbat*, it is the only one recited on *Yom Tov* that takes place on *Shabbat* (*Aruch HaShulchan* 270:3).

Mizmor Letodah: *To Stand or Sit?*

QUESTION: Does one stand or sit during the recitation of the *Mizmor LeTodah* prayer said during *Shacharit*?

RESPONSE: The Talmud notes that when *K'lal Yisrael* recite the Scriptural order of the offerings, God considers it as if they had brought the sacrifices and their sins will be forgiven (*Megillah* 31b, *Ta'anit* 27b). Magen Avraham rules that one should stand while saying the *korbanot* found in the morning prayers to emulate the *korbanot* in the *Bet HaMikdash*, which requires those involved in the process to stand (*Orech Chayyim* 48:1). The *Shulchan Aruch* Harav notes that similar logic would mandate one to stand while chanting *Mizmor LeTodah* (Piskai HaSiddur, *Siman* I:4). Yet, in a subsequent edition, the *Shulchan Aruch* Harav rules (that though some have the custom to stand) it is not necessary to do so while saying the *korbanot* because the person *daven*ing is not a *kohen* performing an actual service of a *korban*. As such, the Ketzot Hashulchan (which analyzes the halachot of the *Shulchan Aruch* Harav) adds that one may sit while reciting the *Mizmor LeTodah* prayer. He also cites the Shar Hakavanot who overtly states that one should say *Mizmor LeTodah* while seated (Piskai HaSiddur, Mahadura Batra, *Siman* 1:9, also *Ketzot Hashulchan, Piskai HaSiddur* p. 2). In terms of common practice, many *hasidim* sit whereas Ashkenazim stand.

Of concern is a necessity to provide a rationale for the custom to stand. Is not the *Shulchan Aruch* Harav correct in that the person *daven*ing is simply not in the *Bet HaMikdash* bringing a *korban* and subject to laws relating to *korbanot*? He is merely *daven*ing. Thus, he need not stand.

The *Aruch HaShulchan* argues that this logic solely applies to anyone who is not a *kohen*. Such a person does not have to simulate the role of a *kohen* in the *Bet HaMikdash*—a role he would never be able to perform. However, a *kohen*, even in contemporary times, is in a completely different situation. He should stand for he should consider the fact that had he been in the *Bet HaMikdash* bringing a *korban*, he would have stood as part of his obligation as a *kohen*. This imposes an obligation on every *kohen* (*Aruch HaShulchan, Orech Chayyim* 1:26). Apart from this mandate for *kohanim* to stand, it should be pointed out that the Magen Avraham never specifically delineated that one should emulate the *kohen* in the *Bet HaMikdash*. He merely stated that recitation of the *korbanot* should require one to stand as during the *korbanot* itself.

Of concern is the issue of who was required to stand while the sacrificial rites took place. The logic of the *Shulchan Aruch* Harav is that a non-*kohen* need not emulate the role of a *kohen* in the *Bet HaMikdash*. The implication is that during the *korbanot* only the *kohanim* were required to stand and everyone else, namely, spectators, was permitted to sit. But this is not so. Indeed, the Talmud rules that only kings who were descendants of King David were permitted to sit in the *azara* (see *Yuma* 25a). Accordingly, everyone present stood. This suggests that any references to the performance of *korbanot* should impose an obligation to simulate the posture of all during that process—namely, all should stand.

The Talmud records that the rule permitting only those who were descendants of King David to be seated did not refer to the *ezrat nashim* (*Sota* 41b). Thus the issue of standing or sitting during *Mizmor LeTodah* would hinge on the issue as to whether the spectators were in the *ezrat nashim* or the *azara* itself.

The Lubavitcher Rebbe (*z"l*) rules that the latter edition of the *Shulchan Aruch* Harav, which contended that one need not stand for *korbanot*, applied only to *korbanot* and not to *Mizmor LeTodah*. Indeed, said the Rebbe, the general principle that recitation of the *korbanot* is deemed as if one brought a *korban* does not apply to *Mizmor LeTodah*. Thus, one should sit while saying the *korbanot* and stand for *Mizmor LeTodah* (see *Likutai Piskai Halachah U'Minhag, Siman* 21). It is apparent that the Lubavitcher Rebbe (*z"l*) disputed the Ketzot HaShulchan's assumption that the posture and stance for *korbanot* equally applied to *Mizmor LeTodah* (appreciation to Rav Mordechai Gutnik for the latter reference).

The Conclusion of Kedushah

QUESTION: General custom is to stand during the recitation of *Kedushah.* Is it necessary to remain standing until the conclusion of the *berachah* that ends with the phrase *Hakail Hakadosh,* or may one move about or be seated before the *hazzan* says the portion that begins with the phrase *Ledor Vador*?

RESPONSE: The *Shulchan Aruch* rules that during the recitation of the *Amidah* both feet should be placed together to emulate the posture of angels (*Orech Chayyim* 95:1). As it pertains to *Kedushah,* the *Shulchan Aruch* notes that "it is preferable to place (one's feet) together also at the period of time one is reciting *Kedushah* with the *shliach tzibur* (*Orech Chayyim* 95:4). The Mishneh Berurah rules that in the event that someone came late to the synagogue services and would not be able to conclude the *Amidah* prior to the *hazzan*'s conclusion of *Kedushah,* he should not start the *Amidah* but, rather, await the chanting of the *Amen* said after the *berachah* of *Hakail Hakadosh.* Why? For the *Amen* of *Hakail Hakadosh* is part of *Kedushah* (literally *Shiy'ach Likedushah*) (*Mishneh Berurah* 109:5).

As such, one may presume that until the *Amen* of *Hakail Hakadosh* is chanted, *Kedushah* is still in effect. This suggests that no movement should take place until the *Amen* is recited. A contrary position may be deduced from the terminology of the *Shulchan Aruch.* The Codes do not explicitly mandate one to place the feet together during *Kedushah*. Rather, it says that such a posture should take place in the period of time that one says *Kedushah* together with the *shliach tzibur*. To the extent that only the *hazzan* says the *Ledor Vador* and not the community at large, perhaps this section relates to *Kedushah* but lacks the requirement to stand as one stands for *Kedushah*.

The Sukkah Berachah

QUESTION: During the recitation of the *Kiddush* on Sukkot, should one be seated after the *berachah* of *laishev basukkah*?

RESPONSE: The question is an issue of concern, for more than one custom prevails. The *Shulchan Aruch* overtly cites the Rambam's ruling that *Kiddush* on Sukkot should be chanted while standing, so that directly after the *laishev basukkah berachah* one should sit down. The Rema, however, demurs. He notes that such is not the custom for "we recite *Kiddush* [while] seated" (*Orech Chayyim* 643:2).

The Rema's position appears to be that since (his) custom was to recite *Kiddush* sitting down, one did not have to alter this stance because of the *laishev basukkah berachah*. That is, the entire *Kiddush* including the *laishev basukkah berachah* may be chanted while seated.

The parameters of the debate are articulated by the Mishneh Berurah as follows: The Rambam's view is that the actual mitzvah of the *sukkah* commences the moment one sits in a *sukkah*. To the extent that a general halachic principle is that a *berachah* is chanted prior to the performance of a mitzvah, it is necessary to sit down subsequent to the *berachah* to portray that one is actually performing the *sukkah* mitzvah after the *berachah*. Rema's rule (cited in the name of the Rosh) is that sitting in a *sukkah* does not represent the onset of the mitzvah; the actual *sukkah* mitzvah begins when one eats in a *sukkah*. Accordingly, should one make *Kiddush* while seated, the fact that one sits prior to the *berachah* of *laishev basukkah* in no way even suggests that the mitzvah was performed prior to the *berachah* (*Orech Chayyim* 643:4).

At issue is the preferable mode for those who make *Kiddush* standing. It seems from the Mishneh Berurah that any change of posture from standing to sitting after the *laishev basukkah berachah* may be frowned upon, for it falsely conveys the impression that by merely sitting one observes the *sukkah* mitzvah. Such is simply not so. The mitzvah of *yeshivat sukkah* does not literally mean sitting in a *sukkah* but, rather, dwelling and/or remaining in a *sukkah*. Since, moreover, we may recite the *berachah* when we eat (certain minimum amounts), perhaps it is wrong to overtly even suggest otherwise. As such, even though many have the custom of reciting *Kiddush* while standing, they should remain standing till the conclusion of *Kiddush* and purposely not sit down so that any erroneous concepts may not be projected.

Such an analysis is a proper logical inference from the Mishneh Berurah's analysis of the position of the Rambam and the Rosh. Of interest is that the *Shulchan Aruch* Harav presents a position that differs from the above premise. He notes that the rationale for sitting after the *sukkah berachah* is not to demonstrate that sitting is the actual mitzvah, but rather to give the impression that one is not imminently leaving. Should one stand, the impression might be that one is not remaining in the *sukkah*. Accordingly one makes the *berachah* seated to dramatically focus that the person is in the *sukkah* to stay. Should, however, the entire *Kiddush* be recited while seated, then it is of course proper (*Shulchan Aruch*, *Orech Chayyim* 743:2). Accordingly, sitting after the *berachah* does not convey a false halachah as to when the mitzvah commences. It is merely a symbolic act to project the image that one is remaining in the *sukkah* and not standing, ready to leave.

A means of demonstrating loyalty to both the position of the

Mishneh Berurah as well as to the theory of the *Shulchan Aruch* Harav would be to recite *Kiddush* while standing (as many do) and then to manifest permanency by sitting down to drink the wine. This probably would satisfy the halachic authorities who maintain that the mitzvah commences when one eats (or drinks wine) in the *sukkah*.

Havdalah

QUESTION: Should one sit or stand while reciting *Havdalah*?

RESPONSE: There are two traditions. The *Shulchan Aruch* rules that *Havdalah* should be chanted while sitting; the Rema demurs and states that common custom is to stand (*Orech Chayyim* 296:6).

The Taz notes that one person generally recites *Havdalah* for the members of the household. Accordingly, the process requires a posture of permanency (*kvi'ut*) that is lacking in a standing position (*Orech Chayyim* 296:5). (The implication is that should a person recite *Havdalah* solely for himself then he need not sit.) The Vilna Gaon, however, made no such qualification and simply rules that *Havdalah* should be chanted while seated (*Orech Chayyim* 296:18).

The Mishneh Berurah says that the rationale for the ruling to stand is that *Havdalah* symbolizes an escort to royalty (the *Shabbat* Queen), and such escort services when royalty departs take place while standing. The fact that people are summoned to gather for the purposes of *Havdalah* endows the process (according to the view of the *Shulchan Aruch*), with the quality of permanency (*Orech Chayyim* 296:26, see *Tosafot Berachot* 43a). Mishneh Berurah notes a preference for the seated position not only for the person chanting *Havdalah* (*Orech Chayyim*

296:26) but also for all assembled who are included in the *berachah* (*Orech Chayyim* 271:46). (Though the Mishneh Berurah states that it is preferable (*lchat'chila*) to sit, implying that ex post facto it is permissible to stand, in his notes (*Shaar HaTzion*, ibid.), he contends that, according to the Vilna Gaon, it is not clear as to whether the requirement to sit is essential or only preferential.) The *Aruch HaShulchan*, however, notes that common custom is to stand (*Orech Chayyim* 296:17).

Of interest is that the *Shulchan Aruch* and the Rema reverse their positions from *Kiddush* to *Havdalah*. Concerning *Kiddush* the *Shulchan Aruch* rules that *Vayechulu* is recited while standing, followed by the blessing for wine and *Kiddush* (*Orech Chayyim* 271:10). The obvious implication is that the entire *Kiddush* is recited while standing. The Rema adds that one may stand for *Kiddush*, but it is preferable to be seated (ibid.), just the opposite of his position for *Havdalah*. The *Aruch HaShulchan* notes that the kabbalah was the main source to stand for *Kiddush* on Friday night and such was the custom of the Ari (*z"l*) (*Orech Chayyim* 271:24). Another reason for standing for *Kiddush* is that it is a form of testimony that God created the world and witnesses must stand (ibid.). Since *Havdalah* does not have such concerns, therefore, the *Shulchan Aruch* (may have) ruled one may sit. The Rema discounts the reasons to stand Friday night but must have held that the mitzvah of escorting the *Shabbat* Queen overshadows all general concerns to perform mitzvot while seated. As such, he records all should stand.

What is fascinating is that the general public disregards such finely honed distinctions. Most Jews equate *Havdalah* with *Kiddush*. Those that stand for *Kiddush* stand for *Havdalah* (standing is deemed a sign of great respect). Those who sit for *Kiddush* also sit for *Havdalah*.

Praying on an Airplane

QUESTION: In the event one is praying while travelling on an airplane, does halachah mandate the *Shemoneh Esrai* to be recited while standing?

RESPONSE: HaGaon HaRav Moshe Feinstein (*z"l*) rules that one may sit. He notes that one may sit even preferentially (*lechat'chila*) during *Shemoneh Esrai* if standing (in an aisle or other section) will disturb his concentration and negatively impact his attention. However, based upon the Rema (*Orech Chayyim* 94:5) he should stand, if able, during those sections that require one to bow (*Iggrot Moshe, Orech Chayyim*, vol. IV, *Siman* 20). This means that he should (if he could) preferably stand during the beginning of *Shemoneh Esrai* and during the *brachah* of Magen Avraham as well as during the concluding periods when one is mandated to bow, namely, *Modim* and *Hatov Shimcha*. Ex post facto, should the entire *Shemoneh Esrai* be recited while sitting (even those sections wherein one must bow) Rav Moshe (*z"l*) rules that the person is not required to repeat the *Shemoneh Esrai* when he arrives to a place wherein he would be conveniently able to stand and *daven* (*Pesak* HaGaon Rav Moshe Feinstein, *LeTorah V'HoRa'ah, Choveret* 5, *Shevuot* 5735).

Gadlu

QUESTION: When the *sefer Torah* is removed from the Holy Ark, the *hazzan* recites the phrase *Gadlu* (namely, "Declare the greatness of HaShem with me and let us exalt His Name together." Psalms 34:4, Art Scroll translation). Should the *hazzan* face the congregation or the Holy Ark when reciting this verse?

RESPONSE: In many *siddurim*, including Art Scroll, the *hazzan* is directed to face the Holy Ark when reciting this verse. Of interest is that in the noted scholarly volume on the *siddur* entitled, *Tz'luta D'Avraham*, in the commentary of HaRav Menachem Mendel Chayyim Landau, (Aimek Berachah), this custom is deemed an error. His rationale is that just as when the *hazzan* recites the *Shema Yisrael* while he faces the congregation, for he wishes to address it, so too should this apply to the verse of *Gadlu*. Lacking any special reason mandating the *hazzan* to face the Holy Ark, no direction is given to the *hazzan* in the *Siddur Tz'luta D'Avraham* and the implication is that he faces the congregation.

The difficulty is that the requirement for the *hazzan* to face the Holy Ark while reciting *Gadlu* is located in a number of *siddurim* noted for their halachic accuracy (see, for example, the *siddur* of the Vilna Gaon). In addition, the *Aruch HaShulchan* specifically rules that the *hazzan* should face the Holy Ark while reciting *Gadlu* (*Orech Chayyim* 134:4).

Scholarship discloses that in the prayerbooks of such ancient sources as the Machzor Vitri, Tur, Kol Bo, and the Abudrahm the *hazzan* recited only the *Gadlu* verse, even on *Shabbat*. Thus, he did not recite the *Shema Yisrael* and *Echad* phrases when the Torah was removed from the Holy Ark (*Likutai Maharich*, vol. 2).

The *Orchot Chayyim*, a compilation of ancient customs by HaRav Aaron HaKohen of Luniel, cites a fact that sheds light on the matter of concern. He contends that *Gadlu* was recited by the *hazzan* when he actually removed the *sefer Torah* from the Holy Ark. At the moment of removal he chanted *Gadlu* and was obligated to lift the Torah high. Indeed, anyone who did not follow this procedure was deemed in violation of the verse that states, "Cursed is he who does not maintain this Torah" (Deut.

27:26). (See *Orchot Chayyim*, vol. 1, Laws of Monday and Thursday.)

According to the above, the *Gadlu* verse was always recited facing the Holy Ark while the Torah was removed. The requirement in our day for the *hazzan* to face the Ark while saying *Gadlu* may simply be a means of remembering the original format for removing the Torah and reciting this verse. Indeed, this may also be the source for the custom of some to bow toward the Holy Ark when reciting *Gadlu* (see Art Scroll *siddur*). The *hazzan* was basically bowing to the *sifrai Torah* in the Holy Ark. This suggests that it is quite proper to not close the Holy Ark until after the *Gadlu* prayer is concluded.

Keriat Hatorah

An Error During Keriat Hatorah

QUESTION: When an error is found in the Torah during the middle of *keriat hatorah*, what is the proper procedure to follow concerning the recitation of the second *berachah*?

RESPONSE: In the case at hand there are three basic theories with a number of modifications. The Mahari Bei Rav rules that the faulty *sefer Torah* should be rolled up, another taken out, and the second *berachah* recited upon the conclusion of the portion read for that *aliyah* in the new Torah. The portions read prior to the error as well as the number of people previously called to the Torah are considered valid *aliyot*. The Mordechai demurs. He contends that once an error is found in a *sefer Torah*, the person who had the *aliyah* should recite the second *berachah* on the faulty *sefer Torah* and then it should be rolled up and another taken out. The Rema provides a compromise position. In the event that the error is located in a section wherein it is not permitted to stop, namely, prior to three verses read, then one rolls up the Torah and chants the second *berachah* at the conclusion of the *aliyah* in the new Torah. Should, however, the error be found in a section where one may stop the reading, then the second *berachah* should be recited over the *sefer Torah pasul* (*Orech Chayyim* 143:4; see Mishneh Berurah and Beur Halachah). My grandfather, the Minchat *Shabbat*, notes authorities who express a preference to recite the second *berachah* over the kosher *sefer Torah*. The rationale is that it is preferable to miss out on an opportunity to recite a *berachah* in its proper sequence than to violate the sin of chanting an unwarranted blessing (*berachah levatalah*) (*Minchat Shabbat* 78:14).

The third position, not so well known, is that of the Vilna Gaon. He rules that once an error is found in a *sefer Torah* it voids all of the readings that *Shabbat*. Accordingly, a kosher *sefer Torah* is brought out and the weekly portion is read from the beginning of the *parsha.* In addition, seven people should be called up in the new Torah. Of interest is that even though the Mishneh Berurah suggests that in a synagogue wherein there is no established *minhag* one should follow the rules of the Rema, he still notes that it is preferable (*lechat'chila*) to call seven people in the kosher *sefer Torah.* In the commentary of the Beur Halachah he cites the position of the Shaar Efra'im, which is a modified view of the Vilna Gaon, namely, when an error is noted, no *berachah* should be recited over the faulty Torah. When the new Torah is opened, the *baal koreh* should commence reading not at the verse where the error was found, but at the place wherein that *aliyah* would have customarily started. Also, even though the first *berachah* was already chanted over the faulty Torah, it should be rechanted before the reading commences. This differs from the Vilna Gaon's position, which requires all the readings to be read again.

Accordingly, should one not make a *berachah* on the *sefer Torah pasul*, one would be observing the halachic ruling of two out of three major customs.

Missing a Word of the Torah Reading

QUESTION: In the event a person does not hear several words from the *keriat hatorah*, is he required to read the Torah once again to make up for the omission?

RESPONSE: Though some halachic authorities contend that there is an obligation to hear every word of *keriat hatorah* (see Mishneh Berurah, *Orech Chayyim, Hilchot Shabbat* 285:14, who notes the concurrence of the Magen Avraham and the Vilna

Gaon), the final halachah is not clear on this matter. Indeed, it appears probable that the mitzvah was a communal obligation and not necessarily a mandate upon every single Jew. In other words, every community has an obligation to read the Torah in the presence of at least ten Jews. No one may walk out, disturb others, or act indifferent to *keriat hatorah*, for such are acts of disrespect (see *Berachot* 8a). It is even probable that in the synagogue one must be attentive to each word read to ensure that at least a minyan hears the *keriat hatorah*. Yet should an individual miss part of the *keriat hatorah* (or even all of it), there is no halachic requirement to take out the Torah and read it again to enable him to fulfill his personal obligation.

Tosafot (*Sukkah* 52a) report that the synagogue in Alexandria was so large that when a person had an *aliyah* to the Torah, a flag would be waved to signal the conclusion of the *berachah* so that the congregation could respond by chanting *Amen*. Now, if the congregation could not hear the *berachot*, it is obvious that they also could not hear the *keriat hatorah*. Yet the synagogue conducted public readings of the Torah knowing full well that not all could hear the proceedings. The logical answer is that as long as a quorum of ten Jews heard the *keriat hatorah*, it was sufficient to meet the requirement. Those who did not hear the *keriat hatorah* were not obligated to reread the Torah. As long as they worshipped in a synagogue where the Torah was publicly read (even if they did not hear it), they were absolved from all personal requirements.

On Purim there is a requirement to read the *Megillah* even without a minyan (*Shulchan Aruch, Orech Chayyim* 690:18, glosses of Rema). There is no such stipulation for *keriat hatorah* throughout the year.

Rabbi Yaakov of Lissa (Chavat Da'at) ruled that those who quietly learn Torah by themselves during the reading of the *sefer Torah* should not be rebuked, for they have halachic authority to rely upon (*yesh lachem al ma lismoch*) (Derech HaChayyim, *Laws of Communal Behavior during Keriat Hatorah*, law 4). Yet he notes that such behavior is not permissible during the reading of *Parashat Zachor* and *Parashat Parah* (ibid., law 6). The distinction is clear: *Keriat HaTorah* is a communal ordinance, but the others are personal obligations.

The *Aruch HaShulchan* (*Hilchot Keriat Hatorah* 146:5) restricts independent Torah study during *keriat hatorah* to advanced professional scholars but concludes, on the basis of the practical consideration that such activities might induce a disrespect for *keriat hatorah* among ordinary laymen, that it should be prohibited. In other words, one must be attentive to *keriat hatorah* for secondary reasons.

Rabbi Henkin, the previous *posek hador* and righteous director of Ezras Torah, explicitly stated, "The reading of the *Megillah* is a more stringent requirement than *keriat hatorah*, for the former is an obligation upon each and every person, while the latter is only a communal requirement. Thus, should a person miss even one word of the *Megillah*, he is required to reread the entire *Megillah*" (*Edut LeYisrael*, p. 134). There is no such mandate for *keriat hatorah*.

Calling Out Chazak, Chazak

QUESTION: Common custom is for all to call out *Chazak, chazak, v'nitchazaik*, "Be strong, be strong, and be strengthened," when any one of the five books of Moshe is concluded. At issue is whether the person granted an *aliyah* when this reading takes place should also so proclaim.

RESPONSE: In a special guide of *dinim* and *minhagim* for soldiers in the Israeli Defense Forces, HaRav Gad Navon, Chief Rabbi of the Israel Defense Forces, rules that the person granted the *aliyah* at the conclusion of one of the five books of Moshe should be silent when all call out *Chazak*. His rationale is that such a person has yet to make the concluding *berachah* of his *aliyah*, namely, *Asher natan lanu*. As such, reciting *Chazak* is an unwarranted interruption (*hefsik*) (see *Luach Lechayal Tzahal* 5749, p. 95).

Most, however, do not follow this custom. Indeed, when the congregation calls out *chazak*, the person who had the last *aliyah* is not silent, but joins the congregation in the vocal proclamation. Of concern is why. Is not such a statement an unwarranted interruption?

The late Lubavitcher Rebbe (*z"l*) rules that the person who has the last *aliyah* may call out *chazak* and it is not an unwarranted interruption. Why? Because it is an integral part of the ritual at the conclusion of one of the five books of the Torah (see *Shaarei Halacha U'Minhag, Orech Chayyim*, part I, p. 282).

Taking Out the Wrong Sefer Torah

QUESTION: A *sefer Torah* that is not properly prepared for the current Torah reading is removed from the *Aron HaKodesh*. May this *sefer Torah* be returned to the *Aron HaKodesh* and another Torah previously rolled up be taken out and used for the current reading? Or must this Torah be utilized even though it necessitates spending considerable time rolling up the Torah to reach the location of the current Torah reading?

RESPONSE: The Kitzur *Shulchan Aruch* notes the following case that may have bearing on this halachic quandary. On a day when two *sifrai Torah* are read, for example *Shabbat* Rosh Chodesh, an error is found in the first *sefer Torah* that mandates removal of that Torah and utilization of another in its place. The *gabbai* is faced with two options: Should he use the second *sefer Torah* that was already removed from the *Aron HaKodesh* and designated for *maftir* (that *sefer Torah* was available on the *bima,* yet was required to be rolled to the proper *Shabbat* reading), or should the *sefer Torah* that was prepared for *maftir* remain for usage at *maftir* and another *sefer Torah* be taken out from the Holy Ark for the regular Torah reading? The Kitzur *Shulchan Aruch* rules that the *sefer Torah* prepared for *maftir* should remain for *maftir* and another *sefer Torah* should be removed from the *Aron HaKodesh* to conclude the *Shabbat* reading. In addition, should two *sifrai Torah* be used on a *Shabbat* and by error the Torah set up for the second reading is opened first, that Torah should be rolled up and the other Torah that should have been first should so be read first (*Kitzur Shulchan Aruch* 78:10). From this it may be deduced that one should not unnecessarily roll up a *sefer Torah.* A *sefer Torah* prepared for reading at a certain period of time should so be read. Accordingly, should by error a *sefer Torah* not previously set up for the *Shabbat* reading be taken out of the *Aron HaKodesh,* perhaps it should be returned to the *Aron HaKodesh* and another Torah previously prepared for the *Shabbat* reading be used. Thus the congregation need not expend unnecessary time waiting while the Torah is rolled to its proper place.

A distinction may be noted between these cases. In a situation where more than one *sefer Torah* is read and the only concern is whether one or the other should be granted priority, then the halachah may be that a *sefer Torah* set up for a specific reading should be so utilized and one should not spend time rolling up the Torah. However, in the event that only one *sefer Torah* is read, the removal of that Torah to the *Aron HaKodesh* to acquire a Torah previously rolled to the proper reading would manifest the impression that the *sefer Torah* was invalid. That impression should perhaps not be imparted.

Of interest is that the question at hand is discussed at length by HaRav Zalman Druk, Rav of the Jerusalem Bet Haknesset Hagadol, in his *sefer* entitled *Mikrai Kodesh* (pp.

27–29). He cites Aishel Avraham, who rules that one should return the *sefer Torah* not properly rolled to the *Shabbat* reading, and another should be taken out from the *Aron HaKodesh*. Though the *Likutai Mahrich* (laws of *Keriat Hatorah*) notes that Rav Yaakov Emden disagrees, it appears that HaRav Druk favors the position of the Aishel Avraham. His reasoning is as follows: As long as one has no intention to use the first *sefer Torah*, one does not violate the talmudic principle of pushing aside mitzvot encountered first to perform other mitzvot (*ain ma'avirim al hamitzvot*). Indeed, the Divrai Malkiel specifically rules that returning a *sefer Torah* not properly rolled is not a violation of the above principle (vol. 1, *Siman* 9). In addition, since the *sefer Torah* was not even opened before it was returned to the *Aron HaKodesh*, there is no concern about false impressions (*a laz*) that the *sefer Torah* was returned because it was invalid (*pasul*). From this halachah it may be gleaned that our Sages were quite concerned with eliminating unnecessary activities that waste the time of the congregation (*tircha d'tzibura*).

Fall of a Sefer Torah Pasul

QUESTION: In the event that a *sefer Torah pasul* falls to the ground, does such a mishap generate the same halachic reaction as when a kosher *sefer Torah* falls to the ground?

RESPONSE: The *Shulchan Aruch* rules that everyone is obligated (*chayav*) to treat a *sefer Torah* with great respect (*Yoreh Deah* 282:1). As such, should a *sefer Torah* (*chas v'shalom*) fall to the ground, it is deemed an act of disrespect. In addition, it is believed to be a bad omen to the person who dropped the *sefer*

Torah as well as to all who had the misfortune of witnessing this mishap.

Chidah cites a number of halachic responses—namely, that the person who dropped the *sefer Torah* should fast (one or more days) and all who witness the trauma should fast. He concludes, however, that the actual halachic response of each community is up to the discretion of the Rav. Thus, the decision may even be not to fast at all, but rather to give charity (see *Shaarei Berachah, Yoreh Deah* 282).

At issue is whether reaction to the falling *pasul sefer Torah* is similar to that of a kosher *sefer Torah.* My belief is that all the stringent customs relating to the fall of a *sefer Torah* do not apply to a *sefer Torah pasul.* Rivash rules that a *pasul sefer Torah* lacks *kedushat sefer Torah* and is not included in the prohibition from selling a *sefer Torah* (Responsa *Rivash* 285). Minchat Chinuch notes that a *pasul sefer Torah* (missing even one letter) not only lacks *kedushat sefer Torah,* but one does not observe the mitzvah of writing a *sefer Torah* with such a Torah (see *Mitzvah* 613). In discussing the obligation to give great *kavod* to a *sefer Torah,* the *Aruch HaShulchan* adds the word *kosher*; thus one is obligated to give special *kavod* to a *sefer Torah kosher.* The implication is that any mandate or special *kavod* is simply not applicable to a *sefer Torah pasul.*

Indeed, there are a number of items associated with a *sefer Torah* that are granted a degree of sanctity (*kedushah*) but certainly not the high level of sanctity of a kosher *sefer Torah.* The Talmud, for example, rules that the cover of a *sefer Torah* should not be utilized as a cover for a *Chumash* (*Megillah* 27a). Thus a cover used for a higher-level *kedushah* should not be used with items of lesser *kedushah.* Yet, no one would suggest that a fall to the ground of a *sefer Torah* cover would generate a requirement to fast or give money to charity.

Of interest is that the *Aruch HaShulchan* notes that common practice is to invalidate any usage of a *pasul sefer Torah* (even when no kosher *sefer Torah* is available) but to permit in an occasional emergency situation (not on a permanent basis) usage of a *Chumash* (a scroll of parchment containing any one of the five books of Moshe). His rationale is that such a *Chumash* is halachically kosher for Torah readings but not utilized because it is not *kavod hatzibbur* to read from a Torah scroll lacking all five books of Moshe (*Aruch HaShulchan* 143:7). Thus a *Chumash* would at least have *kedushat sefer Torah*, but a *pasul sefer Torah* would not. This again suggests that reaction to the fall of a *pasul sefer Torah* would be much less somber than that when (*chas v'shalom*) a kosher *sefer Torah* falls.

A Minor Baal Koreh

QUESTION: May a minor below the age of bar mitzvah serve as a *baal koreh* for a youth minyan in a Day School?

RESPONSE: No. The Magen Avraham rules that a minor may only receive the *aliyah* of *maftir*. He may not serve as a *baal koreh* for the Torah reading nor acquire an *aliyah* when only three persons are called to the Torah (for example, on Mondays and Thursdays) (*Orech Chayyim* 282:6). Mishneh Berurah cites the Pri Megadim, who notes that in the event that no one else but the minor knows how to read the Torah, then perhaps a minor may do so (*Mishneh Berurah* 282:13).

In the Mishneh Berurah's notes entitled *Shar Hatzion*, the Mishneh Berurah discusses the basis for the ruling of the Pri Megadim. He says that the Pri Megadim was concerned with the fact that the Talmud does permit a minor to receive an *aliyah* (*Megillah* ch. 4, *Mishnah* 6). The fact that in talmudic times each person who had an *aliyah* also read the Torah himself indicates that a minor actually served as a *baal koreh*. To this the Mishneh Berurah demurs by noting a major distinction between ancient times and serving as a *baal koreh* in the contemporary scene. In the times of the Talmud a minor was included within the seven *aliyot*, but at no time did they permit all seven *aliyot* to be given to minors. To serve as a *baal koreh* for the entire Torah reading would be like having a Torah reading where only minors were called to the Torah (*Shar Hatzion* 282:16).

The halachic scholar Tehilla L'David advances the same distinction between talmudic and contemporary times, yet concludes that logic would at least support a minor reading the Torah for his own *aliyah*. In other words, a minor could not serve as a *baal koreh* for all of the *aliyot*, but at least he could replicate the talmudic example of reading the Torah for his own *aliyah*.

Yet this argument may not be applicable to the reading on Mondays and Thursdays. Firstly, perhaps, permission was granted to a minor to read the Torah only in the middle of seven *aliyot* but never when only three *aliyot* were operational. Scholars do make a distinction between the sanctity of different sources for *keriat hatorah*.

The Talmud (*Bava Kamma* 82a) states that Ezra ordained that the Torah should be read (publicly) on *Shabbat Mincha* as well as on Mondays and Thursdays. Concerning the latter two periods of time the Talmud notes that even prior to Ezra there was such a practice, for indeed the early prophets (Moshe Rabbenu: see Rambam) enacted that the Torah should be read on *Shabbat* as well as on Mondays and Thursdays. To this the Talmud responds that the original decree was that "one man should read three verses or that three men should together read three verses corresponding to *kohanim*, *levi'im*, and *yisraelim*. Ezra then came and ordained that three men should be called up to read in the Torah and that ten verses should be read." Based upon this, the Tzemach Tzedek ruled that a minor may only serve as a *baal koreh* on *Shabbat* afternoon, for such reading was ordained by Ezra and was not part of the original decree (Commentary on *Megillah*, ch. 3). The implication is that at other times the Torah reading has a greater degree of sanctity and a minor should not serve as a *baal koreh*. The Meiri notes that a minor should have an *aliyah* only after adults so that the ordinance of Moshe should be concluded (*Kiryat Sefer*, *Ma'amar* 5:1). This suggests that only after three verses or three *aliyot* may a minor serve as a *baal koreh*.

Consequently, not only is the general practice not to permit a minor to serve as a *baal koreh*, but sources do not support such a practice, especially for Mondays and Thursdays.

Part V

Kohanim *Concerns*

Blessing Jews

QUESTION: Is a *kohen* permitted to use the (verses of the) *Birkat Kohanim* to (by himself and not during *tefila*) bless another Jew? May a *kohen* bless another with a prayer other than *Birkat Kohanim*?

RESPONSE: The Talmud (*Rosh Hashanah* 28b) states:

> How do I know that a *kohen* who goes up to *duchen* (the platform whereupon the *kohanim* stood) should not say, "Since the Torah granted me permission to bless [*k'lal*] *Yisrael*, I will add a *berachah* of my own; for example, 'May God, the God of your fathers, add to you a thousand times as many as you are now.' [Deut. 1:1]?" [Because such action is prohibited by the verse] *Lo tosefu* ("You mayest not add") (Deut. 4:2).

The *Sefat Emet* (ibid.) remarks that one should not infer from this citation that a *kohen* is prohibited from greeting other people with the blessing of *Shalom*. Such action would certainly not be within the purview of the biblical injunction. Why? Because the Talmud specifically disallows only the adding of an extra blessing to the act of performing the mitzvah of *Birkat Kohanim*. Indeed, the Talmud relates to a *kohen* who "went up to *duchen*" to bless the people. The implication is that the biblical injunction applies to an extra *berachah* appended to the regular *berachot* during the actual observance of the mitzvah. Thus, a *kohen* may extend personal blessings to friends throughout the day, not during the regular prayers, without qualms about violating biblical mitzvot.

This theory appears to be essential to an understanding of the practical application of *Lo tosef*. If someone made *tefillin* with five *parshiyot* and/or *tzitzit* with five strands but did not put on the *tefillin* or wear the *tzitzit*, he would not be violating the biblical law. The violation occurs only during the performance of the mitzvah and not during its process of preparation. Accordingly, there is nothing wrong with a *kohen* extending even *Birkat Kohanim* as long as it is not during the regular prayer service.

Washing Hands of the Kohanim

QUESTION: Who should wash the hands of the *kohanim* prior to *Birkat Kohanim*?

RESPONSE: The *Shulchan Aruch* rules that *levi'im* should wash the hands of the *kohanim* (*Orech Chayyim* 128:6). Two reasons are presented: (1) The *Zohar* contends that washing the hands of *kohanim* is a form of *kedushah* (sanctity). As such, the process of increasing the *kedushah* of the *kohanim* should be generated by those (such as the *levi'im*) who have *kedushah* themselves (*Prisha*, *Tur*, *Orech Chayyim* 128; *Zohar*, *Naso*). (2) The *Aruch HaShulchan* suggests that the usage of *levi'im* is a form of remembrance of the service of the *Bet HaMikdash* wherein *levi'im* guarded the *Mikdash* and served under the rule of the *kohanim* (*Orech Chayyim* 128:15).

Should no *levi* be available, then a *bechor* (firstborn) should be utilized for a *bechor* also is classified as holy [Magen Avraham, citing the Bach, *Orech Chayyim* 128:7].

Should neither a *levi* nor a *bechor* be available, then each *kohen* should wash his own hands rather than use the services of a non*bechor Yisrael* (Mishneh Berurah, *Orech Chayyim* 128:22). The *Shulchan Aruch HaRav* suggests that in this case the reason it is preferable for the *kohen* to become sanctified through his own efforts (i.e., to wash his own hands), rather than through the services of a *Yisrael*, is that he has personal *kedushah*, while a *Yisrael* lacks any *kedushah* (*Orech Chayyim* 128:10). Yet the Minchat Yom Tov (my grandfather) cites rabbinic authorities who maintain that in such an instance the *shamash* (sexton) of the synagogue should be utilized for he was appointed to provide all services of *kedushah* for the congregation (*Minchat Yom Tov* 100:3). The Beur Haitiv cites Rabbi David Oppenheim (Nishal David, no. 60) who discusses the propriety of one *kohen* washing the hands of another *kohen* (*Orech Chayyim* 128:8). Of interest is the role of a minor *kohen* in this process. The Sages do not suggest that a minor *kohen* be utilized when neither a *levi* nor *bechor* are available.

Washing the Levi's *Hands*

QUESTION: Should the *levi* wash his own hands prior to washing the hands of the *kohanim*?

RESPONSE: The *Shulchan Aruch* mandates *levi'im* to wash their own hands but the Rema rules that such is not the general custom in that they rely upon the *netilat yada'yim* performed in the morning on their own hands (*Orech Chayyim* 128:6). The Mishneh Berurah notes that the Rema's ruling is contingent upon two conclusions: (1) the *levi'im* did not distract their minds from the morning washing, and (2) the *levi'im* did not touch any thing or place that renders them unclean. In the event these two conditions are not met, then the *levi'im* should also wash their hands prior to washing the hands of the *kohanim* (*Mishneh Berurah, Orech Chayyim* 128:23). Since most *levi'im* are unaware of the above precautions, perhaps it is preferable for them to wash their hands before they wash the hands of the *kohanim*. Such is halachic logic, yet not halachic practice.

Kohanim *Honoring* Kohanim

QUESTION: When a *kohen* is granted the honor of leading the *zimun* for *Birkat HaMazon* should he honor other *kohanim* by reciting the phrase, *Birshut HaKohanim*?

RESPONSE: *Birshut HaKohanim* is said when one leads the *zimun* for *Birkat HaMazon* (see Ateret Z'Kainim, *Orech Chayyim* 201, who cites this usage). However, when a *kohen* leads the *zimun*, the practice is not to request permission from other *kohanim*. The rationale may be that the mitzvot of *V'kidashto* ("And you shall make him holy") (*Vayikra* 21:8) is presumed to be an obligation solely for non-*kohanim* to honor *kohanim*. It is not an obligation imposed upon *kohanim* to sanctify other *kohanim*.

Of concern is that at a *brit milah* there are a number of special phrases chanted by the person leading the *zimun*. One of them is the expression *Birshat HaKohanim*, namely, a request for permission from the *kohanim* to lead. What is evident from the introductory phrase is that at a *brit milah* it was quite proper to request permission from fellow *kohanim*. This suggests that perhaps it was customary for a non-*kohen* to lead the *zimun* at *brit milah*.

As such, pragmatically a *kohen* honored to lead the *zimun* at a *brit milah* is placed in a halachic quandary. The issue is whether he should say *Birshut HaKohanim*. On the one hand since in general he does not make such a request, perhaps he should simply skip over this phrase while leading the *zimun*. Yet, to delete a well-known, accepted introductory phrase is somehow also not proper. Or, lacking direction, perhaps *kohanim* should refrain from leading *Birkat HaMazon* at a *brit milah* altogether.

A resolution may be noted in the following question posed by the *Aruch HaShulchan*. He asks if the mandate of *V'kidashto*—"And you shall make him holy"—is an obligation imposed solely upon non-*kohanim*? Or does it pertain also to *kohanim* who are obliged to ensure that their fellow *kohanim* are to be treated with *kedushah*? (*Orech Chayyim* 129:72). According to the first part of this question, requesting permission from fellow *kohanim* would not be a normal procedure. Yet, should the halachah be the second consideration, then of course it would be necessary to request permission from the other *kohanim*. The *Aruch HaShulchan* does not resolve the dilemma. Yet, as long as it is even faintly possible that the mitzvah applies also to the *kohanim* (themselves) to honor other *kohanim*, it may be proper for *kohanim* to recite such phrases.

On the other hand, after I made public the above quandary someone consulted a number of sages in Israel about this matter and was told that at a *brit milah*, a *kohen* may skip the phrase *Birshut HaKohanim*. This is not the common practice.

A Kohen *and a Divorcee*

QUESTION: A *kohen* marries a divorcee (*gerushah*). May he *duchen* and receive an *aliyah* to the Torah as a *kohen*?

RESPONSE: Such a marriage could not take place at a ceremony performed by an Orthodox Rabbi. As such, the marriage must be a civil ceremony, or one performed by a non-Orthodox Rabbi.

HaRav Samson Rafael Hirsch rules that a *kohen* who marries a *zonah* (a woman who practiced indiscriminate sex) should not *duchen* nor receive the *kohen aliyah* (*Responsa Shemesh Marpech*, *Siman* 2). As such, a *kohen* who marries a divorcee, which is overtly prohibited by the Torah (*Vayikra* 21:7), should be classified as comparable to the above case and not be treated with the special accord of *kedushah* provided to *kohanim*. The implication is that anyone who profanes the sanctity of *kohanim* by marrying a woman prohibited by biblical law has by such personal action removed himself from the *kedushah* of *kohanim*. That is, one cannot disregard biblical law and simultaneously expect or request special honor due a *kohen*. The honor is granted only to those *kohanim* who respect the code of prohibited marriages imposed upon them by the Torah.

Marriages Prohibited to Kohanim

QUESTION: In a spirit of candor, a woman admits to her fiancé, a *kohen*, that she previously had sexual relations with a Gentile. Does this information create halachic problems?

RESPONSE: Biblical law explicitly prohibits a *kohen* from marrying a woman classified as a *zonah* (Leviticus 21:7). Though common parlance interprets the term *zonah* to refer to a prostitute or a promiscuous woman, such is not the accepted halachic definition as it relates to the prohibition of a *kohen* marrying a *zonah*.

Indeed, having premarital sexual relations with a Jewish man does not automatically brand a Jewish woman as a *zonah* and thus prohibited from subsequently marrying a *kohen*. What does crystallize a status transformation to *zonah* is having sexual relations with a person that a Jewish woman is not permitted to marry. The classic example, without dispute, is that having sexual relations with a Gentile transforms the woman's status into that of a *zonah* and thus generates a biblical prohibition against a *kohen* marrying her. Even though promiscuous sex between a Jewish woman and a Jewish man is immoral, marriage between the partners would be condoned. Accordingly, such a woman may marry a *kohen*, for she is not deemed a *zonah*. Since marriage to a Gentile can never be sanctified or condoned, such a liaison classifies the woman as a *zonah* and precludes a *kohen* from subsequently marrying her (see *Shulchan Aruch*, *Even HaEzer* 6:8). It must be noted that the *pesak* of the *Shulchan Aruch* relates only to the strict rabbinic definition of a *zonah*, and not to the morality of promiscuous behavior nor the extra prohibitions against such practice. In addition, the Beit Shmuel disputes the *Shulchan Aruch*. He cites the Semag, who contends that promiscuous behavior of a woman invalidates her from marrying a *kohen* also.

Though the female offspring of a relationship between a Jewish woman and a Gentile is definitely classified as a Jew, such a child is prohibited from marrying a *kohen* (*Even HaEzer* 7:17; see *Chelkat Mechokek* 7:26 and Ba'er Haitev, who states that this prohibition applies only *lechat'chila* (ab initio), yet *b'dieved* such a woman is not classified as a *chalalah*, and should she marry a *kohen*, a divorce is not required).

Should a woman inform her husband, a *kohen*, that she was raped, halachah contends that her testimony need not be accepted or believed. The assumption is that such a woman may desire a divorce and that the tale of the illicit act was untrue and merely a device to obtain a divorce from her husband. In fact, even if one witness corroborates her statement, the *kohen* may still live with his wife. Should, however, the *kohen* wish to believe his wife's testimony, then the *kohen* should divorce her (*Even HaEzer* 6:12).

In a case where a woman tells her husband, a *kohen*, of an illicit affair and subsequently the husband dies, such a woman may not marry any *kohen*. Even though while the husband was alive halachah does not accept her testimony to force a divorce, we do accept her statement subsequently, for she has in effect proclaimed herself a *zonah* (*Even HaEzer* 6:13).

Thus, a woman's statement that would disrupt or invalidate an existing marriage is not believed, yet a statement after her husband's death is believed and it disqualifies her from marrying a *kohen* in the future. Accordingly, she definitely is to be believed when her statement will disqualify her from *initially* marrying a *kohen*.

Facing the Congregation

QUESTION: When should the *kohanim* turn to face the congregation?

RESPONSE: There is a debate on this issue. Many sages contend that the *kohanim* should not turn from facing the *Aron HaKodesh* to facing the congregation until after completion of the entire *berachah* of the *kohanim*. This is the position of the Rambam. The Minchat Pitim responds that such is the majority viewpoint (*Minchat Yom Tov* 100:19). Another view is that upon hearing the call of *kohanim*, they immediately turn to face the congregation and then commence reciting the *berachah*. The *Aruch HaShulchan* notes that this was the position of the Tur and such was the custom in his area (128:20). The Mishneh Berurah offers a compromise procedure. Namely, the *kohanim* begin their *berachah* facing the *Aron HaKodesh* and turn in the middle of the *berachah* when they recite the world *v'tzivanu*. Thus, they face the congregation for the conclusion of the *berachah* (*Mishneh Berurah* 128:40; see also Kitzur *Shulchan Aruch* 100:8). Of interest is that the *Aruch HaShulchan* notes this "compromise" procedure and concludes that it is highly questionable. He asserts that the custom should be to turn facing the congregation prior to the *berachah* itself (128:20). Local *kohanim* inform me of a *minhag* to turn while chanting the last word of the *berachah*, *b'Ahava*. Chabadniks turn while reciting the beginning of the *berachah*. This appears to be a modification of the Mishneh Berurah's custom. The terminology of the *Shulchan Aruch* also somewhat supports this theory. The *Shulchan Aruch* rules, "When they turn to face the people they recite the blessing" (128:11). The implication appears to be that the blessing is said while they turn. This could also be the basis for the *minhag* cited by the Mishneh Berurah.

What is the basis of the debate? Some say that the *kohanim* face the *Aron HaKodesh* during the *berachah*, for the *berachah* is to HaShem and not the congregation. As such, they turn only after the *berachah* (see Minchat Pitim, *Daf* 41). The other position may be that the *berachah* is an integral part of the *duchen*ing process. To the extent that *duchen*ing must take place *panim el panim* (face-to-face as a friend converses with a friend), the *berachah* must also replicate this format.

To the extent that almost every *kohen* follows the practice of his parent, divergent customs emerge. The fact that the congregation does not look at the *kohanim* during *duchen*ing permits *kohanim* to practice different procedures during *duchen*ing. In other words, nobody is watching, whether they all turn at the same time or not.

Proper Posture for Birkat Kohanim

QUESTION: Should either *kohanim* or the congregation bow or prostrate themselves during *Birkat Kohanim*? What should be the proper posture?

RESPONSE: Traditional sources indicate that no one bowed or prostrated during the blessing of the *kohanim*. Indeed, the Talmud reports that bowing did take place at a different period of time. On Yom Kippur, for example, the *kohanim* and the people who overheard the *kohen gadol* (high priest) recite the Holy Name of God prostrated themselves (*Yuma* 66a). This tradition is part of the contemporary Yom Kippur liturgical service wherein all prostrate themselves when this historical incident is noted in the *machzor* (prayerbook).

HaGaon Rav Yitzchok Hutner (*z"l*), former Rosh HaYeshivah of the Rabbi Chaim Berlin Rabbinical Academy, noted that this communal mandate did not take place at *Birkat Kohanim*. Why? The Talmud specifically states that at *Birkat Kohanim* the *kohanim* faced the people "like a man who talks to his companion" (*Sotah* 38a). Accordingly, any form of bowing or prostration would violate this principle. For this reason, suggests Rav Hutner, the Talmud (and *machzor*) overtly note that when the *kohen gadol* recited the Holy Name, the *kohanim* were together with the people in the audience. This implies that when the *kohanim* were separated from the others as during *Birkat Kohanim*, no one bowed—neither *kohanim* nor congregants (Pachad Yitzchak, *Yom Kippur, Ma'Amar* 5:27).

This has some practical ramifications. (1) A general concern is whether a rabbi is permitted to preach facing the congregation with his back to the Holy Ark? Is this not disrespectful to the *sefer Torah*? The Taz (*Yoreh Deah* 282:1) rules that such behavior is permissible, for the *sefer Torah* in the Holy Ark is considered as if it is in a separate domain. The *Aruch Hashulchan* (*Yoreh Deah* 282:2) notes that the *derashah* of rabbis is basically a form of *kavod hatorah* for the rabbi is teaching the community Torah and its mitzvot. Just as *Birkat Kohanim* must be a process whereby the *kohanim* face the congregation, so too should the rabbi preach facing the people. Indeed, the midrash contends that it is a form of *kavod* to the community for the rav to face them during the sermon. (2) At a wedding, the *Aruch HaShulchan* contends that whoever chants the *Sheva Berachot* should face the bride and bridegroom for all blessings should simulate the posture of *Birkat Kohanim* whereby the *kohanim* face the people (*Even HaEzer* 62:9).

Lifting the Hands

QUESTION: When should the *kohanim* lift up their hands for *nesi'at kapa'im* at *duchen*ing?

RESPONSE: The *Shulchan Aruch* HaRav specifically rules that the *kohanim* should lift their hands only after the conclusion of their *berachah* (128:20). The Meharshom clarifies this by noting that the lifting of the hands is an integral aspect of the actual *duchen*ing process. In other words, it is part of the mitzvah itself. As such, the *berachah* should take place prior to the onset of the mitzvah. Thus, the *kohanim* should not start *nesi'at kapa'im* during the *berachah*. An alternate custom relies on the theory that the *berachah* of the *kohanim* is not a preparation prior to the mitzvah but is part of the *duchen*ing. As such, hands should be extended during the *berachah* itself. Indeed, the Torah directs such a custom. It is written *S'u yedaichem kodesh, u'varchu et HaShem* ("Lift up your hands . . . and bless HaShem" (*Tehilim* 134). In other words, there is a command to first lift up hands and only subsequently a requirement to make a blessing. Accordingly, one lifts up the hands prior to the *kohanim berachah* (*Minchat Yom Tov* 100:22). Those who differ would contend that the lifting up of the hands in the verse refers to the process prior to the blessing of *Yevarech'che'cha* and not to the actual *berachah* itself.

Part VI

Women

Women's Morning Berachah

QUESTION: The *siddur* records a special *berachah* for women to recite each morning. Are there any halachic qualms about this *berachah*?

RESPONSE: The *Shulchan Aruch* rules that each morning women recite the blessing *Baruch . . . she'asani kirtzono* ("Blessed . . . that You made me according to His will") (*Orech Chayyim* 46:4). The earliest reference for this practice is the Tur *Shulchan Aruch*, who says that women have a custom of reciting *she'asani kirtzono*. In other words, women do not recite the male *berachah*. Of interest is the terminology utilized: The Tur does not say that the Sages mandated women to make a special *berachah*. The Tur does not even say that the Rabbis formulated the text of the *berachah*. He says, rather, that women have such a practice. The implication is that women by themselves initiated this *berachah*. Indeed, prior to the Tur there is no earlier source relating to this special women's *berachah*. This in itself generates halachic concern. The rationale for its absence in early sources may be the general consensus to refrain from reciting *berachot* not found in the Talmud. Though there are exceptions to this rule, it may have served as the reason several scholars have severely limited its usage. Indeed, contrary to popular opinion, which assumes all rabbis support its recitation, the views of the following Sages should be considered.

1. The *Aruch HaShulchan* contends that since this *berachah* is not mentioned in the Talmud, many women simply do not recite it altogether (*Orech Chayyim* 46:11).

2. HaRav HaGaon Rav Baruch Epstein (author of *Torah T'mima*) cites the Talmidai Rabbainu Yona (Commentary, *Rif*, *Berachot*, ch. 6) that any *berachah* not mentioned in the Talmud should not be recited using *Shem U'Malchut* (any reference to

God's Name or His Kingdom). As such, he suggests that women should, therefore, recite a curtailed version. They should say *Baruch ata she'asani kirtzono* ("Blessed are You Who made us according to His will") (*Baruch Sheamar*, Commentary on the Siddur).

3. Both the Pri Chadash and HaRav HaGaon Rabbi Yaakov Emden rule that since this *berachah* is not located in the Talmud it preferably should not be chanted. Since, however, it is noted in the *Shulchan Aruch* and a widespread practice of saying it has developed, some suggest that one should not protest its recitation. Women who, therefore, do recite this *berachah* should say the well-known phrase that is chanted whenever a questionable *berachah* is said (*Baruch shem kavod malchuto l'olam vaed*) (*Likutai Maharich, Birkot Hashachar*).

4. The Nusach Ari Siddur of Chabad Chasidim does not contain this women's *berachah.* It was reported to me that the recent Chabad *rebbetzen* (*z"l*) was asked her custom on this matter. Tradition has it that she responded that neither she nor the women in *Bet HaRav* recited this *berachah.*

It was previously suggested that the terminology of the Tur implied that the special *berachah* for women was not actually decreed by the Sages. This concept is based upon the talmudic principle that the terms used to describe customs direct attention to the origin and parameters of its observance. The Gemorah says that should the word "halachah" be used to note a custom, then it should be publicly taught to the community at large. In the even the term *minhag* is utilized, one should not publicly preach its observance, but should individuals request information then one should rule according to the custom. Should, however, the phrase *nahagu* be used to describe the custom, then the implication is that the Rabbis never ordained its practice but, rather, the people took upon themselves its observance. Rashi contends that in such a case one is not even mandated to so rule to those who personally request information regarding observance; one merely does not deter people from such a practice, should they so desire to follow the custom (*Ta'anit* 26b).

Of interest is that the term used by the Tur to note the existence of the women's *berachah* is the phrase *nahagu.* In other words, women assumed this custom by themselves; it was not specifically ordained by the Sages. Accordingly, this may serve as an additional reason why scholars curtailed its observance. Thus, apart from a number of qualms concerning the essence of this *berachah*, there are serious halachic issues involved with its recitation.

Women Davening in Synagogues

QUESTION: Is there any halachic imperative indicating a preference for women to *daven* together with the congregation in the synagogue rather than to pray privately at home?

RESPONSE: From the responsa of HaGaon HaRav Moshe Feinstein (*z"l*) it appears that women as well as men should always seek to *daven* with the *tzibur* in the synagogue rather than at home by themselves.

The following two questions were posed to HaGaon HaRav Moshe (*z"l*): (1) A person contended that he was able to have great *kavana* only when he *daven*ed at home. In the synagogue, the rush to conclude prayers as well as the noise and multitude of people simply mitigated against intense *kavana* in his prayers. Accordingly, this person wished to know whether it was preferable for him to *daven* at home rather than to attend *shul* services. (2) Of concern was a person who felt that attending synagogue services took away precious time that could have been spent learning Torah. At issue was whether such a person should refrain from attending synagogue services so that more time could be devoted to Torah studies. In both of the above cases justification was requested to *daven* at home rather than in *shul*.

HaGaon Rav Moshe (*z"l*) ruled that *daven*ing with the *tzibur* (the congregation) always takes priority over *daven*ing at home, even if it mutes one's ability to have greater *kavana* or reduces time to spend learning Torah. His argument is as follows: The Talmud rules that the prayers of a congregation are never rejected; they always are heard by the Almighty (*Berachot* 8a). In other words, when a person prays at home his prayers may or may not find favor in the eyes of God. Even righteous people—even sages—cannot guarantee that their personal, private prayers will be automatically accepted. Accordingly, it is always preferable to pray with the congregation, for in such a case the prayers are always heard by God. Indeed, when a person is praying it should be done in a place where there is almost a guarantee that the prayers will be accepted (*Iggrot Moshe*, vol. III, *Orech Chayyim* no. 7 and *Orech Chayyim* vol. II, no. 27).

The argument mandating men to attend synagogue worship appears to be equally compelling to women. Namely, they too should seek to pray only in a venue wherein their prayers are guaranteed to be heard. This suggests that women should make every effort to attend synagogue communal services.

Pesach Clothing for Women

QUESTION: Does halachah mandate husbands to see to it that their wives have new clothes for Pesach?

RESPONSE: Yes. Indeed, it may be shown that the acquisition of clothes for women is interrelated with the very essence of the Exodus from Egypt.

The Bible states, *Ve'atem lo teitzu ish mipetach baito ad boker*—"And no man [none of you] shall go out of the door of his house until morning" (Exodus 12:22). This means that during the Tenth Plague, while the Egyptian firstborn were killed, no Jew was permitted to leave his house. This decree extended until the morning, even though the plague had ended at midnight, and Pharaoh set the Jews free (Exodus 12:29–32).

Two questions may be posed: First, why does the Bible specify that no man should go out of the door of his house until the morning? Why the emphasis upon the man leaving his home? The Bible could simply have noted that no one should leave home until the morning.

Second, Scripture states, "And so it shall come to pass that when ye go, ye shall not go empty. Then every woman shall ask of her neighbor vessels of silver and vessels of gold and raiment which ye shall put upon your sons and upon your daughters, and ye will make the Egyptians divest themselves of everything" (Exodus 3:21–22, Hirsch translation).

Accordingly, serious concern must be raised as to when the Jews actually borrowed the gold, silver, and clothing from the Egyptians. Three positions are presented: (1) The process took place prior to the night when the firstborn were killed. However, at such a time the Egyptians probably were not in a generous mood to give gifts to the Jews. Indeed, prior to the Plague of the Firstborn, no one truly believed that the Exodus would occur. (2) The Jews borrowed gifts during the night of the plague. This is impossible, for the Bible specifically states that no one was permitted to leave his house until the morning. (3) The Jews borrowed gifts from the Egyptians during the morning of the Exodus. This, too, is problematic, for the actual Exodus began during the morning (see *Berachot* 9a and Numbers 33:3).

Rav Pinchas Halevi Horowitz (Rav, Frankfort On The Main) therefore suggested the following novel approach: The Bible specifically states that no man was permitted to leave his home until the morning. This means that only adult men were prohibited from leaving their homes. The prohibition did not include women and children. Consequently, what may have happened is that men borrowed gifts prior to the evening. However, their success was not great. The preponderance of the wealth taken from the Egyptians was culled through the efforts of women and children. Therefore the Bible specifies that women may borrow (Exodus 3:23; *Panim Yafot*, *Parshat Bo*).

Based upon this interpretation, Jewish wealth was to a great extent the result of the brave efforts of Jewish women. It was they who entered the homes of the Egyptians amidst the death of the firstborn to borrow items of value. The role the women played was not forgotten by our Sages.

The halachah states that one way to observe the biblical mandate to be happy on *Yom Tov* is to purchase beautiful clothes for women (*Orech Chayyim* 529:2). Does this not presume that Jewish women are concerned only with clothing and not spiritual values? And if so, does this not denigrate the religious character of women? No, for this rule may be intertwined within the same concept. Women bravely brought home beautiful clothing from the Egyptians on Passover. They, too, made their husbands wealthy. So on *Yom Tov* the past is remembered by purchasing clothes for women. It is a symbolic form of appreciation for past historic services.

A Girls' Choir Performing for the General Public

QUESTION: Is it proper for an Orthodox day school to promote and encourage an all-girls choir of young ladies above the age of Bat Mitzvah to perform at a public mixed event?

RESPONSE: The talmudic injunction against a man listening to a woman sing is well known (*Berachot* 24a). At issue is whether the same prohibition is operational not only in the event that one young lady sings a solo, but also when a group of young ladies sing together in a choir.

The halachic propriety of women singing together with men is discussed by Rav Yechiel Yaakov Weinberg (the last Rosh HaYeshivah of the Hildesheimer Rabbinicial Seminary). He noted that upon his arrival in Berlin he was quite perturbed over the common practice of allowing young men and women to sing *zemirot* together on *Shabbat*. His concern was that such a custom appeared to violate a basic halachah in *Shulchan Aruch* that prohibits men from listening to women singing, (*Kol b'isha ervah*) (*Orech Chayyim* 75:3; see Magen Avraham). Upon enquiry concerning the propriety of this matter, he was informed that both HaGaon Rav Azriel Hildesheimer, the founder of the yeshivah and the former rav of the Adas Yisrael congregation in Berlin, as well as HaGaon Rav Samson Raphael Hirsch, the rav of Frankfurt, had formally permitted such a custom. The rationale presented was that when people sing together, one is not listening to the voices of the other (*Trai koli lo mishtami*) and consequently there is no prohibition. In addition, the Sedai Hemed cited a Sephardic rav who ruled that there is no prohibition against men and women singing holy *zemirot* together.

Though Rav Weinberg clearly stated that the East European rabbinate ruled otherwise and was generally quite stringent on this issue, he personally supported the position articulated by Rav Hildesheimer and Rav Hirsch. Why? He felt that the spirit of the times necessitated such a rule. The general social scene was such that many of the Jewish youth had become alienated from Judaism altogether. Indeed, German Torah *chinuch* was known to be successful in the rearing of observant young men and women, while other communities lost a great deal of influence over their youth. Accordingly, he felt that permission for young men and women to sing holy *zemirot* together on *Shabbat* was a vehicle for infusing within them an elevated feeling of *Shabbat* joy and spirituality (*Responsa Seridei Esh*, part II, no. 8).

The problem with this decision is that it appears to be based primarily upon the perception of lifestyle and cultural milieu rather than a purely halachic source. Of interest also is that no lenient consideration was granted to the fact that a number of women were singing together.

I suggest that Rav Hildesheimer and Rav Hirsch derived their halachic ruling from a specific talmudic citation, *Sotah* 48a. It is written: "When men sing and women (subsequently) join in, it is licentiousness; when women sing and men (subsequently) join in, it is like a fire in tow. For what practical purpose is this mentioned? To abolish the latter before the former."

In discussing this text, Rashi makes the following comments: When women commence a song and men respond, then the respondents must pay attention to the women's voices. Such attention to women singing is a violation of halachah and arouses male desire. Yet when men are the leaders of a song, even though women subsequently respond, such a situation does not excite sexual thoughts, for the leaders do not pay too much attention to the respondents. In a situation wherein the people will not desist from both practices, it is a priority to seek to eliminate the case wherein women originate the song and men subsequently respond.

The implication is that both cases should be abolished. Yet, should one not have such power (for people simply will not eliminate both practices), then effort should be made to eliminate the second case rather than the first. In other words, the first case is not deemed as reprehensible as the second. What is clear is that the prohibition against women singing is not alleviated by having several women sing together. Indeed the Talmud relates to women singing as a group.

Of further interest is that there is a third case that the Talmud neglects to mention, namely, when men and women sing together in unison. This situation is not recorded at all. Why? When men and women sing in unison no one is listening to another's voice; each group or person is doing his or her own "thing." As such, the Talmud has no qualms whatsoever about this practice. Indeed, this may be the source for permitting the custom in Germany in which everyone sang together. Accordingly, there may not be any halachic qualms even for an audience to hear a choir of men and women together, for in such a case there is no concentration either upon a singular woman's voice or that of a group of women. Indeed, this may be the meaning of the phrase *Trai koli lo mishtami*. The specific concern in the Talmud regarding the case where men led the song and women responded was that in such a situation, the women sang as a unit by themselves. This is objectionable. Yet even this was considered to be a situation that the sages could live with, for the men who led the song did not pay too much attention to the respondents.

Consequently, a mixed choir of young men and ladies should not generate halachic qualms. However, a choir composed solely of women would be objectionable, an endeavour that a religious institution should not promote. (A viable option for a girls' choir is to ultilize only young ladies before the age of Bat Mitzvah.)

Working Wives

QUESTION: Is it proper for a married woman to work outside of her home?

RESPONSE: "Our Rabbis taught: He who looks for the earnings of his wife or of a mill will never see a sign of blessing (*siman berachah*)" (*Pesachim* 50b). This suggests that a man should not depend on his wife's income. A man should be able to support himself. A corollary may be that one should not marry a woman in anticipation of an income from her.

Thus the phrase "will never see a sign of a blessing" may be interpreted as a form of a curse. Do not marry for wealth; do not depend upon your wife's income. Should one violate this principle, no blessing will come from such money. Yet this interpretation is false, for the Talmud itself limits its parameters. "'The earnings of his wife' means (she goes around selling wool) by weight. '(The earnings of) a mill' means its hire. But if she makes (i.e., woollen garments) and sells them, scripture indeed praises her, for it is written, 'She maketh linen garments and selleth them' (Proverbs 31:24)" (*Pesachim* 50b).

Rashi notes that the first case relates to a woman who takes a scale and goes to the market to sell wool. Such a process is deemed difficult and poorly rewarded. A woman engaged in this pursuit is considered as one degrading herself for a minimum profit. The second case refers to a salary as a laborer in a mill, which is considered extremely arduous work with meager financial benefit. But, suggests Rashi, should one buy and sell a mill, such is considered to have the status of conducting business. The implication is that there is nothing wrong with a man being supported by his wife. The Talmud takes a pragmatic view of the situation. A man who relies on the funds acquired by his wife working as a laborer in a mill or selling wool will not see a blessing from such funds. Why? For such pursuits are arduous and provide meager sustenance. As such, they are not a blessing. However, should his wife be a businesswoman, then he may be content, for this activity generates high levels of income.

Rabbenu Hananel adds that "since the wages are low one does not see a blessing in such an endeavor (*bezah haderech*)." Again, such types of labor are not financially sound. *Tosafot* cite Rav Hanenel, who contends that such labor shames women in that they uncover their arms while making the wool. It is clear from this statement that women labored in mills for meager wages, sold wool in the markets, and conducted business. In fact, the last is lauded for its ability to generate high income.

A scholar who believes that his wife's income as a laborer in a mill will enable him to concentrate upon his studies is warned that such a pursuit will not benefit him at all. Indeed, this may explain a phrase used in another portion of the Talmud. In a debate as to whether one should first seek marriage and then devote himself to study or just the opposite, Rabbi Yochanan noted, "A mill on his neck and he is to learn Torah?" (*Kiddushin* 29b). In other words, the obligation to support a wife is a burden that will hinder Torah study. Note the phrase "a mill on his neck." Perhaps the allusion is to young women who labored in mills and assumed that their income would be sufficient to support a husband. Rabbi Yochanan suggested that even should the wife work, the income would still not suffice.

At any rate, the original citation clearly demonstrates that women labored outside the home to earn funds. Indeed, some women were so industrious that they performed four jobs simultaneously. Rashi (also Ran) notes that some women (1) guarded cucumbers, (2) kneaded flax, (3) taught music to other women, and (4) held silkworms to their chests for warmth, all at the same time (*Ketubot* 66a).

Sharing Income

QUESTION: May a wife refuse to share her income with her husband?

RESPONSE: The Talmud rules that since a husband must provide his wife with food and sustenance, her earnings were granted to the husband (*Ketubot* 58b). That is, a husband might claim that it was unfair to require him to support his wife if she was permitted to keep her wages to herself (Shitah Mekubbetzet, quoting Talmidei Rav Yona, *Ketubot* 58b). Nevertheless, a woman is permitted to contend that she would rather support herself with the fruits of her own labor than have her husband's financial support (*Ketubot* 58b).

Accordingly, during the talmudic era, it was a normal procedure for married women to have sources of income outside of the house. The implication was that the woman had the decisive role in determining whether the money she earned was to be given to her husband or kept for herself. Should the source of income be small, then most probably it was not to her advantage to withhold such funds from her husband, for she would thereby forgo his requirement to feed and clothe her. Should, however, her income be substantial, it might be to her advantage to retain her earnings and forgo her husband's support.

The halachic mechanism granting her this right is of interest. The Ritva contends that a woman is permitted to inform the *bet din* of her desire to retain the fruits of her labor and forgo her husband's support and subsequently to change her mind. That is, she may return to the *bet din* at a later date and proclaim that she prefers that her husband support her and that all income she earns be granted to him. The rationale is that each day generates a new obligation of a husband to support his wife. Accordingly, a woman may at any time alter the financial contractual relationship with her husband. HaRah (Rabbi Aaron HaLevi) disagrees with this procedure. He contends that once a woman renounces the support normally provided to her by her husband, she no longer may commit him to provide such sustenance. Otherwise, a wife could make a mockery of the rabbinic obligation of men to support their wives. Rabbi Betzalel Ashkenazi supports this position (Shitah Mekubbetzet, *Ketubot* 58b).

Providing a Profession for a Jewish Woman

QUESTION: Is a Jewish father mandated to provide a profession for his daughter?

RESPONSE: The Talmud rules that a father is obliged to provide that his son learns a profession or craft. The source, says Chizkiyahu, is the verse that states "See, life with the woman whom you love" (Ecclesiastes 9:9). Thus the word "life," which has the connotation of "livelihood," is juxtaposed to the word "woman." This teaches that "just as one is obligated to take a wife for his son, so too is he obligated to teach him a craft" (*Kedushin* 30b). Of concern to the great sage HaRav Pinchos Horowitz, Rav of Frankfort and author of *HaMakneh,* was whether this ruling also applied to daughters. He suggests that talmudic citations indicate that a father is required to provide a similar training for his daughters. His logic is as follows: The obligation to provide a profession for one's son is derived from the obligation to see to it that one's son gets married. Yet the Talmud specifically notes that a father has an obligation to see that not only his sons get married but also his daughters. This concern is emphasized by the Gemorah, which specifically remarks that a father should expend funds to clothe his daughter so that suitable young men may find her attractive for marriage (*Kedushin* 30b). As such, based on the principle that if a father is obliged to marry off his son he is also obliged to provide him with a profession, the same logic is applicable to daughters. Indeed, continues the *HaMakneh,* common sense also suggests that daughters should have professions. "Do only sons need a livelihood and not daughters?" he asks. Even though a married women is to be sustained by her husband, questions the *HaMakneh,* "How will she survive or who will sustain her in the event she becomes a widow or divorcee?" (see *HaMakneh Kedushin* 30b).

Thus, though Jewish fathers traditionally did not provide professions for their dauaghters, the above commentary provides the logic for the contemporary practice of women entering professions.

A Women's Holiday

QUESTION: Is there any holiday or special commemoration in which women are more observant than men?

RESPONSE: Yes, Rosh Chodesh. The Tur *Shulchan Aruch* (*Orech Chayyim* 417), citing the Pirkei d' Rabbi Eliezer, contends that since Jewish women did not give up their jewelry for the fabrication of the Golden Calf, God granted them the observance of Rosh Chodesh. That is, they would not perform work on Rosh Chodesh, while men do. Rav Yehuda, the Tur's brother, suggested that the twelve annual Rosh Chodesh celebrations were intended to symbolize the twelve tribes of Israel. When, however, the tribes sinned by worshipping the Golden Calf, the reward for Rosh Chodesh was granted to women.

The Darchei Moshe (Rema), in the name of the Or Zerua, notes that Rosh Chodesh symbolizes the rejuvenation of women after their menstrual cycle. Just as the moon is reborn each month, so too when women monthly immerse in a *mikvah* are they as dear to their husbands as on the day of their marriage. Thus, Rosh Chodesh is a *Yom Tov* for women.

The Perishah comments in the name of his teacher that tradition has it that a time will come when old, righteous women will be rejuvenated as were Yocheved and her children. Rosh Chodesh was, therefore, granted as a special holiday for women to symbolize this belief.

The Be'ur Halacha (Mishneh Berurah, *Orech Chayyim* 417) rules that an ancient custom was for women to observe Rosh Chodesh differently than other days; i.e., some refrained from all work, others from partial forms of work.

Thus the consensus of authorities was that Jewish women refrain from some form of work (*melachah*) to distinguish the day. This suggests an obligation to inform women of the time of Rosh Chodesh and to publicize their unique role in its celebration so that they may properly observe this "women's holiday."

Jewish Singles

QUESTION: Does halachah encourage events geared for single men and women to meet each other?

RESPONSE: The Mishnah relates that on the fifteenth day of Av the unmarried girls of Jerusalem would dance in the vineyards and call out to young men to take notice of them for purposes of marriage. So as not to embarrass anyone, Rashi notes, all wore borrowed garments and even the wealthy girls borrowed clothing from others (*Ta'anit* 26b). The Talmud states that any man who had no wife would attend this event. The young ladies would call out to the men specific statements regarding their personal qualities. The beautiful or those with *yichus* (respected lineage) would emphasize these traits. Those girls who felt they had no such superior qualities would request the men to seek a mate for the sake of heaven (*leshem shamayim*) (*Ta'anit* 31a). Thus, the Mishnah and Gemorah fully sanction an event where women take the initiative in publicly calling attention to themselves to attract suitors.

Is this not somewhat bizarre? Does this appear contrary to the traditional modesty expected of Jewish women? Does this suggest that sages approved of women parading themselves for purposes of marriage and initiating contact with men? Doesn't it demonstrate that there are no halachic qualms about unmarried men gazing at such women to select a proper wife?

Rabbi Aaron Hakohen of Luniel, an ancient codifier of Jewish law and custom (cited by the Bet Yosef on numerous occasions), contends that this custom did not apply to young women whose parents had the ability to arrange for them a proper marriage. It was, rather, a custom for young ladies who could not otherwise find a suitable mate. Indeed, Rabbi Aaron Hakohen conjectures that without this custom, perhaps, "They would sit alone until their hair turned white." Even though Rabbi Aaron Hakohen himself notes that the custom is strange, for it gives the impression that Jewish women were somewhat *hefker* and men just "grabbed" those whom they wished to marry, he says that the sages sanctioned the event to provide a vehicle for unmarried women to acquire mates. Those parents who were able to marry off their daughters properly, he adds, simply did not send them to those events (*Orchot Chayyim, Chamisha Asar B'Av* 23).

Of interest is that this interpretation appears to be contrary to the talmudic discussion of the festivity. The Gemorah states that "The daughter of the king would borrow a garment from the daughter of the *kohen gadol*." She, in turn, would borrow from the daughter of someone in a lesser status, and so on (*Ta'anit* 31a). It is highly improbable that the king and the *kohen gadol* were not able to arrange a proper *shidduch* (match) for their daughters. Yet the Talmud rules that they too borrowed garments. This suggests that all unmarried women, even those able to acquire suitable mates, participated in the dance in the fields.

Upon reflection however, it may be noted that Rabbi Aaron Hakohen's ruling is in harmony with the Talmud and suggests an unusual nuance of Jewish morality. If women who could not acquire a suitable *shidduch* (match) were the only ones to borrow clothes for the dance, such a practice would highlight the problem and be a source of embarrassment. Indeed, the moment a young lady borrowed clothes for the Chamisha Asar B'Av dance, it would pinpoint her tragic inability to find a *shidduch*. Everyone would know of her plight even prior to the event. To mitigate such concerns, every unmarried girl would borrow clothes, even the daughter of a king. Thus, until the event no one knew who was, indeed, planning to be at the dance and no one knew who was relying on the dance to acquire a mate. The Talmud does not state that the daughter of the king danced in the fields. It was a device for sustaining the integrity of all unmarried Jewish women.

Thus, a public event for Jewish singles who cannot otherwise select suitable mates is definitely sanctioned by tradition.

Part VII

Circumcision

Attendance at a Brit Milah: *Spectator or Participant?*

QUESTION: Is someone who attends a *brit milah* merely a spectator or considered one involved in the actual performance of a mitzvah?

RESPONSE: It is known that the *kohen gadol* performed several functions on Yom Kippur. He read from the Torah and also brought a number of sacrifices. The Mishnah reports that "He who sees the high priest when he reads (the Torah) does not see the (sacrifices of) the bullock and he-goat that were being burnt. . . . (Why?) Not that he (the observer) was not permitted but because the distance apart was great and both rites were performed at the same time" (*Yoma* 68b). Commenting upon this Mishnah, the Gemorah was concerned with the necessity to detail that it was permissible (should it have been possible) for a person to observe both the ritual of the burning of the *korban* (sacrifice) as well as the *kohen gadol*'s reading of the Torah. Was it not self-evident that both acts were permissible for observers to watch as well as to go from one to another? The Talmud notes that there is a precept that might appear to be violated. It is the rule that one does not leave one mitzvah to attend another. Of this the Talmud questions, "And what mitzvah is here?" Namely, spectators are not performing any mitzvah. The Talmud responds that there is the mitzvah of "in the multitude of the people there is the king's glory (*berov am*)." Rashi notes that generally it is prohibited to leave one mitzvah to perform another. The reason why it is permitted to leave from observing the mitzvah of burning the sacrifices or watching the *kohen gadol* is that the spectators were not actually involved in the performance of the mitzvah itself (*Yoma* 70a).

Indeed, the above indicates that had the people observing

the *kohen gadol* been actual participants in the mitzvah, then they would not have been permitted to leave. Accordingly, a spectator observing the performance of a mitzvah need not remain till the mitzvah is concluded. This is not the case when one actually performs a mitzvah. When a person actually performs a mitzvah there is a general rule that "Whoever commences a mitzvah should conclude it (*HaMatchil b'mitzvah, omrim lo gemor*)."

Of interest is the following observation of the B'Nai Yessaschar concerning the function of those who merely attend a *brit milah*. Citing a midrash as the source, he contends that God decreed that Eliyahu, the prophet, should be in attendance at every *brit milah*. To this Eliyahu demurred, saying that it is known that his character is such that he cannot tolerate sinners. Accordingly, should the father of the child be a sinner, Eliyahu would not be able to tolerate such sin (the implication was that Eliyahu might attack the father of the child for being sinful). To this the Almighty responded that He would forgive the sins of a father who has his child circumcised. Eliyahu further was perturbed about the status of religious observance of those who merely attended the *brit milah* by being present at the performance of the circumcision. Perhaps, suggested Eliyahu, there would be in the audience Jews who sinned and would incur the prophet's anger (again implying Eliyahu's presence might cause more harm than good). To this question God responded that He would forgive the sins of all who observed the performance of the circumcision. Another midrash is quoted that maintains that whoever stands and observes the child placed on the chair of Eliyahu (*kisai shel Eliyahu*) is forgiven from all sin (B'Nai Yessaschar, *Maamarai Tishrai Maamar* 4, *Derush* 7).

This midrash strongly suggests that a witness to a circumcision is not just a spectator to a mitzvah. No, a *brit milah* has the unique power to transform the sins of all in attendance. All guests in attendance are involved with the mitzvah of *teshuvah* (repentance). Who would leave such a scene? Indeed, all would no doubt be obligated to remain until the mitzvah was concluded to be graced with the special powers of atonement.

She'hecheyanu *at a* Brit Milah

QUESTION: Why is it that the *berachah* of *She'hecheyanu* is not recited at a *brit milah* in the Diaspora?

RESPONSE: In *Eretz Yisrael*, common practice is to follow the ruling of the Rambam, who maintains that such a *berachah* should be recited at a *brit milah*. Outside of Israel, Ashkenazim do not chant this *berachah* at a *brit milah*. Of concern is the rationale for not saying this *berachah*. The Vilna Gaon cites a number of theories and refutes each of them. One such hypothesis is that *She'hecheyanu* is only recited at happy occasions, not those that are sad or replete with pain. To the extent that the child suffers pain as a result of the circumcision, it would appear not proper to recite a *berachah* reserved for joyous events (see *Yoreh Deah* 265:7, *Biur HaGra* 36). The Vilna Gaon refutes this argument by citing the talmudic ruling that upon hearing news of the death of a parent who left a large inheritance, the son recites two blessings: one, *Dayan ha'emet*, over the sad news of the death, and the second, *Hatov u'maitiv* (a *berachah* comparable to *She'hecheyanu*, which is reserved for good tidings), over the wonderful, happy news of the inheritance (*Berachot* 59b). This aptly demonstrates that the sadness of death does not mute the joy over the inheritance. Accordingly, the pain of the child at the circumcision should not mute or in any way prevent the joy of the mitzvah.

One may, however, articulate a major distinction between the cases of a *brit milah* and that of a death coupled with an inheritance. The Talmud discusses the following situation: A river overflows onto a person's property and ruins his crops. Yet because of the overflow the soil will be quite fertile in future years. Does one assess the scene as a loss because of its present predicament and chant *Dayan ha'emet*, or is one to be future-oriented and feel joy over the future benefit to his field and recite *She'hecheyanu*. The Talmud rules that one is to be concerned with the loss of the present, not the future gain (*Berachot* 60a). This, therefore, is the difference between an inheritance and a *brit milah.* At the death of a parent two diverse sentiments simultaneously take place; the trauma of the death occurs at the same time as the joy of the inheritance. Consequently, two diverse *berachot* may be recited. At a *brit milah,* however, the pain to the child takes place prior to the joy of the mitzvah. In such a circumstance, the pain mutes the subsequent joy and no *berachah* for joy is to be recited. The Rambam's position would be that there is no difference whether the joy is simultaneous with the pain or subsequent to the pain; as long as joy takes place a *berachah* for happiness may be recited.

Priority in Circumcision

QUESTION: On a given day two circumcisions are to take place. One child is in the eighth day from birth and is classified as a normal *brit milah* in its regular time frame. The other child for one reason or another could not have his circumcision on the eighth day from birth. Which circumcision has priority?

RESPONSE: Of concern is which type of circumcision has a greater urgency to be performed at the earliest possible moment. Tradition has it that HaGaon Rav Chayyim Soloveitchik (Brisk) contended that commonsense logic suggests that a circumcision delayed from a previous eighth day mitzvah has priority over a circumcision of a child born but eight days ago. Why? A circumcision may be performed at any time throughout the eighth day. Though the zealous perform *mitzvot* as early in the day as possible (*z'rizim*), should the circumcision take place in the afternoon of the eighth day, no sin occurs. When, however, a circumcision is delayed to a time beyond the eighth day, any delay beyond when it becomes feasible to perform the mitzvah—even if just a few hours (says Rav Chayyim)—is sinful. Consequently, such a circumcision has priority even over a circumcision to be performed on the eighth day after birth (see *Ma'atikai Shmuah* [Torah recited in the name of the Brisker Rabbonim, p. 144]; see *Responsa D'var Avraham*, vol. II:1).

Many mistakenly believe that if a child is not circumcised on the eighth day from birth then the parents may delay the circumcision until any convenient time. The above position of Rav Chayyim Brisker disputes such a custom. His ruling teaches us that the first day or moment a child may be circumcised after postponing the performance on the eighth day must be utilized without delay. Thus it is not normative halachah to contend that once the eighth day is not used for circumcision then the discretion as to when circumcision should take place is within the dictates of the parents and/or convenience.

A Mohel *and* Tachnun

QUESTION: Should a *mohel* who performs at least one *brit* a day pray regularly in one synagogue?

RESPONSE: No. The *Shulchan Aruch* rules that *Tachnun* is not recited in a synagogue wherein a bridegroom is present or a *brit milah* takes place (*Orech Chayyim* 131:4). The Mishneh Berurah notes that should the *mohel* pray in a synagogue, no *Tachnun* is recited even if the *brit milah* takes place outside of the synagogue (*Orech Chayyim* 131:22). The Mishneh Berurah contends that it is preferable for a bridegroom not to go to the same synagogue the entire first week after his wedding, for such would withhold the congregation from saying *Tachnun* (*Orech*

Chayyim 131:26) The Bair Haitiv records this principle but does not state it as a preference. Rather, he simply rules that a bridegroom should not withhold the congregants from reciting *Tachnun* (*Orech Chayyim* 131:14). As such, a *mohel* with a regular schedule of performing a *brit* each day definitely should be in the same category as a bridegroom. Accordingly, in a large city, he should frequent different synagogues for prayer. I believe such was also the *pesak* for procedure in major *yeshivot.* This suggests that a synagogue should not seek options to excuse themselves from reciting *Tachnun.*

Tefillin *and* Brit Milah

QUESTION: Should *tefillin* be worn by those involved in a circumcision?

RESPONSE: The Shach rules that one should not remove *tefillin* prior to a *brit milah.* Why? Both a circumcision and *tefillin* are deemed heavenly symbols, or "signs." Accordingly, the spiritual sign of *tefillin* should be worn to reinforce the spiritual sign of circumcision (see *Yoreh Deah* 265:24; also cited by the Bair Haitiv, 265:18).

Though the Shach deals with a circumstance in which the *brit milah* generally occurs prior to the recitation of *Aleinu* (*Yoreh Deah* 265:24), which is almost at the conclusion of the *Shacharit* service, his rationale is applicable to cases where the circumcision takes place long after all morning prayers are concluded. As such, perhaps, one should endeavor whenever possible to "double up" on holy signs. In fact, this occurred at the *brit milah* of my oldest son. HaGaon Rav Yitzchak Hutner (*z"l*), my Rosh HaYeshivah (Yeshivat Rabbi Chaim Berlin), was to serve as the honored *sandak* at my son's *brit milah,* but due to a snowstorm he arrived a few hours after *Shacharit* services were concluded. When he arrived the *mohel* and I were still wearing our *tallits* but had removed our *tefillin*. Rav Hutner personally instructed me to don the *tefillin* once again for the *brit milah*.

This is not the general custom. The *Aruch HaShulchan* rules that in his era the common practice was for people to remove *tefillin* prior to the *brit milah* even when the circumcision took place in a synagogue. His rationale was that since most circumcisions took place in homes, therefore even on the infrequent occasions when the circumcision took place in a synagoguge, *tefillin* were not worn (*Yoreh Deah* 265:38). The *Aruch HaShulchan* does not even mention the Shach's theory of doubling up on holy signs. Indeed, the *Aruch HaShulchan* appears to rule that when a *brit milah* takes place in a private home, after *Shacharit*, there is not even an intimation that *tefillin* should be worn.

This suggests that the Shach's theory has application only when the *brit milah* takes place within the *Shacharit* service. The *Shulchan Aruch* rules that *tefillin* may be removed each morning after the recitation of *Kadosh, kadosh, kadosh* in the *Uva l'tzion* prayer. Other scholars extend this until after either *Aleinu* or the subsequent *Kaddish* (*Orech Chayyim* 25:13; see Mishneh Berurah 25:55, 56). Accordingly, this may be the reason behind the *Aruch HaShulchan*'s position. The ancient custom was to have the *brit milah* prior to *Aleinu*. Though normally one may remove *tefillin* before *Aleinu*, on the day of *brit milah* perhaps one should not do so in order to double up on holy signs. But in a situation where a *brit milah* takes place in a home, after a period of time following *Shacharit*, there is no reason to put on *tefillin* at all. For this reason, even when on occasion a *brit milah* takes place in a synagogue after services, no *tefillin* are worn. This would limit the wearing of *tefillin* to cases in which the *brit milah* occurs prior to the conclusion of services. Coupled with this, quite a number of Hasidic rebbes were known to *not* wear *tefillin* purposely during a circumcision.

Moreover, the Chida rules that the doubling up custom is

not applicable to *tefillin*. Indeed, one reason *tefillin* are not worn on *Shabbat* is because *Shabbat* itself is classified as a sign and needs no additional sign. This theory even suggests that the wearing of *tefillin* at a circumcision may be a form of (*chas v'shalom*) belittling the sacred sign of circumcision (*ma'rit ayin*) (Halek Halikutim, *Siman* 2).

In light of such conflicting theories and customs, it seems preferable pragmatically to restrict the Shach's custom as outlined, and not wear *tefillin* at a *brit milah* that takes place much after *Shacharit* services. Should however, the *brit milah* take place directly after services, then the wearing of *tefillin* depends on one's personal custom.

Circumcision or Megillah: *Which Comes First?*

QUESTION: When faced with the double obligation of a circumcision and the *Megillah* reading, which mitzvah is to be performed first?

RESPONSE: The Rema overtly rules that priority is to be granted to the circumcision. The rationale is that the Book of Esther describes the joy of the Jews over their salvation from Haman by the statement (*laYehudim*) "The Jews had light and gladness, joy (*sasson*) and honor" (8:16). The term *sasson* traditionally is interpreted to refer to the mitzvah of circumcision. This seems to suggest that circumcision is granted an element of importance and priority (*Shulchan Aruch, Orech Chayyim* 693:4, Mishneh Berurah 693:12).

The matter is further elaborated by the Machatzit Hashekel. Two interpretations are presented: (1) The word signifying light (*ora*) traditionally relates to Torah. Hence, a circumcision should immediately follow the reading of the Torah on Purim, which takes place before the reading of the *Megillah.* (2) Since Jews were granted light (*ora*), it is important to circumcise the child to enable him to be immediately included in the community of Jews (*Yehudim*) for such a blessing (Machatzit Hashekel, citing the *Maharil* 693:3).

The Vilna Gaon disagrees with this ruling. He contends that the reading of the *Megillah* should take priority over the mitzvah of circumcision. His reasoning is as follows: It is well known that the reading of the *Megillah* takes priority over the public mitzvah of *Avodah*—the sacrifices in the *Bet HaMikdash* (see *Megillah* 2a). Accordingly, it certainly should be granted priority over the mitzvah of circumcision, which may take place at any time throughout the day and is performed early only because of the concept of *z'rizim* (namely, the zealous perform mitzvot at the earliest period of time).

Further elaboration of the Vilna Gaon's position may be the following: The Talmud notes that a public mitzvah (*mitzvah d'rabbim*) has a priority over a private mitzvah. Rashi defines a public mitzvah as a situation where one may include another (*motzi*) in a mitzvah. *Tosafot* disagree. They contend that a public mitzvah is one in which the public celebrates a mitzvah as a communal entity, namely, everyone performs the mitzvah together or performs the same mitzvah. An example is the mitzvah of making a bride and bridegroom happy (*Berachot* 47b). Accordingly, reading the *Megillah* in a synagogue should have the status of a public mitzvah, while a circumcision is a private mitzvah. In such a case, the public mitzvah should have priority over the private mitzvah.

The Rema's position may be based upon a unique understanding of the talmudic citation deriving from biblical verses, that there are two basic mitzvot pertaining to circumcision: (1) A father is commanded to circumcise his male child on the eighth day from birth. (2) In the event this does not take place, then the *bet din* is obligated to circumcise the child (*Kiddushin* 29a). The commentaries contend that the latter obligation is imposed upon *k'lal Yisrael*, and the *bet din* is merely *k'lal Yisrael's* instrument for implementing the mitzvah. At issue is the relationship of the father's mitzvah to that of *k'lal Yisrael.*

There are two ways to view the matter. The basic approach is that the mitzvah is a personal, private commandment of the father and in his absence or lack of action, the *bet din* becomes the agent of the father to fulfill the mitzvah. An alternate view is that when a child is born, the mitzvah of circumcision is imposed upon the entire Jewish community and they are responsible to see to it that the child receives a proper circumcision. However, the father is granted priority in performing the mitzvah. According to this orientation, circumcision is a form of a public (biblical) mitzvah. This may be the reason why the Rema rules that the mitzvah of circumcision takes precedence over the reading of the *Megillah.*

Part VIII

Health Issues

Heart Transplants

QUESTION: Does halachah permit heart transplants?

RESPONSE: Assume a person has been informed that should he receive a heart transplant, he has a good chance at living for many years. In the event, however, that he does not acquire a new heart, his medical condition is such that in terms of statistical probability, he may not live past a few months. Such a person may be classified as one who is in a life-threatening condition (*pikuach nefesh*). Indeed, the Talmud rules that "There is nothing that stands before [the duty] of saving life, with the exception of idolatry, incest [including adultery], and murder" (*Yoma* 82a). Thus, should the above three items be lacking, then every effort must be utilized to save one's life. Even such sacred Jewish values as *Shabbat* and Yom Kippur must be violated to save a life (ibid.; also see 84b).

At issue is whether the process of acquiring the (new) heart is in fact an act of bloodshed upon the donor. The Talmud specifically states that a person is not permitted to save his life by murdering another. The rule is recorded as follows: "A man came before Raba and said to him: The lord of my village told me: kill so-and-so, and if you will not, I shall kill you. He [Raba] answered: Let him kill you, but do not kill. What makes you see that your blood is redder than his? Perhaps the blood of that man is redder than yours" (*Yoma* 82b). As such, it is necessary to assess whether the taking of a heart from a person violates the above cardinal principle of Judaism.

HaRav Moshe Tendler, a major halachic advocate for utilization of heart transplants, permits the removal of a heart from a person who is deemed "brain (stem) dead." Based upon the understanding of a ruling of the great decisor of halachah, HaGaon Rav Moshe Feinstein, he and others contend that a person who is "brain dead" is for halachic purposes considered dead. As such, the removal of the heart in such a case therefore violates no commandment and is considered a meritorious act.

Of concern is that a number of scholars do not necessarily agree with the above-mentioned definition of death. They rule that life continues until the heart stops beating. As such, the removal of a heart from a person deemed "brain dead," whose heart is yet beating and respiration is operational, may be a form of murder that cannot be sanctioned by halachah. Indeed, the Talmud overtly rules that *Shabbat* is to be violated to save a person who has only "a short while to live (*chayai she'ah*)" (*Yoma* 85a). This rule is interpreted to mean that even should a person have but a few hours to live, one must still violate the *Shabbat* to save his life. In other words, the fact that a person is considered "brain dead" and may have only a short period of time left to live does not declassify such a person from the living. He is yet deemed alive, according to this definition of death. This is of major concern, for once the heart stops beating, it is for all practical purposes useless as a transplant. As such, utilization of heart transplants will depend upon which definition of death emerges as sanctioned by halachic authorities.

A means of resolving this issue may be gleaned from an understanding of the following talmudic incident: "When Ulla went up to the land of Israel, he was joined by two inhabitants of Hozai, one of whom arose and slew the other (he simply murdered him). The murderer asked of Ulla: 'Did I do well?' 'Yes,' he replied, 'Moreover, cut his throat clean across.' (See commentaries of Rosh and Ran, who note that such an action would hasten the death of the dying person.) When he came before Rabbi Yochanan, he asked him, 'Maybe, God forbid, I have strengthened the hands of transgressors?' He replied, 'You have saved your life'" (*Nedarim* 22a).

Of major concern is the rabbinic approval granted Ulla by Rabbi Yochanan. Is there not a general rule that one is not permitted to save one's life by killing another? Ulla had no right to protect himself from a potential or probable danger by sacrificing the life of the person close to death. The fact that the victim was close to death should not alter the objection to hasten death. As previously noted, the Talmud ruled that life of even a short span of time is still a life that requires violation of *Shabbat* to sustain. So why was Ulla permitted to hasten another's death to save himself from a *sakana*? This question was posed by the Tiferet Yisrael. His response generates a unique halachic perspective. He contends that the fact that one is mandated to violate *Shabbat* to save a dying person who has but a few hours to live does not mean that such a person's life is equal to one who may live for quite a number of years. When the choice is between saving a person who has but a few hours to live versus violating *Shabbat*, then the life of the dying person takes precedence over the sanctity of *Shabbat*. When, however, the choice is between someone who will die imminently and someone who has many years to live, then it is proper to sacrifice the person who will shortly die so that the other may have a normal lifespan. This is why Rabbi Yochanan approved Ulla's actions (see commentary, *Peah*, *Mishnah* 1; see also *Yoma* 8:4).

Based upon the above consideration, one may find additional halachic support for heart transplants from "brain dead" donors: (1) Once the donor is deemed "brain dead," then according to some scholars he is halachically dead. As such, from this perspective there are no halachic qualms over utilizing his heart for transplant. (2) Even should one subscribe to the halachic position that "brain stem death" is not the halachic definition of death, it is certain that such a person would be classified as one in the category of *chayai she'ah*, namely, as one who has only a short time to live. According to the Tiferet Yisrael, the long, probable life of another takes precedence over such a life. It would, therefore, appear that one may rely upon the Tiferet Yisrael's position where the potential donor is "brain stem dead" and another life may be saved.

Critical Comment I

The Minchat Chinuch makes a distinction between cases relating to *ones* (compulsion or duress) and *choli* (illness or sickness). He maintains that acts permitted to one under duress may not necessarily be also permitted to people who are sick (see Minchat Chinuch, *Mitzvah* 295). Since the Tiferet Yisrael's theory is based on a case dealing with compulsion, one may not assume that the same halachah holds true in a case relating to sickness. To rule upon "heart transplants" by citing the Tiferet Yisrael's position is a blurring of a major distinction between Ulla's duress and the illness of a patient. As such, the citations supporting the Tiferet Yisrael would not justify the removal of a patient's heart for a transplant.

It is vital to understand the context under which the Minchat Chinuch formulated his distinction between cases of duress and illness.

The talmudic sages were interested in ascertaining the scriptural reference that served as the source for the concept that *Shabbat* may be violated to save a life. Seven theories were presented; three are relevant to our discussion. Rabbi Yishmael contended that the verse permitting one to kill a thief who enters a home at night is the source ("If a thief be found breaking in" [Ex. 22:1; *Im B'Machteret*]). "Now if in the case wherein it is doubtful whether he [the thief] has come to take money or life . . . it is permitted to save oneself at the cost of his life, how much more may one suspend the laws of *Shabbat* to save human life?" (*Yoma* 85a). Rabbi Shimon ben Menassia derived the rule from the verse "And the children of Israel shall keep the *Shabbat* (*V'shamru*)" (Ex. 21:16). "Profane for his sake one *Shabbat* so that he may keep many Sabbaths." Shmuel noted that the source was the biblical mandate that says, "And he shall live by them (*V'chai bahem*)" (Lev. 18:5). The Talmud further notes that except for the source delineated by Shmuel, all the other theories may be refuted. In other words, only Shmuel's position has halachic validity.

Of concern to the Minchat Chinuch was the position of Rabbi Yishmael. There is a general rule that three mitzvot take priority even over life itself, namely, the prohibitions against *Avodah zarah*, murder, and adultery. However, Rabbi Yishmael disputes this cardinal rule. He maintains that the verse *V'chai bahem* implies that life is even more important than the prohibition against idol worship. This, moreover, only relates to the violation of the sin of *avodah zarah* in private. Even Rabbi Yishmael would prohibit a public act of *avodah zarah* in that such would be a *chilul HaShem* (a public desecration of God's Name) (*Avoda Zara* 27b, Lev. 22:32).

At issue to the Minchat Chinuch was the necessity of Rabbi Yishmael to seek a verse other than *V'chai bahem* to support the rule that *Shabbat* may be violated to save a life. As demonstrated, Rabbi Yishmael derives from this verse the rule that life is even more important than violating *avodah zarah* privately. As such, he should have used the same verse to note that life is more important than *Shabbat.* In response to this question, the Minchat Chinuch formulated a distinction between duress and sickness. Accordingly, the verse *V'chai bahem* deals with a person under compulsion to do *avodah zarah* privately to save his life. Yet one may not automatically assume that what was permitted to a person under duress would also be permitted to someone who is sick. Consequently, Rabbi Yishmael sought support from another source. To Shmuel, however, there is no necessity for a distinction between duress and sickness. The verse *V'chai bahem* supports violating all mitzvot (except the three cardinal laws of *avodah zarah*, murder, and adultery) regardless of whether the case related to duress or sickness. Since all the theories of the sages on this matter were rejected from halachah except for that of Shmuel, a distinction pertaining to Rabbi Yishmael's view has no halachic standing.

The Or HaChaim contends that one may not violate the *Shabbat* to save a person who is judged to be unable to live past that *Shabbat.* His reasoning is that Rabbi Shimon ben Menassia ruled that *Shabbat* may be violated to save a life based on the premise that this *Shabbat* should be violated so that the person may observe other Sabbaths. To the extent that the sick person will not live past this *Shabbat* and will not have an opportunity to observe future Sabbaths, there is no valid reason to permit violation of *Shabbat* in his behalf (*KiTissa*). The Minchat Chinuch takes strong issue with this position. He explicitly notes that the fact that the Talmud rules that all positions except that of Shmuel may be refuted implies that the halachah is not as delineated by any one but Shmuel. Thus, the position of Rabbi Shimon ben Menassia is deemed rejected from halachah (Minchat Chinuch, *Mitzvah* 39; see also *Daat Torah, Orech Chayyim* 329:4).

The same argument may be applied to Rabbi Yishmael's position. It is rejected from halachah, and distinctions based upon it have no halachic bearing. Accordingly, the Tiferet Yisrael's theory has relevance to our case at hand.

Critical Comment II

The Rambam rules that in the event that Jews are told by enemies that one Jew should be given to them to be killed or else all the Jews involved will be killed, it is not permitted to save the group by surrendering a Jew to be murdered. In case the enemies designate a specific Jew that they wish to be given over to them to kill, unless the designated (fingered) Jew was already judged guilty of a capital offense, it is still prohibited to deliver such a Jew to his death (*Yesodai HaTorah* 5:5). The Kesef Mishnah cites Yerushalmi wherein the above second case is recorded as a debate between Rav Yochanan and Raish Lakesh. Rav Yochanan rules that once the enemies designate a Jew to be killed, then even if the Jew so "fingered" was not guilty nor judged guilty of a capital crime, it is permissible to hand over that Jew to the enemies who wish to kill him. Raish Lakesh, however, does not permit handing over to enemies any Jew, even one "fingered" by enemies unless the Jew so designated was guilty of a capital crime. The Kesef Mishnah notes that it is apparent that the Rambam rules in favor of Raish Lakesh rather than Rav Yochanan, even though the accepted practice throughout the Talmud is to rule like Rav Yochanan whenever others debate his decisions.

In an attempt to understand the rationale underlying the decisions of the Rambam in the above cases, the Kesef Mishnah notes the following: A Jew is not permitted to save his or her life by killing another person. The Talmud specifically states that this prohibition is not based upon a biblical reference or mandate but is a moral principle mandated by logic (*sevara*). That is, no one has the right to determine that his life is more important than another. Perhaps, it is just the opposite—maybe the other's life is more valuable than yours. As such, there is no moral license to kill another to save one's own life. This logical principle is termed *my chazit* (*Yoma* 82b).

Based upon the above concept, it is understandable why Jews are not permitted to hand over a Jew to be killed who was not specifically requested by the enemies. For any Jew whom Jews themselves select to give over to enemies one may contend that the principle of *my chazit* applies: Why this Jew more than another? To the extent that the concern would revolve around this moral issue, no Jew may be given over to enemies.

The second case may not be so understood. In the second case, the enemies designate a specific Jew whom they wish to kill. They contend that should that Jew not be handed over to them, then they will kill all the Jews involved. It may even be a situation wherein the lives of a thousand or more are at stake. At issue, notes the Kesef Mishnah, is that logic dictates that one thousand Jewish lives are more important than one Jewish life. Since the enemies "fingered' the victim, the argument of *my chazit* simply does not apply. Accordingly, Rav Yochanan's ruling appears to be more logical and credible than that of Raish Lakesh. To this the Kesef Mishnah concludes that the basis for forbidding one to kill another is not solely the logic of *my chazit*; it is also an ancient *mesorah*, an old tradition. As such, even when the logic of *my chazit* does not apply, one still may not save one's life at the expense of killing another. That is why it is prohibited to save even an entire town by handing over a Jew designated by the enemies.

From the above it is clear that logical distinctions demonstrating the superiority of certain lives over others may be against the position of the Kesef Mishnah. This strongly suggests that the Tiferet Yisrael's comparison between a *chayai she'ah* and a long, normal life may be disputed by the Kesef Mishnah. In addition, just as the Rambam rules against Rav

Yochanan in the case at hand (*Yesodai HaTorah*), so too does it suggest that the Rambam would rule against Rav Yochanan's position regarding Ulla (*Nedarim* 22a).

Indeed, it may be demonstrated that Rav Yochanan does make logical distinctions negating the value of *chayai she'ah* when such may mitigate against the concern for a prolonged lifespan. The Talmud discusses the propriety of using apostate, Gentile doctors who were suspected of murdering Jews. In the event that a Jew had a sickness from which without utilizing medical help he would definitely die, such a person was permitted to use the services of a doctor suspected of murdering Jews. Why? Because without the doctor the man would die anyway. The doctor, however, may either kill him or cure him. Since there is a chance that the doctor may cure him, it is proper to seek out even the services of a doctor suspected of murdering Jews. To this the Talmud poses the question: What about *chayai she'ah*? In other words, even though the sick person may die within a few days or weeks without medical help, such is more of a life than the possibility of dying immediately at the hand of a murderous doctor. The response is that compared to the hope of living a full, long life, the concern for *chayai she'ah* is not considered important. For proof of this position, the Talmud cites the case of four leprous men who lacked food and drink and decided it was prudent to enter an enemy camp to acquire their needs. Their argument was that should they remain where they were, they would starve to death; should, however, they enter the military camp of the enemy, then the soldiers would either kill them upon sight or have mercy on them and give them food. Thus the concern for a long life took priority over the *chayai she'ah* of death by starvation. The author of this talmudic rule is Rav Yochanan (*Avodah Zarah* 27b; see also II Kings 7:4).

At issue is whether the Kesef Mishnah and the Rambam dispute the theory of the Tiferet Yisrael.

Tosafot suggest that the general prohibition against saving one's own life by taking another (*my chazit*) relates only to a situation wherein it is necessary to do an action against another person in order to save one's own life. In the event, however, that no action need be taken at all against any other person, then it is not prohibited to save one's life at the expense of another. The example presented is one in which a person is told that unless he permits himself being thrown upon the body of an infant (wherein the infant will definitely die) then he himself will be killed. Since he performs no action at all and is simply passive, the situation is not comparable to the classic case of *my chazit* and such a person may permit himself being thrown upon the infant even though such an action will kill the infant (*Tosafot Yuma* 82a). The Rema cites this distinction in his rulings (*Yoreh Deah* 157:1).

The Tosafot Yom HaKipurim of Rav Moshe ibn Haviv was quite concerned with the ruling of *Tosafot* and the Rema. His problem was that neither the Rambam, the Tur, nor the *Shulchan Aruch* cite this distinction of passive behavior that appears to override the prohibition of *my chazit*. At the same time from a purely logical comparison to the classic case of *my chazit*, the position of *Tosafot* appears to be correct. Namely, when no action is required, then one's own life takes priority over the life of another. In such an instance, *chaiyecha kodem*, your life is more important than the life of another. He suggests that the Rambam, Tur, and Kesef Mishnah (*Shulchan Aruch*) dispute the theory of *Tosafot* and the Rema. Their position is the theory expounded by the Kesef Mishnah (in *Yesodai Hatorah* 5:5), namely, the prohibition against saving one's life by taking the life of another is not solely based upon logic and rational thought; it is an ancient tradition, a *mesorah*. Accordingly, even when logical distinctions may be developed between the case at hand and the concept of *my chazit*, the prohibition is still operational. Thus the above scholars would prohibit a person from saving his life by allowing himself to be thrown upon an infant. *Tosafot* and the Rema, however, believe that the prohibition of *my chazit* is purely a logical imperative and any case wherein distinctions may be drawn may be permissible. In terms of a decisive ruling on this matter, the Tosafot Yom HaKipurim notes that in such a difference of rabbinic opinion one should take the lenient position because whenever there is a question of life or death, the lenient position prevails. In the event of *kiddush HaShem* then one may be stringent (see Tosafot Yom HaKipurim, *Yuma* 82).

It is evident that the Tosafot Yom HaKipurim believes that the person involved in the decision has an obligation to view his case from a lenient viewpoint even though from the view of the infant, for example, it is a stringent decision. Also, it is well known that the Ashkenazic sphere of halachah follows the Rema and not the position of the *Shulchan Aruch* (Rabbi Yosef Caro). As such, the position of the Tiferet Yisrael, which makes logical distinctions between cases, is in accordance with accepted halachah.

Of special interest is the ruling of the Rambam in accord with the theory of Raish Lakesh and not Rav Yochanan. Such a decision is contrary to the accepted practice of ruling like Rav Yochanan. On this issue, perhaps, the theory of the Lechem Mishnah may be utilized. He contends that the Rambam ruled like Raish Lakesh only in such an instance wherein there was an opportunity for an escape. In the event that no escape was available, then even the Rambam would rule like Rav Yochanan. Accordingly, the position of the Tiferet Yisrael is neither refuted nor rejected—just the opposite, Rav Yochanan's position is not even disputed by the Rambam.

Critical Comment III

The position of the Tiferet Yisrael may not be the accepted halachic ruling. Indeed, in the general debate concerning the halachic propriety of heart transplants, the sages involved make no reference to the Tiferet Yisrael.

According to the Tiferet Yisrael (as utilized to permit heart transplants), it may be permitted to kill a *traifah* (one with a punctured lung) to save the life of a person who may live (with, for example, the heart of the *traifah*) for a long period of time. A *traifah* is definitely a person classified as a *chayai she'ah*. Yet, the halachic rule is that one is not permitted to kill a *traifah* to save the life of another. This demonstrates that the position of the Tiferet Yisrael is not basic halachah.

Instead of chiding the Tiferet Yisrael for citing a unique talmudic and halachic reference, not generally noted by others, I would have assumed that *b'nai torah* would laud the fact that a new halachic perspective was brought to the debate. Indeed, the ruling of the Tiferet Yisrael adds an important dimension that must be considered. It simply cannot be rejected because certain rabbis did not refer to it.

A review of commentaries on the incident of Ulla (*Nedarim* 22a) indicates the following: Both the Rosh and the Ran contend that Ulla requested the murderer to hasten the death of the victim. The Meiri, however, demurs. He suggests that the victim was actually dead. Ulla's words were merely exaggerated statements to express feigned approval and joy over the murder. The request to open the throat of the victim did not, therefore, relate to the taking of a life, even a life of a *chayai she'ah*. The difficulty with this interpretation is that it means Ulla did nothing wrong except to laud the murderer. Did he not realize that such was permissible to save himself from being killed? Was such a situation so difficult that he needed to solicit the guidance of his Rebbe, Rabbi Yochanan? Also, most of the *rishonim* disagree with the Meiri's observation. Apart from those already noted, the Shita M'kubetzet cites two sages who explicitly concur with the Rosh and the Ran. The Ritz (some contend that it is the M'hari Mintz) says that the victim was not able to live as a result of the initial blow by the murderer; Ulla suggested that the murderer hasten the pace of the victim's death. A second position is noted that implies that the case deals with killing, not exaggerations. As such, the majority position appears to discuss the fact that Ulla was responsible for hastening the death of the victim.

HaRav Shlomo Kluger poses similar questions to those of the Tiferet Yisrael. Indeed, he attempts to respond the same as the Tiferet Yisrael, namely, that the projected long life of Ulla takes priority over the *chayai she'ah* of the victim. To this HaRav Kluger notes that Ulla was not faced with certain death. Rather,

Ulla was faced only with a doubtful (*safek*), life-threatening condition. Yet, the previous victim (whose death was hastened) was a case of a certain death. Perhaps, he suggests, the halachah mandates that even a case of long life threatened only by an uncertain death takes precedence over a *chayai she'ah*. HaRav Kluger concludes that the matter requires further consideration (*tzorech iyun*) (*Sefer Nidrai Z'rizim*). The implication is that the person with the potentially long lifespan is only doubtfully in a life-threatening situation. Should, however, such a person be in a condition wherein his probable long life is definitely threatened, then there would be no hesitation over sacrificing the life of the *chayai she'ah* for his life.

To suggest that the Tiferet Yisrael's position may be extrapolated to condone the killing of a *traifah* is not an issue of pragmatic concern. My contention is that only in a case where a person is deemed "brain dead" and the heart was yet beating could one rely upon the Tiferet Yisrael's position to remove the heart to save the life of another who would die without such a heart. Only in such a situation, where by one group of rabbinic scholars the person was already categorized as dead, should reliance upon the Tiferet Yisrael be considered. In other words, only in such a traumatic scene should the Tiferet Yisrael be utilized to mute the opposing theory. To discard the Tiferet Yisrael's position because of a "slippery slope" concern that it may be wrongfully used is a *gezairah* (a rabbinic ban) that is in the realm of a value judgment of personal preference.

The Crime of Suicide

QUESTION: Why is suicide deemed by Jewish law to be a grave sin? Does not each person have an inherent right to do whatever he so desires with his own body?

RESPONSE: This question was posed to the great sage HaGaon HaRav Shlomo Kluger who articulated the following response: Every person is brought to this world to serve the Almighty. This is the mission of each person, the raison d'etre of every human being. No one has the authority to decide that he or she no longer wishes to continue in this role. No one may by fiat terminate the amount of time available to serve HaShem. Whatever amount of time is allotted for one's life is a schedule determined by God. To commit suicide is to reject God's will. It is an affirmation that one's personal sensitivities are more important than the Divinely decreed amount of time available for the service of God. For this reason tradition has it that a suicide has no share in the world to come. A suicide is, therefore, an apostate. He simply refuses to serve God in the time granted to him. He feels that his schedule for life takes priority over that decreed by God. Accordingly, he loses the reward granted the faithful (*Avodat Avoda*, vol. III, *Siman* 157).

Part IX

Social and Ideological Concerns

Wearing a Yarmulka

QUESTION: Why do Jews cover their heads by wearing a *kippah* (yarmulka)?

RESPONSE: The Talmud (*Kiddushin* 31a) notes that "Rav Huna son of Rav Yehoshua would not walk four cubits bareheaded, saying 'the Divine Presence is above my head.' Thus, the covering of one's head is a formal symbolic manifestation of the constant presence of God. As the psalmist states (Psalm 23): "Yea, though I walk through the valley of the shadow of death, I shall fear no evil for Thou art with me." My God is always above me. I am covered by the protection of my God. It is a constant reminder that the Jew is never alone; he walks with God. It is a feeling of assurance and comfort, and at the same time an ever-present conscience to withhold one from going astray.

But a head covering has another role: It is a symbol of humility. How enlightening it is that the Talmud presents the concept of covering one's head directly adjacent to a statement prohibiting one from "walking with the haughty." The most distinctly human quality of man is his mind. It is his essence, yet it must be controlled. It is constantly covered as a shield against arrogance. The greatest treasure of man—his mind—is always withheld from public scrutiny hidden like a priceless heirloom controlled by the presence of God. Yes, the bareheaded man is a symbol of pride and perhaps, arrogance. His head is in the clouds. Not so the Jew. His head is covered to remind him of his limits, frailties, and even dependence upon God. The hat or yarmulka is the daily implementation of the rule in Proverbs (1:17) that "The fear of the Lord is the beginning of knowledge." It is the intertwining of religion and wisdom.

Since the presence of God permeates our existence (and is not only experienced in the synagogue), tradition has been to cover the head throughout all pursuits of life in and out of the synagogue and home. This custom has for so many centuries been the mark of the Jew, that one great halachic sage has even ruled that to be bareheaded was an overt simulation of Gentile practices (Taz, Codes, *Orech Chayyim* 8:3). Of interest is that not one Jewish scholar throughout Jewish history has ever dismissed the custom as irrelevant or lacking religious merit. Its compulsory requirement has been discussed but never its value questioned.

In talmudic times, moreover, the type of hat worn was a visible means of determining status. A married man wore a different covering than a single person (*Kiddushin* 29b). A scholar, too, had a distinctive hat (ibid. 8a, Rav Kahana; also 30a, Rav Yeshoshua ben Levi; see Rashi).

The Talmud notes that the placing of a covering on one's head is as natural to the Jew as rising in the morning and getting dressed with clothes. In *Berachot* (60b) the Talmud contends that each process of awakening has a concomitant blessing. For example: "When he opens his eyes, he should say: 'Blessed is He Who opens the eyes of the blind.' . . . When he dresses, he should say 'Blessed is He Who clothes the naked.' When he places a covering on his head, he should say: 'Blessed is He Who crowns Israel with glory.'" In other words, the covering of one's head is part of the process of getting dressed in the morning. It is inconceivable that the Jew would not place a covering on his head.

Indeed, the significance of the blessing relates to the primary religious role of the hat (or the yarmulka). The Jew makes numerous *berachot* (blessings) throughout each day. Prior to the performance of any mitzvah, the Jew acknowledges its sanctity by chanting a blessing. Why is it that the all-pervasive mitzvah of believing in God has no *berachah* each day? A partial response is that blessings were instituted as preparatory statements prior to specific actions. Blessings were never set up for the obligations of the heart or the mind. Yet, by placing a covering on one's head each day one is concretely and actively manifesting the presence of God. Thus the blessing of covering one's head is, in reality, the *berachah* of belief, for God is . . . the glory of the Jew.

Is it no wonder that a Jew covers his head. It is his tag of identification; it overtly stamps him as a believing Jew. It is the essence of belief.

Frumkeit

QUESTION: How is *frumkeit* viewed in terms of halachic standards?

RESPONSE: I never considered the word *frumkeit* to be a positive term to describe religious observance. The word seems to exude overtones of excessive piety. A person considered *frum* was one who generally went "overboard" in displaying extreme ritual stringencies. Thus the *frum*ie, namely one who excelled in *frumkeit*, was a pejorative description of personality, certainly not one to be emulated or praised. The common joke was that one could not "out*frum*" the "*frum*ie." No matter how sincere or stringent a person was, the "*frum*ie" would concoct a never-before-heard-of stringency that would outdo anything anyone else would observe. The normal concern was, therefore, to ascertain the basic halachah and not to seek out or practice unwarranted stringencies (*chumrot*).

This was my approach. I remember it said once that someone asked the Gaon HaRav Shlomo Kluger of Brod to detail the stringencies that he followed. His response was that he did not practice any stringencies. Indeed, he added that he considered himself fortunate to be able to follow the rules of the humble Jews who observed the laws set up in the *Shulchan Aruch.*

A *dvar Torah* by the Lubavitcher Rebbe (*z"l*), however,

truly altered my perspective on this matter. The Rebbe's brief analysis forcefully demonstrated the theological value of *frumkeit* and provided a moral imperative to perform mitzvot in a manner above and beyond that which is required. The Talmud reports that all the Divine acts of reward and punishment benefit the human deeds; they are "measure for measure." For this reason the captain at the gate of Samaria who refused to believe in a specific prophecy that abundance would follow famine was not privileged to enjoy the bounty when the prophecy was fulfilled (*Sanhedrin* 90a, b). In other words, God's response to human behavior appears to us a reaction to the manner in which we perform mitzvot. Explaining this quote, the Rebbe noted that should we only observe mitzvot according to their basic halachic requirements, then God, in turn, will respond to us in the same fashion. We will be granted only that which the law mandates is the basic response to the mitzvah—nothing more. We have no right to beseech special favors or considerations. We receive a legal response—a reward for our mitzvot and a just punishment for our sins. In the event, however, that we perform mitzvot in a manner above and beyond that which is required, we can anticipate that God will so respond in a comparable manner, which will be above and beyond what we deserve.

This concept is the meaning of the talmudic citation wherein God states that it is permissible to show favoritism to *k'lal Yisrael* in that the Torah mandates a blessing after one is sated and Jews undertake to make a blessing even after eating (bread in) the amount of an olive or an egg (*Berachot* 20b). Thus, a self-imposed stringency is rewarded by a special Divine consideration. Indeed, rabbis of the Talmud who were known for their scrupulous concern for the dignity of others were deemed worthy of miraculous responses from the *Rebbono Shel Olam* (ibid., 20a) (see Lubavitcher Rebbe, "Chidushim on Chanukah," *HaMoar*, vol. 46, nos. 5–6 [October–November 1993], pp. 7–8).

This concept radically alters one's reaction to *frumkeit*. "*Frum*ie" should not be a term evoking negative sensitivities, but rather a means of seeking better treatment in cases of need.

It is a positive theological approach to ensure better Divine treatment. Of course, this principle should not be exclusively relegated to the realm of ritual, but should also be applied to the sphere of morals and ethics. This suggests that the "*frum*ie" should also find it necessary to be excessively stringent concerning the feelings and concerns of others.

There is, however, one aspect of *frumkeit* that must be clearly noted. It requires one to be learned in the intricacies of halachah. *Frumkeit* can be transformed into a theological force mandating special treatment in that it is an action or behavioral pattern above and beyond that which is required by law. This definitely indicates that the person involved recognizes the obligation of the basic halachah and the fact that he (or she) is observing the mitzvah in a manner that is beyond the minimum required. In other words, the "excessive" behavior is an act of devotion to set in motion God's special treatment. Otherwise, the performer of the mitzvah is not displaying an attitude of extra concern. This cogently suggests that perhaps, in the performance of each mitzvah, it is necessary to note the distinction between what is required and what is done as a means of total devotion.

Accordingly, the performance of even "so-called *chumrot*" is not a matter of concern. At issue is the attitudinal basis of the person performing the mitzvah. As long as the person believes that he (or she) is performing above and beyond that which halachah demands so that special Godly consideration should take place in return, then the entire process has merit. If, however, the person performing the excessive element of the mitzvah feels that such is the normal requirement, then the entire performance lacks the recognition that is beyond the cause of duty. Perhaps, in such a situation, this ignorance does not trigger special Divine care.

Honor to Grandparents (Part I)

QUESTION: Who merits greater *kavod*, a father or a grandfather?

RESPONSE: The Rema rules that one owes greater respect to a father than to a grandfather (*Yoreh Deah* 240:24). The simple interpretation is that deference is owed to both, with the father being granted priority over the grandfather. The source for this ruling is the verse in Genesis that states that Yaakov made a sacrifice to the God of his father Yitzchok (*VaYigash*, Genesis 46:1). Citing a Midrash, Rashi says that Yaakov made no reference to his grandfather (Avraham). The reason, he notes, is that the obligation to give *kavod* to a father is greater than the obligation to a grandfather. Consequently, only the father is mentioned in the Torah. A pragmatic halachic application would be to rule that in the event both a father and a grandfather request service, preference should be granted to the father.

Of interest is that HaGaon HaRav Akiva Eiger suggests that in the above case wherein both a father and a grandfather request service, priority must be granted to the grandfather. His rationale is as follows: The Talmud rules that in the event both a father and a mother request a service, priority is to be given to the father's request. Why? For both the child and mother are obligated to pay homage to the father (husband) (*Kedushin* 31a). So too should be the case wherein a father and grandfather request service. Both grandson and father are required to give *kavod* to the grandfather. Accordingly, the ruling of the Rema granting greater *kavod* to a father over a grandfather is interpreted to apply to a circumstance wherein both parents are no longer alive. In such a case (after death), *kavod* to a father takes precedence over *kavod* to a grandfather. Again reference is made to the previous citation in *Kedushin*. Therein it is ruled that in the event a father and mother are divorced and both request service, no priority is granted to the father. For once a divorce takes place, the mother is no longer obligated to give *kavod* to her (former) husband. Death, says HaRav Akiva Eiger, should be comparable to a state of divorce. That is, once death occurs, the obligation of the father to the grandfather is null and void (Responsa HaRav Akiva Eiger, vol. 1, no. 68).

One may question HaRav Akiva Eiger's logic by noting a major distinction between the request of a father and mother and the request of a father and grandfather. In the former case the son has an independent obligation to his father as well as to his mother—and she, the mother, has an independent obligation to honor his father, her husband. In the latter case, however, perhaps the son's obligation is merely to honor his father and his father has an obligation to honor *his* father. Thus the obligation to the grandfather is only via the father and the son has no independent obligation to honor the grandfather.

One may, however, diffuse this argument. The Bach articulates a novel rationale for an independent obligation of a grandchild to honor grandparents. The Talmud reports that a grandparent is mandated to teach Torah to his grandchild (*V'hodatem levanekcha v'livnai vanecha*—"You shall make them known to your sons and grandsons") (Deuteronomy 4:9, *Kiddushin* 30a). Reasons the Bach: If a grandparent is obliged to teach Torah to a grandchild, is not such a grandchild obligated to grant *kavod* in return? (*Tur, Yoreh Deah* 240). Thus, the mandate of the grandparent generates a reciprocal obligation upon the grandchild. This obligates the grandson to honor his grandfather separate and distinct from his obligation to his father. As such, HaRav Akiva Eiger's comparison of the case of parents and grandparents to a mother and father is substantiated. Namely, the grandfather takes precedence while both the father and grandfather are alive.

Honor to Grandparents (Part II)

QUESTION: Does the Talmud present any actual cases in which grandchildren did not provide *kavod* to a grandparent?

RESPONSE: Yes, there appears to be a talmudic citation that severely limits the *kavod* granted to a grandparent. The Talmud relates the following incident (*Sotah* 49a):

Rabbi A'ha ben Yaakov reared in his own home his grandson, Rabbi Yaakov, the son of his daughter. When Rabbi Yaakov grew up, his grandfather requested that he bring him some water. Rabbi Yaakov responded, "I am not your son," and this is the source for the popular saying "Revi, revi, I am the son of your daughter."

Rashi says that *revi* means "Support me, rear me, but I am only your daughter's son and not obliged to serve you." Some authorities utilize this citation to substantiate the view that a grandson is not obliged to provide acts of service to his grandfather. Others make the distinction that it applies to a daughter's son, while still others contend that *kibud* to a grandfather is required only during the parent's lifetime and not subsequent to it (see commentaries on *Yoreh Deah* 240:24).

This debate misses the essence of the incident. Was the grandfather, Rabbi A'ha, ignorant of the halachah? Why, in fact, did he request service from his grandson? Also, the popular saying indicates that the grandson's retort was immoral. In other words, Rabbi Yaakov's contention was an act of the greatest chutzpah. To request support and sustenance and then reject any obligation of service is a travesty of morality. Rabbi A'ha's position may have been that when a grandparent actually sustains and rears a grandchild, such sustenance crystallizes a special obligation of service. It is for this reason that Rabbi A'ha made the request, and the popular saying jeered Rabbi Yaakov's response.

In other words, the case is an example of what should not be done. Rather, grandparents must be honored.

The Lawful Use of Lethal Force

QUESTION: Does halachah permit a Jew to use lethal force?

RESPONSE: Scripture (Exodus 22:1) notes an interesting case. It states that if a thief is found breaking into a person's home in the middle of the night and the owner kills the intruder, the owner is innocent of any charges of murder. But why is that so? Did the thief come with a weapon? Did the thief threaten the life of the homeowner? What are the circumstances of the case?

The Talmud (*Sanhedrin* 72a) suggests that this case is based upon a number of presumptions that provide the homeowner with a license to exercise even lethal force.

The first presumption is that a homeowner, awoken by a thief in his own home in the middle of the night, would probably defend his home and property even with lethal weapons. The thief must be aware of this presumption and yet still be prepared to overcome the owner even though it may mean an eventual murder of the homeowner. In other words, the presumption is that the thief is prepared to combat the owner and kill him. Accordingly, the owner is allowed to stop the thief by killing him, on the grounds of self-defense.

In the event, however, where the presumption of a life-threatening condition is not operational, then the homeowner may not use lethal force. For example: a case wherein a father breaks into the home of his son. The Talmud presumes that should the son awaken and catch his father in the act of stealing, no father would ever normally seek the death of his son. As such, there is no presumption of jeopardy to life. Consequently, the homeowner has no license at all to kill the intruder.

Of interest is that once there is such a presumption of a life-threatening situation, not only may the victim lawfully use lethal force but this right is granted even to spectators who observe the incident.

The Talmud classifies the following case as the law of the pursuer (*rodef*): Should A run after B, and A is carrying a weapon and threatening to imminently kill B, in such an event should B save his own life by killing A, it is deemed self-defense. Moreover, should a spectator observe the spectacle of A running after B and threatening to kill B, the spectator is not permitted to disassociate himself from the problem or pretend it does not concern him but is mandated to help the potential victim, as it is written: "Thou shalt not stand idly by the blood of thy neighbor" (Lev. 19:16, *Sanhedrin* 73a). Accordingly, should the bystander save B by killing A, he is not charged with murder. The Talmud, however, makes an interesting distinction. It says that one may kill a pursuer only if the death of the pursuer is the only way to save the victim. In the event one may save B by destroying a limb of A, then A's murder is not justified (*Sanhedrin* 74a).

In other words, the legal usage of lethal force requires two essential elements: (1) a presumption of a life-threatening condition, and (2) a second presumption that the only means available to avert the life-threatening condition is through the use of lethal force.

In rabbinic literature there is an interesting debate on this latter issue. One Sage (*Mishneh L'Melech*, Maimonides, Laws of *Choval U'Mazik* 8:10) contends that the judgment that lethal force may be exercised only if such is the only means of saving the victim is a limitation imposed only on the spectator's involvement, not on the response of the victim himself. The argument is as follows: A spectator, an individual not pursued or attacked, has the capacity to assess a situation and to coolly and wisely determine the amount of force necessary to save another from a threatened attacker. A victim, however, is not in such a state of mind to make fine distinctions as to how to save himself.

The victim is frightened for his life. His life is in danger; he wishes to save himself. His concern is how to save himself from death, not how to minimally hurt the murderer. To the victim, says this sage, once the presumption of jeopardy to life is a reality, then any act, even a lethal act, is absolved from punishment even if an objective outsider might have merely shot the attacker in the foot, for example.

Some scholars even maintain that the rule of self-defense demands that one does not take chances with one's life. If there is even a scintilla of a possibility that a nonlethal act would not avert the life-threatening condition, then it is prohibited to attempt to injure a limb of a person to save oneself.

Use of Nonlethal Force Against Another Jew

QUESTION: Does halachah ever permit the use of nonlethal force against another Jew?

RESPONSE: The Talmud (*Bava Kamma* 27b) says as follows: There was a well of water that belonged to two people. Each used it to draw water on alternate days. A, for example, drew water on Monday and B used it on Tuesday. One of them came and used it on a day not his. The other person said to him, "This day is mine, not yours." But the latter paid no attention, so the person to whom the water belonged that day took a hoe and forced the other off the land and away from the well. The matter came before the Rabbis, who ruled that there is a general debate as to whether a person may take the law into his own hands. Even scholars who contend that one may not take the law in one's own hands agree that in a case where an irreparable, irreplaceable loss is pending, one may legally use force to protect one's interests.

Say Rashi and other commentators, the case of the well cannot await a decision by a court, for until such time as a court convenes, the usurper may take as much water as he desires and there would be no way of knowing how much he used. He may even take so much that no water is left at all. Since courts cannot assess A's loss or determine the exact extent of his losses, A is permitted to use force to protect his interests. As such, should one feel that until such time as court convenes a litigant may hide, steal, ruin, or destroy the contested property, then one may use force to avert such a problem.

Later sages contend that this right to use force is granted only to one who has sufficient documentation, witnesses, and deeds to support his claim. Then he may use force to protect his position. Accordingly, force is granted only to those who wish to save time and secure property from losses (*Aruch HaShulchan, Choshen Mishpat* 4:1–2). In the event, however, that one has no such corroborating documentation or evidence then no physical force may be used against another person.

Jewish law thus provides the utilization of force in situations wherein the delay of time might benefit the wrongdoer and becloud losses.

Theft of a Large Sum of Money

QUESTION: Is it a greater sin to steal a large sum of money than to steal a small amount?

RESPONSE: Yes. It is well known that it is prohibited to steal the value of a *perutah* (i.e., penny). HaRav HaGaon R. Yitzchak Ze'ev Soloveitchik, the Brisker Rav, contends that a person who steals one thousand *perutot* commits one thousand sins. His rationale is based on the following: The Talmud rules that should a person on *Shabbat* carry from a private home into a public thoroughfare food within a vessel, then, the person is deemed as if he committed two sins: one for carrying the food, and one for carrying the vessel (*Shabbat* 93b). Yet why should this be so? The sinner made only one action: He carried items on *Shabbat*. Why is he liable for two sins? Thus we see that once one carries more than the minimum prohibited, each additional amount generates another sin. Each amount is classified as if an additional sinful action occurred. So too is the case by theft of more than a *perutah*. Though one act of robbery may have transpired, each multiple of a *perutah* is classified as an independent sinful theft. (See *Ma'tikai Shmuah*, [Torah recited in the name of the Brisker Rav]. This particular *d'var Torah* is cited by HaGaon HaRav A. M. Shach, p. 73.)

Accordingly, one may gauge the severity of sins by the quantitative amount of the transgression. Thus one who eats (*chas v'shalom*) an entire nonkosher meal acquires a sin for every multiple of the amount of an olive that he eats. One act of theft of a large sum of money may actually translate into a massive quantity of sins.

The above formulation engenders a major distinction between Jews and Gentile regarding the severity of the crime of theft. Let us assume both, for example, steal one thousand *perutot*. The Jew is charged with one thousand sins. The Gentile has committed only one crime of theft. Since Gentiles have no minimum measurements, he is not culpable for each and every multiple of a *perutah* (ibid.).

American law does, of course, consider a theft of a large amount of money to be more onerous a crime than a theft of only a few dollars (i.e., grand larceny). Though halachah does not consider stealing a large sum qualitatively distinct than stealing a small amount it does, as noted, quantify the crimes based on the multiples of the *perutah* stolen.

Honoring Parents

QUESTION: May one observe the mitzvah of honoring parents via the services of a surrogate?

RESPONSE: The Talmud reports, "Eleazer ben Mathia said: If my father orders me, 'Give me a drink of water,' and I have a commandment (mitzvah) to perform, I disregard my father's honor and perform the mitzvah. (Why?) Since both my father and I are bound to perform commandments. Issi ben Yehudah maintained: If the mitzvah can be performed by others, it should be so performed by others, while he should care for his father's honor (by fulfilling his request). Said Rabbi Mattena: The halachah agrees with the position of Issi ben Yehudah" (*Kiddushin* 32a).

HaRav HaGaon Rav Zevi Pesach Frank, former Chief Rabbi of Jerusalem, cites a rabbinic scholar who derives from the above citation proof that the mitzvah of honoring parents may not be delegated to others nor observed through the usage of a surrogate. Issi's position in the Talmud is that a judgment must be made as to whether the mitzvah competing for the time and service of the son may be observed by anyone other than the son. Yet at no time does the Talmud even suggest that an assessment be made as to whether the request of the parent may also be fulfilled via the services of another person. This strongly indicates that the mitzvah of honoring parents simply cannot be delegated to others (see Har Zevi, *Al HaTorah, Parshat Yitro*).

An interesting personal anecdote may shed light on this issue. Over two decades ago my father, HaRav HaGaon Reb Meir Cohen (*z"l*), former Menahail of the Agudat HaRabbonim, was ill. My older brother, Rabbi Dr. Shmuel Cohen, and I would rotate the responsibility of transporting our father to and from his appointments with his doctors. My father lived in Boro Park, Brooklyn. I lived in Forest Hills, and my brother resided in Far

Rockaway. The difficulty was that our father's doctor was in Washington Heights, Manhattan, a three-hour-minimum round-trip, not including the time spent at the doctor's office. After consultation together, my brother and I approached our father with the following plan of action: To save precious time, our father was asked to inform us when he scheduled a medical appointment and we would arrange for a taxi to transport him all over New York City. Of course, the taxi would be available to return him home at his convenience. Our father (*z"l*) was perturbed as well as astonished at our plan. His response: "I should take a taxi when I have sons?" We did not subsequently offer any alternatives.

Punishing Those Who Dishonor Parents

QUESTION: Is there any special punishment given those who dishonor parents?

RESPONSE: Honoring parents is such a special mitzvah that the Torah itself explicitly promises a reward of long life for its observance, as it is written: (*kibaid* . . .) "Honor thy father and thy mother that thy days may be long" (Exodus 20:12, Hirsch translation). The basic interpretation is that long life is a reward granted those who honor parents. As such, anyone who dishonors parents simply loses out on the bountiful blessing of long life but does not necessarily receive any additional punishment.

The Vilna Gaon, however, suggests that the mitzvah of honoring parents contains within it the seed of a curse (*chas v'shalom*) as well as a blessing. It's a two-edged sword.

The Torah records that the biblical Yosef died at the age of 110. The Midrash notes that Yosef should have lived to the age of 120 years. His death ten years earlier was a punishment because Yosef heard his father Yaakov insulted ten times, and throughout Yosef did not protest the dishonor. What happened? Yosef's brothers referred to their father, the patriarch Yaakov, five times as "your servant," as if Yaakov was the obedient servant (or slave) of Yosef (see Genesis 43:28; 44:24, 27, 30, 31). In addition, the *mailitz* (translator) repeated in the Egyptian language each reference (Genesis 42:23). Thus, Yaakov was called a "servant" ten times in the presence of Yosef. Yosef heard the belittlement—ten times—and said nothing in return. For each negative statement spoken before Yosef to which he was silent, he lost one year of his projected span of life.

This position of the Vilna Gaon adds a unique nuance to the observance of the mitzvah to honor parents. We learn that any infringement of proper respect to a parent generates a curtailment of life itself. Of interest is that it is not even necessary to utter an ungracious word to parents or to perform an uncivil action in order to receive such a punishment. From the story of Yosef it is self-evident that even silence in the face of an insult to parents is sufficient to trigger the Divine punishment of curtailing life. (For full discussion of this concept, see HaRav Moshe Shternbach, *Ta'am V'daat*, vol. I, *Braishit* 42:23.)

The Role of a Gadol Hador

(In memory of HaGaon R. Yitzchok Hutner (*z"l*), Rosh HaYeshivah, Yeshivah Rabbi Chaim Berlin Yahrzeit 20 Kislev)

QUESTION: Does a *gadol hador* have a specific role? Must a *gadol hador* be treated in a special way?

RESPONSE: The Talmud reports that Shmuel HaNavi as a youngster was castigated for making a halachic ruling in the presence of his Rebbe, Eli, the *kohen gadol*. *Tosafot* question the propriety of the condemnation, for Shmuel was not known to have studied with Eli prior to this incident. Accordingly, Eli was not his Rebbe and Shmuel's behavior was, therefore, proper. *Tosafot* respond that Shmuel's action was still not right for Eli was the *gadol hador* and Shmuel had come to learn (Torah) from Eli.

From *Tosafot* it is evident that Shmuel's improper behavior was due to (not one but) two considerations: (1) Eli was a *gadol hador*, and (2) Shmuel desired to learn Torah from Eli. This suggests that even though Eli was the *gadol hador*, Shmuel's ruling would not have been wrong had he not desired to learn Torah from him. Yet, why is this so? Why must both elements be necessary?

HaGaon Rav Hutner (*z"l*) made the following analysis: The Rambam records that Eli was the head of the Sanhedrin (introduction to *Yad HaChazakah*). Each leader of the Sanhedrin (called the *nasi*), says the Rambam, serves "in the place of Moshe Rabbenu" (*Hilchot Sanhedrin* 1:2). The implication is that Moshe Rabbenu had a specific role and each *nasi* in succeeding generations should replicate Moshe Rabbenu's role.

What is this role? The Torah informs us that *k'lal Yisrael* was frightened at the revelation on Mount Sinai. They feared that they might die due to the unique encounter with God (see Deuteronomy 5:21 and 23). Therefore, they gave Moshe Rabbenu an unusual mission, as it is written: "Approach thou and hear all that God, our God shall say, and speak thou unto us all that God, our God shall speak unto thee, and we shall listen to and do it" (Deuteronomy 5:24, Hirsch translation). The Rambam says that the verse teaches us that Jews relinquished direct personal encounters with God to receive His holy Torah. Rather, they authorized Moshe to serve as their surrogate. Subsequently Moshe directs *k'lal Yisrael*: "Go back to your tents" (Deuteronomy 5:26). The Rambam comments that Moshe Rabbenu informed *k'lal Yisrael* that God had accepted their suggestion that Moshe be used as the vehicle to inform them of God's wishes and Torah. From this we see that acceptance of Moshe by *k'lal Yisrael* as the spokesman for God and the people was an integral aspect of *Kabbalat HaTorah.* Indeed, *Kabbalat HaTorah* did not conclude until *k'lal Yisrael* accepted Moshe as the Divinely inspired authentic teacher of Torah.

To serve as a *nasi* of a Sanhedrin or a *gadol hador* implies that *k'lal Yisrael* has previously accepted upon itself that such a person is to serve as the spokesman for Torah. That acceptance imposes upon the *gadol hador* the special obligation of not only teaching Torah but insuring the authenticity of the *Torah Mesorah* (*Lishmore v'la'asot*). (*Lishmore,* says the Brisker Rav, is the obligation to insure the purity of the *Mesorah*—see *Pachad Yitzchok, Shevuot* 38:3, *Chiddushai HaGriz, V'etchanan.*)

Tosafot's position regarding Shmuel and Eli now becomes clear. A Rebbe is a person who actually teaches Torah to a student. Prior to such a process of learning Torah a potential student has no special obligation to a future Rebbe. Commitment to learn Torah from a Rav at a future date does not create a Rebbe (denoting a "master")-student relationship. The exception is if the Rav is a *gadol hador.* A *gadol hador* has a status of a Rebbe even prior to one's learning Torah from him. It is he who has the obligation of insuring the *Torah Mesorah.*

An important requisite is that one must accept the Rav as a *gadol hador.* This commitment transforms the Rav into the role of Moshe Rabbenu, which is a Rebbe-student relationship, even prior to learning any Torah at all. Shmuel HaNavi had come to learn from Eli. This meant that he accepted Eli's status as the *gadol hador.* For this reason Eli became his Rebbe even before he taught Shmuel any Torah.

From the above it appears that once one accepts a Rav as a *gadol hador,* then it is prohibited to disagree with him even when one has never learned any Torah from him. Just as an ordinary Jew may not disagree with Moshe Rabbenu, who is charged with imparting authentic Torah, so too cannot one disagree with a *gadol hador,* who has the same mission.

HaGaon Rav Hutner (*z"l*) once noted that the phrase "Long

live the king (*Yechi HaMelech*)" has a special dimension. It is a commitment to follow the decrees of a king even under circumstances in which one may not always agree with the king's pronouncements—for otherwise, should a person always agree with a king, then there is no subordinate relationship to a king. "Long live the king" is a commitment to follow the king even should one disagree with his policies. That commitment is the essential element for enthroning a king. It may also be the pivotal ingredient in an acceptance of someone as a *gadol hador*.

[The author accepts all responsibility for any errors resulting from the above expansion of basic Torah principles tersely articulated by HaGaon Rav Hutner, (*z"l*).]

Moral Qualities of a Rosh HaYeshivah

QUESTION: Must a Rosh HaYeshivah manifest specific moral qualities?

RESPONSE: The Torah notes: "And he sent Yehudah before him unto Yosef so that he should direct him (*lehorot*) to Goshen" (Genesis 46:28). Commenting on this verse, Rashi says that Yehudah was given a mission to establish a *Bet Talmud* (a yeshivah) in Goshen. At issue was the necessity to select Yehudah to serve as the Rosh HaYeshivah. Was not Yosef already in Egypt? Could not Yosef establish a yeshivah? Also, why was Yehudah selected for this sacred task over his brothers?

HaGaon HaRav Yaakov Nayman (*shlita*), my father-in-law, the famed disciple of the Brisker Rav, made the following comments:

Yehudah had a number of special moral qualities that made

him the most proper person to serve as a Rosh HaYeshivah for *k'lal Yisrael.*

1. Yehudah had compassion. When the brothers desired to kill Yosef, "Yehudah said to his brothers, 'What profit is there if we kill our brother?'" (Genesis 37:26). This teaches us that not only did Yehudah not wish to kill Yosef, but he also would not allow his brothers to physically harm Yosef. A Rosh HaYeshivah must be able to protect his students and to see to it that no harm comes their way. Someone who is able to stand up and openly defend his brother has the moral fiber to be a Rosh HaYeshivah.

2. Yehudah had the ability to recognize his own shortcomings and admit to error. In the incident with Tamar, Yehudah overtly states, *Tzadka Mimeni*—"She is more righteous than I" (Genesis 39:26, Hirsch translation). She is right; I am wrong. Yehudah does not hide from the truth when he sins or commits a wrong; he acknowledges his mistake.

Yehudah was privileged to be selected to serve as the Rosh HaYeshivah to establish the *Mesorah* of *k'lal Yisrael* because of his inherent moral qualities as noted above. He cared for the young, was able to protect them from harm, and personally had the strength of character to admit to his own errors. That is the type of Torah leader that should be entrusted with caring for children.

A Temporary Baal Teshuvah

QUESTION: Is there any value to a person who becomes a *baal teshuvah* for a short period of time and then reverts to committing sins?

RESPONSE: Yes, according to HaGaon HaRav Moshe Feinstein (*z"l*). He derives this concept from the biblical story of the twelve spies (*meraglim*) sent to assess the land of Israel. Each person sent was a leader in his own right. Their role was to prepare the people for the invasion of Canaan. Ten brought back a negative report; two were positive about the Jewish people's ability to conquer the land. Speaking of Kalev's role, the Torah says: "My servant Kalev had another spirit in him (*ruach acheret imo*)" (*Bamidbar* 14:24). God praises Kalev for a special positive spirit. What did he do that was so special or unique? Rashi contends that when the spies returned from viewing Israel, the first report was that of Kalev. As the Torah says, *V'yas Kalev et ha'am* (*Bamidbar* 13:30)—"And Kalev stilled the people, saying we can go to the land of Israel." For calming the Jews, for giving them hope, for eliminating their fears over war and defeat, Kalev was to be rewarded by God. Of interest, says HaGaon Rav Moshe Feinstein, was the fact that Kalev's influence was only transitory. Indeed, once Kalev concluded his uplifting remarks, the ten spies spoke their words. Their reports were negative. They bemoaned their own weakness and dramatically enhanced the might, the power, the strength of the enemy. In other words, there was a debate, a dialogue between Kalev and the ten spies who gave negative reports. This means that Kalev was successful in calming the people and forestalling any fears for only a short period of time. Accordingly, the Jewish people's resolve to go to war to acquire the land of Israel lasted only until the spies had an opportunity to speak and overturn the feelings of the people. And yet God still lavished praise upon Kalev for calming the people, teaching us that a resolution to do good is rewarded even if the resolution lasts for only a short period of time.

This concept may be bolstered by an understanding of a talmudic text dealing with life, death, and the violation of *Shabbat*. The Talmud rules that if debris massively fell upon a person on *Shabbat* and there was a major task to remove it, involving the violation of many *Shabbat* laws, one is mandated to violate the *Shabbat* to save the person in jeopardy. The Talmud goes further: This obligation is required; it is not optional. It is a mitzvah even if it is doubtful whether someone underneath the debris (say from an earthquake) is alive or dead, Jew or non-Jew. If one finds the person underneath alive, one should continue to remove the debris on *Shabbat.* If, *chas v'shalom,* the person is dead, then the work should cease until *Shabbat* is over. Now, on the phrase "If he is alive, one should continue to remove the debris," the Talmud rules, "Is not this self-evident?" In other words, as long as the person is alive one must violate *Shabbat* to save the life. Why must the Talmud delineate this concept? To this the Talmud responds, the statement is necessary in the event the person is judged to have only a short while to live (*chayai she'ah*). This Gemorah (*Yoma* 85a) teaches us that it is necessary to violate the *Shabbat* to save a person who may never even live to observe another *Shabbat.* Furthermore, it is obligatory to save a person who may yet live only for a few hours.

From this talmudic citation, HaGaon Rav Moshe Feinstein (*z"l*) derives the following: We see that the extension of one's physical life, even for a very brief period of time, is so important that *Shabbat* is violated. We do not dismiss the case by contending that two or three more hours of life are meaningless. Just the opposite, we judge them so important, in fact, they are deemed more important than *Shabbat.* If so, reasons Rav Moshe (*z"l*), how much more important and valuable is the spiritual life of the soul of the Jew? If an extension of a physical life even for a brief moment is meritorious, then of course a period of pious observant behavior, even a temporary one, is rewarded by God (*Kol Ram* vol. 1, Torah by HaGaon Rav Moshe Feinstein, recorded and edited by Rabbi Avraham Fisheles, Parshat Shelach).

Naming A Child "Nimrod"

QUESTION: May the name of a known sinner, such as Nimrod, be given to Jewish children?

RESPONSE: The Talmud reports that the verse stating "The name of the wicked shall rot" is interpreted to mean "Rottenness enters their names." Their names are not to be used (*Yoma* 38b). There are two basic considerations to this ruling.

1. Rashi says, "A man should not name his son after a wicked person" (*Yoma* 38b). This suggests a practical means of expunging the names of the wicked from Jewish usage. No Jew should be called by such a name. The implication is that there is a general ban against using the names of the wicked, and the practical vehicle to curtail such usage is to not name children after them. In the event that a father inadvertently so named his child, logic would dictate that the general community substitute a different name for the child. In other words, the prohibition may not be only upon the father, but upon the community at large.

2. Rabbenu Hananel notes that the prohibition against using the names of the wicked means that "Any person so named (by the name of the wicked) will not be successful." This suggests a form of a curse. The general community may not incur any sin by calling a person by his given name even if such is the known name of a sinner. The rule is basically a curse upon the child so named. He will not have a successful life. What parent would wish to overtly disregard this concern? What parent would waive all tradition in favor of a name that would brand a child a loser?

In matters pertaining to halachic problems there is a general rule that issues of potential danger (*sakana*) are viewed more stringently than cases of potential violations of Jewish law. According to Rabbenu Hananel, this issue has an aura of *sakana*. This suggests a probable responsibility to protect the individual from his name

As such, even if a child is named by his parents "Nimrod" it would be halachically proper to change or alter his name.

Advice of Daat Torah

QUESTION: Common custom is to seek *daat Torah,* namely, the advice and guidance of great rabbinic scholars or sages in matters pertaining to religious as well as personal, business, and family concerns. Do such rabbis err? Are their decisions fallible?

RESPONSE: It is the nature of humans to err. Nevertheless, *daat Torah* is not only meritorious but also the proper vehicle for Torah decisions.

The Talmud states: "Rabbi Yosi Haglili says: The righteous are judged by the good inclinations (*yetzer tov shoftan*) . . . the wicked are judged by their evil inclination (*yetzer hara*) . . . average, ordinary people (*bainonim*) are judged by both the good and evil inclination" (*Berachot* 61b).

The Vilna Gaon cites his brother, Rabbi Avraham, who notes that the word "judged" (*shoftan*) means that the character, decisions, or behavior (*hanhaga*) of a person is impacted by the relative influences of either the *yetzer tov*, the *yetzer hara*, or a combination of both. As such, a righteous person is guided by the direct influence of the *yetzer tov*. Of concern is the measuring rod to provide an assessment as to whether a person is guided by the *yetzer tov* and not otherwise.

The Talmud reports that Torah is the best medicine to mute or weaken the power of the *yetzer hara*, for it is written: "My children, I have created the *yetzer hara*, but I (also) created the Torah for its antidote. If you occupy yourselves with the Torah you will not be delivered into his hand" (*Kedushin* 30b; see commentary, Vilna Gaon, *Berachot* 61b; see also *Sefer Maalot Hatorah*, authored by the Vilna Gaon's brother, Rabbi Avraham, p. 18).

This suggests that a Torah sage has weakened the power of the *yetzer hara* by virtue of his Torah knowledge. Accordingly, he would be the most likely person to be influenced by the *yetzer tov*. For this reason, it is proper to seek the advice of *daat Torah*.

Why? For Torah sages will provide decisions as well as guidance on a variety of issues guided mostly by the heavenly directive of the *yetzer tov*. The degree of Torah of the individual insures the probability that the *yetzer tov* will be the guiding light of the decision-making process. To the extent, however, that no one ever totally eliminates the *yetzer hara*, a degree of fallibility may always be present.

Mourning a Parent

QUESTION: Why is it that halachah mandates a longer period of mourning for a parent than for a child?

RESPONSE: It is reported that when the Rosh HaYeshivah of Yeshivah University, HaRav HaGaon Yosef Dov Soloveitchik (*z"l*) was sitting *shivah* for his wife, the following interesting discussion took place. Many rabbis came to pay their respects and to offer condolences. To the extent that it became an assemblage of great Torah scholars, a theoretical question was posed relating to the laws of mourning.

Jewish law requires a mourner of a parent to demonstrate acts of mourning far in excess of that required when mourning over the loss of a mate or a child. For example, mourning for a mate or a child lasts for a period of thirty days (*shloshim*). Mourning rituals for a parent are for a period of a year. Yet, such mourning patterns appear to be contrary to logic and nature. Parents, by their very existence and nature, are older than children. It is, therefore, self-evident and normally anticipated that parents will die while their children are yet alive. It is normal and natural for such to take place. On the other hand, it is not so normal or natural for children to die in the lifetime of their parents. It is certainly not anticipated for such to occur. In fact it is an unusual, shocking, tragic experience when a child dies. So it seems the halachah should reflect this concept: The duration of mourning should depend upon the quality of the trauma. To the extent that the loss of a child galvanizes and crystallizes a more massive unexpected trauma than the loss of a parent, the mourning period for a child should be greater and longer than that imposed upon the death of a parent. And yet, that is not the case. Everybody knows that Jewish law imposes a longer mourning period for the loss of a parent. Why is this so? Why does halachah deem the loss of a parent to be so unique and so traumatic?

Of interest is that two great rabbis were present during this discussion. One was HaRav HaGaon Yitzchak Hutner (*z"l*) the Rosh HaYeshivah of the Rabbi Chaim Berlin Rabbinical Academy. The other was the great pulpit rabbi, the Chief Rabbi of Elizabeth, New Jersey, HaRav HaGaon Pinchas Teitz (*z"l*). Both expressed thoughts as to why Jewish law considers mourning for a parent so much more tragic than any other loss.

Rav Hutner's position was that the tragedy of parental loss is that such a death formally places the children yet another generation further away from the revelation of Mount Sinai. It is a formal recognition that an era has ended. The children are totally on their own, one more generation further removed from the lessons of Sinai. The message of Torah is therefore fainter and less clear than what was available to the previous generation.

We mourn the distance from the source of Torah. Torah is a *mesorah*, a tradition whereby one generation hands down the eternal truths to another generation (*Moshe keebal Torah mi Sinai umsaraha le Yehoshua*—Moses accepted the Torah from Sinai and gave it over to Joshua; and he to the elders and they to the prophets). Each generation learned from the past what to give to the future.

The death of parents formally signifies that the past is no longer here to help us. We are the ones to transmit the future. The death of a parent signifies that the new transmission will be weaker than the past. We are now on our own. A Judaism based upon tradition and *mesorah* is not overjoyed when a past generation is no longer available to help us. The goal of the Jew is to become closer to Sinai, not further away.

Rav Teitz, however, gave a more concrete psychological response to our problem. His contention is that the loss of a parent is in a class of its own, for in no way is it comparable or replicated by any other situation. Parents are unique. A person could have more than one brother or sister. A person could conceivably remarry at the loss of a mate. Of course it may not be the same, but the status of a mate could be replaced. A person could, perhaps, have several children. Though each child is unique, it is still clear that a person could have several children and be consoled by that very fact.

When it comes to parents, however, there is no replacement. A human is born but once. When parents die they are simply irreplaceable. There is no way to make up this loss. It is for this reason that halachah demands greater periods of mourning for a parent than for any other person. The Torah is teaching us that we have to care for with greater appreciation and unusual sensitivity that which cannot ever be replaced. A priceless relationship is one that is unique. It stands alone.

Addendum:

HaRav Yosef Blau, Mashgiach Ruchani, Yeshivah University, informed me that HaRav Soloveitchik added a personal observation that provided a compelling reason to mourn parents more than children. He noted that when parents become old, a role-reversal takes place. The parent who cared for the child, sustaining him and protecting him, is no longer physically capable of such a function, and now requires a support system himself. The child takes on the role of the parent—caring, protecting, and sustaining—while the parent is now the recipient of such care. In the latter stages of illness the parent is almost like a child. Accordingly, sufficient time to mourn is needed and provided by halachah to overcome the visions of the invalid, childlike parent in order to remember the parent as vigorous and strong and fulfilling his or her parental role. That requires a considerable period of time.

Determining the End of the Mourner's Shivah

QUESTION: A Jew dies Friday afternoon in Los Angeles, California. The family decision is that burial will take place in Israel. Accordingly, Sunday morning, the daughter and her husband escort the *aron* (casket) on a flight to Israel. That Sunday afternoon, the widow, who is too ill to travel, performs the mitzvah of *kriya* (rending of the garment) and begins sitting *shivah* in the home of her daughter. The burial takes place Monday night in Jerusalem. Tuesday morning, the daughter and her husband board a flight home and return to Los Angeles late Tuesday evening. At issue is when the daughter concludes sitting *shivah.*

RESPONSE: When a person is not buried in the town where he (or she) lived but, rather, in some distant area the following rules prevail: The mourners present at the interment commence *shivah* from the time of the burial. Those mourners who are not able to attend the funeral, however, commence *shivah* when they conclude escorting the *aron* (see Rav Avraham Danzig, *Chachmat Adam Hilchot Availut Kelal* 162:3).

HaGaon Rav Moshe Feinstein discusses a case in which a burial took place in Belgium, attended by some mourners, while a number of other mourners remained at home in New York City. He notes that the New York mourners started *shivah* immediately upon leaving the New York airport (or when the plane departed) while those who escorted the *aron* started *shivah* several days later at the time of the actual interment. This method of calculating dual *shivah* periods occurs only when the burial is not in an area adjacent to or near the mourners who do not attend the funeral (Iggrot Moshe, *Yoreh Deah* I, Responsum 253).

Based upon the above considerations, the calculating of

shivah observance in the case at hand should be as follows: The widow started her *shivah* observance on Sunday. As such, her seventh day falls on *Shabbat*. Thus her *shivah* concludes Friday, *Erev Shabbat*, a short period prior to *Shabbat*. The daughter, however, was present at the burial of her father, which took place on Monday night. This means that the first opportunity she had to sit *shivah* was Tuesday morning. Accordingly, she should sit *shivah* until Monday morning.

Of practical interest is that the Chachmat Adam rules that the above calculation would not be operational in this matter. In our case the daughter who attended the funeral returned home to the place where her mother had already started sitting *shivah*. As such, the daughter's period of *shivah* is deemed to be the same as that of her mother. Accordingly, both mother and daughter conclude Friday, *Erev Shabbat*. Indeed, the Chachmat Adam even notes that this method of reckoning takes place regardless of whether the head of the household (*gadol habayit*) stayed at home or was at the funeral. As long as those who attend the funeral return to a residence wherein *shivah* has already started, all count from the date that those in the home started observing *shivah*. Had the daughter stayed in Israel, then her *shivah* would have started from the time of the burial (Chachmat Adam, *Kelal* 162:15; see notes). The implication is that one does not observe two periods of mourning in the same house. Had the mother not observed *shivah* at her daughter's home, but at her own home, then daughter and mother would have observed different periods of time for *shivah*.

Bar Mitzvah Parties

QUESTION: A bar mitzvah is generally celebrated with a festive meal, a party. But why is this so? Is not a bar mitzvah a religious celebration? As such, it should be celebrated with special attention to religious concerns, extra *daven*ing, more *mitzvot*, and not by a major banquet.

RESPONSE: It should be noted that the bar mitzvah party is not an innovation of modern life. It is firmly based in tradition, and is cited by ancient *chachamim* as a significant celebration of the bar mitzvah itself.

The Talmud notes that Rav Yosef, who was blind, was troubled as to whether a person in such a condition was obliged to observe mitzvot. He said, "Now that I have heard Rabbi Hanina's halachah that he who is commanded and fulfills the command is greater than he who fulfills it though not commanded, if anyone should tell me that the halachah does not agree with Rabbi Yehudah (who ruled that the blind are exempt from mitzvot), I would make a *Yom Tov* for the rabbis" (*Kiddushin* 31a). Rashi interprets the latter phrase to mean a "banquet."

Rabbi Shlomo Luria (the Rashal, Yom Shel Shlomo, Bava Kama) derives from this the general rule that an initial obligation to observe mitzvot crystallizes a celebration. The reason is that Rav Yosef in the Gemorah expressed a desire to have a banquet to celebrate his obligation to observe mitzvot. A similar thing happens at a bar mitzvah. The thirteenth birthday of a boy is a form of status transformation. The bar mitzvah is the date wherein the boy assumes obligations to perform mitzvot in his own right. Accordingly, the banquet celebrates this new obligation, comparable to Rav Yosef's declaration. Though this suggests an ancient source, a rationale (*sevara*) is yet necessary to comprehend its religious significance—in other words, what is the source of Rav Yosef and Rashi's position?

The Rema rules that common custom is to permit haircuts on Lag b'Omer and (that it is proper) to increase (somewhat) happiness (*marbin ketzat simcha*) on that day (*Orech Chayyim* 493:20). *Aruch HaShulchan* adds the notion that Lag b'Omer necessitates added happiness for it is deemed a semi-*Yom Tov* (*Yom Tov Ketzat*) (*Orech Chayyim* 493:7).

Yet, why is this so? Why is Lag b'Omer classified as a partial *Yom Tov*, which necessitates added joy and happiness? The source, says the Vilna Gaon, is the Gemorah citation that reports that on the fifteenth of Av the Jews who departed from Egypt and were destined to perish in the wilderness finally ceased dying (*Ta'anit* 26b). The implication of the Vilna Gaon's position may be as follows: the Mishnah reports that to the Jews the most joyous holidays were Yom Kippur and the fifteenth of Av. Yom Kippur was considered a joyful period of time, for Jews were granted an opportunity to have their sins forgiven. The fifteenth of Av was deemed a happy time because, on that day, the Jews who wandered forty years in the wilderness and were destined to perish stopped dying (*Ta'anit* 29b). Since the Mishnah designates the fifteenth of Av as a *Yom Tov*, it indicates that when large-scale communal deaths cease, the day is classified as a *Yom Tov*. To the extent that custom has it that Rav Akiva's students ceased to die on Lag b'Omer, that day also may be deemed a partial *Yom Tov*.

This halachic conclusion may be challenged on a variety of levels. The Talmud notes that not just one good thing happened, but a number of happy events transpired on the fifteenth of Av (*Chamisha Asar b'Av*). Indeed, the following took place: "It was the day on which permission was granted to the tribes to intermarry. . . . It was the day on which the tribe of Binyamin was permitted to re-enter *k'lal Israel*. . . . It was the day when the generation of the wilderness ceased to die out. . . . It was the day when Hosea ben Elah removed the guards that Yerovam ben Nevot had placed on the roads to prevent Israel from going (up to Jerusalem) on pilgrimage. . . . It was the day when permission was granted for those killed at Betar to be buried. . . . It was the day on which (every year) they discontinued to fell trees for the *mizbei'ach*." (*Ta'anit* 30b, 31a) In other words, six wonderful events took place on that day. As such, its status as a semi-holiday may be the result of the convergence of all of these events and not just one. It is evident, however, that the Vilna Gaon rules otherwise. He considers each event by itself as sufficient to merit the fifteenth of Av as a partial holiday.

Otherwise, there would be no basis to support the contention that Lag b'Omer is a semi-holiday due to the singular fact that students ceased to die on that day.

There is another issue of contention. The ceasing of the deaths of those who departed from Egypt implied that the Jewish people were ready to enter the holy land. So, perhaps, the stopping of death by itself is not indicative of a *Yom Tov* status. The holiday classification was due to the fact that *k'lal Yisrael* was ready to acquire the land of Israel. Again, since the Vilna Gaon made no such notation regarding the reason for the ceasing of deaths, this suggests that each act by itself regardless of ultimate purpose is sufficient to classify a day as a semi- or partial holiday.

Based upon the concept that a holiday may be established with the rationale of just one of the six items noted in the Talmud, it is important to relearn the sixth item that the *chachamim* maintained was cause for celebration on the fifteenth of Av. It was the day that Jews stopped cutting down trees for wood to be used in the *mizbei'ach*. The reason that they stopped was that the sun ceased being powerful on that day. In fact, from that day onward Jews were to devote more time to Torah study in the evening. This means that the happiness of the fifteenth of Av was that there was more time each evening to learn Torah.

Now, if our Rabbis decreed a holiday simply because there were greater opportunities to learn Torah, would not a holiday be granted to one who has the joy of being obligated in *kol hatorah kulo* in observing mitzvot altogether? For this reason Rav Yosef held that a party was important. Now we can understand the position of the Rashal that a bar mitzvah obligates a party.

Reactions to Sinners

QUESTION: How is one to relate to sinners? Is it permissible to hate the nonobservant?

RESPONSE: The Talmud notes that testimony concerning adultery requires two witnesses. In the event only one witness comes to the *bet din* and gives testimony in a case relating to adultery, the *bet din* would have no legal recourse to act upon it, and the witness is deemed a talebearer (a *lashon hara'nik*) and it is permitted to hate him. Proof is deduced as follows: "It is written, 'If thou see the mule of thine enemy lying under its burden . . .' (Exodus 23:5). But is it permitted to hate him? Surely, it is written, 'Thou shalt not hate thy brother in thy heart.' (Leviticus 19:17) So how is it possible for a Jew to hate an enemy? Again, if there are witnesses that he had committed wrong, then all indeed may hate him! Why particularly this person [i.e., why does the Torah declare the person to be your personal enemy]? Hence it must surely apply to such a case where he had seen something indecent (and testified), knowing full well the testimony had no legal standing, and merely was a form of slander. Rav Nachman ben Yitzchak said, 'It is a mitzvah to hate him'" (*Pesachim* 113b).

The above quote delineates the proper reaction to sinners. The prohibition against "hating Jews" relates only to Jews who observe mitzvot. Personal hatred may be directed toward individuals of whom one witnesses an act of sin but there is not sufficient evidence to convict. In the event the *bet din* convicts a sinner, then all have the right to hate him.

It is important to recognize that halachic scholars have severely limited the above blanket license to hate sinners.

1. The *Tosafot* pose an apparent contradiction. Talmudic law mandates that should a person have the choice of either helping a friend unload a burdened animal or an enemy reload a burden on his animal, it is preferable to help the enemy, so that

one may overcome the emotion (of hatred) (*Bava Metzia* 32b). Now if it is a mitzvah to hate sinners, why should one even attempt to overcome such an emotion? To this the *Tosafot* respond that people act toward each other in a mirror-like fashion. Should one, therefore, manifest (actual) hatred, the other will reciprocate, and true hatred will emerge (*Tosafot Pesachim* 113b). The meaning may be that the mitzvah to hate sinners is only a halachic permission to internally vent emotion and experience the personal sensation of hatred, but under no circumstances is anyone ever granted license to act upon such hatred or to express it to another. An internal catharsis is permitted, not hateful action, for acts of hate generate warfare.

2. The Torah mandates Jews to love fellow Jews (*v'ahavta lere'acha*—and thou shalt love they neighbor) (Leviticus 19:18), as well as not to hate them (*lo tisnah*—thou shalt not hate your brother) (Leviticus 19:17). So, why is it permitted to hate sinners (*Pesachim* 113b)? Is there not a responsibility to correct sinners from sin, to make them aware of the error of their ways and direct them to *teshuvah*? Does not the Torah say, "Rebuke thy neighbor" (Leviticus 19:17)?

HaRav Moshe Shternbach cites the Chazon Ish, who made the following distinction: Halachic permission to hate sinners is an option provided only after a sinner is rebuked or reproached for committing a sin and he refuses to repent. It is not the act of sin, rather it is the rebellious rejection of *teshuvah* subsequent to reproach that crystallizes the permission of hatred. Accordingly, prior to rebuke the mitzvot of love and the prohibition against hate are operational, even to a nonobservant Jew. The Talmud, moreover, notes that no one knows how to properly rebuke (*Arachin* 55a). Now, if in the talmudic age no sage knew how to properly rebuke sinners, in our contemporary era we certainly lack such ability. This suggests that sinners may not automatically be deemed rebellious violators of Jewish law, and thus generate permission of hatred. They are wrong, they are violators of Jewish law, but until properly rebuked, they cannot be hated (*Taam V'Daat*, HaRav Moshe Shternbach, *Parshat Emor*, *Vayikra*).

Obligations of a Charity Collector

QUESTION: Someone makes a request for support from community charity funds. May the *gabbai tzedakah* discuss the case with family members who are reasonably well-to-do? That is, may the *gabbai* disclose to a member of the family that one of them is in need of help? In addition, should the *gabbai* request that family members contribute to the support of the indigent family member?

RESPONSE: The Talmud states that "Anyone who falls (into a state of poverty) falls to the community agent first" (*Niddarim* 65b). *Tosafot* note that the primary responsiblity to care for a poor person is incumbent upon the impoverished person's family, not the *gabbai tzedakah.* As such, any action of a *gabbai tzedakah* would not come into place until after an assessment was made of the family's reaction to the impoverished family member. This suggests that the *gabbai tzedakah* has full authority to discuss the plight of the individual with his or her family, prior to any action taken by the community representative. The implication, moreover, is that the authority to discuss the matter with family members as well as to seek their financial support is not dependent upon whether the claimant for funds gives such permission.

Halachic sages rule that family poor should take priority even over local poor who may have greater needs. The family members always have priority (*Panim Yafot,* Deuteronomy, *Parasha Re'eh*; also cited by Responsa Chatam Sofer, *Yoreh Deah* 231).

Relating to the Semiobservant

QUESTION: How does halachah relate to Jews who observe some mitzvot but not all? Are they hypocrites?

RESPONSE: Hypocrisy is to be shunned. No one likes a hypocrite, and certainly no one wishes to be so labelled. It is of interest that the desire to be innocent of any aspersions of hypocrisy is utilized as a major excuse for the nonobservance of Jewish traditions.

When Jews who have strayed somewhat from the religious path are asked to observe a specific ritual, the rationale they offer—not only for their nonobservance but also to cut short any further enquiries—usually goes as follows: (a) How can I maintain a kosher home when I do not discriminate outside the home? (b) Why pray in your synagogue on *Shabbat* when I do not observe the *Shabbat* at all? (c) Why observe the traditional laws of mourning when I do not follow any other precepts? Accordingly, any request for increased observance is countered by an admission of nonobservance in another area. The response generally includes the statement, "I am not a hypocrite." What irks is the final charge: "Rabbi, are you asking me to be a hypocrite?" Such encounters can definitely faze a rabbi. Some rabbis, as a result, have simply given up and preach only to the committed.

What is unique is that intellectual honesty and purity are generally demanded only of religion. Only in the sphere of Jewish ritual observance is hypocrisy held to be a (legitimate) defense against partial commitment. People never claim that since they do not always tell the truth, therefore they must always tell lies. No one contends that since they cheat occasionally, all honesty is to be scorned. Likewise, lack of ability to ascend all rungs of religious life does not mean that partial ascent should be castigated. The higher the goal, the more difficult it is to achieve. In fact, true religious passion and spiritual fervor require years of training. One does not become a religious, spiritual Jew overnight. One cannot succeed in religion by attempting to accomplish everything in one period of time.

Certain items, however, do require a plunge. *Kashrut*, for example, does necessitate commitment for one cannot become kosher dish by dish. Yet, inability to do all does not negate the value of what is or has been accomplished. The human personality is not perfect, and it is normal for people to assume obligations and express thoughts that are not part of a total, holistic approach. That is not hypocritical—that is the real world.

The following tale of the Chafetz Chaim suggests a pragmatic approach to the problem: An old woman who made a living selling bagels had an accident. Some youngsters jostled her basket of wares, and all her bagels fell to the ground. Numerous children pounced upon the strewn bagels, grabbing as much as they could carry, and then ran away. The old woman, sitting on the street, began to cry and bemoan her plight. "Foolish woman," called out a man to her. "If you sit and cry, you'll end up with nothing. Chap (grab) some bagels too."

How true. How realistic is this approach! Should Jews merely bemoan their inability to observe all the mitzvot, then they will end up like the old woman with nothing. "Grab bagels!" A *kaddish* . . . a *yahrzeit* . . . a mitzvah . . . *succah* . . . something!

Expressing Thanks for a Loan

QUESTION: Does halachah permit the expression of "Thank you" to a person who is kind and gracious enough to extend to you an interest-free loan?

RESPONSE: The Talmud and the Codes record that it is prohibited to extend *Shalom* to a person who loaned one money if prior to the loan one never was accustomed to do so. This is deemed a form of "oral interest" (*ribit dvarim*) that many believe is a rabbinic prohibition (*Bava Metzia* 75b and *Yoreh Deah* 160:11). Based upon the above, several scholars have contended that it is prohibited to express "Thank you" to the person who provided the loan. The "Thank you" is deemed a prohibited expression of *ribit.*

Of concern is that the famed *Darkai Teshuvah*, by the Gaon Rav Tzvi Hirsh Shapira of Munkatsh, limits severely this prohibition. He contends that it is not proper to say "Thank you" prior to the repayment of the loan. Thus, while the funds borrowed are still within the possession of the borrower, then and only then is it prohibited to express "Thank you" (*toda*). (This concept is specifically noted in the Codes, wherein it is stated that "One may not teach the person who extended the loan during the period that the funds are still in the possession of the borrower, providing, of course, that such was not the procedure prior to the loan" [*Yoreh Deah* 160:10].) Nevertheless, he suggests it is proper to wait some period of time after the return of the funds before one expresses appreciation for the loan. The minimum time span he rules is the time it takes to recite approximately four words (see *Darkai Teshuvah* 160:88).

HaGaon Rav Shlomo Zalman Auerbach (*z"l*) contends that it is not at all prohibited to say "Thank you" for a loan. His argument is that "Thank you" is a common decency that should be expressed to all who do good and gracious acts of kindness. He believes that it is as if there is a specific pact set up by the person who extends the loan that the borrower should not be an ingrate (*kafui tova*) to anyone who is nice to him, inclusive of the person who loaned him money (*Responsa Minchat Shlomo, Siman* 27:1). The implication is that appreciation is the basis of a moral personality and Jews should not be withheld from its expression. Accordingly, should the expression of appreciation be withheld until a period of time after the loan is repaid, such a custom would meet even the halachic standard of the *Darkai Teshuvah.*

The Honor of a King

QUESTION: The Talmud rules that a father may renounce his honor, a rebbe may renounce his honor, but a king may not renounce the honor due him (*Kedushin* 32a and b). Why is the king's honor different from the honor due a parent or a rebbe?

RESPONSE: It is a blessing to have a living parent. In the event, however, that a parent should die, the child incurs no sin whatsoever for the lack of a parent. It is important to have a dynamic relationship with a rebbe. In a case wherein the rebbe or the student no longer wishes to maintain the relationship, no sin takes place. A person may change his rebbe. A person may become his own rebbe. A person may, without transgressing any sin, not have a rebbe at all.

A king is a qualitatively distinct concern. There is a mitzvah to have a king. A king that renounces his honor is as one who removes that person (or persons) from the mitzvah altogether. No one has the right to eliminate a mitzvah. No one is permitted to make inoperational a mitzvah that is incumbent upon every single Jew (Hamakna, commentary on *Kedushin* 32).

Counting Jews

QUESTION: Is it permitted to take a census of the Jewish people? Is it permissible to count a segment of Jews?

RESPONSE: The Bible notes that a census of those over twenty years of age was taken via usage of a half shekel (Exodus 30:12–14). Thus, it appears that there is nothing wrong with counting Jews. As such, the Ramban was perturbed as to why King David was punished for counting the Jews in his reign (see II Samuel, ch. 24). Perhaps, suggests the Ramban, King David erred in that he did not realize that permission to take a census of Jews was solely on the condition that Jews themselves were not counted but, rather, it was done by usage of a half shekel or some other matter (see commentary, Exodus 30:12–14).

The difficulty with this position is that the Ramban himself, in another section, rejects this theory. Indeed, says the Ramban, it is hard to believe that King David was unaware of the necessity to count Jews via a half shekel. Moreover, even should it have occurred that King David forgot the biblical requirement of half a shekel, Yoav ben Tzrura, who was commanded to implement the census, should have recalled the halachah. Maybe, says the Ramban, King David's sin was that he had no real necessity, no need for the census (it was without a *tzorech*). Also, contends the Ramban, the Torah permitted a census only of those above age twenty. King David took a census of those even thirteen years of age. Thus, King David extended the number of people to be counted (see Ramban, Numbers 1:3). The theories of the Ramban suggest that with certain restrictions, it appears permissible to count Jews.

Of concern is that the Prophets specifically state that it is wrong to count Jews. Indeed, in Hosea it is written: "The number of the children Israel shall be like the sand of the sea, which cannot be measured or numbered" (Hosea 2:1). Based upon this verse, a talmudic sage ruled that a Jewish census is forbidden (*Yoma* 22b).

To resolve this issue, one may suggest that to take a census of the entire Jewish nation may be prohibited based upon the verse in Hosea. This sin would relate even to a census that was conducted via means of a half shekel. Counting all Jewish males from a certain age level would relate to the restrictions stipulated by the Ramban.

To count a segment of Jews would be permitted providing it was not done by actually counting the head of each Jew. Indeed, common custom is to assess the number of Jews available for a minyan by assigning each to be counted as a word of a ten-letter verse. Thus, upon conclusion of the verse, it would be evident that a minyan was present. (The verse most commonly used is *Hoshea et amecha* [Psalms 28:1].) Yet, even this method need not be utilized. The Talmud records that the *kohanim* in the *Bet HaMikdash* would vie with each other to serve on the altar. To eliminate problems the leader of the shift would select an arbitrary number. He would then ask that the *kohanim* present lift up one or two fingers, which he would count. When he arrived at the prearranged number, the *kohen* upon whom the count concluded would have the honor of serving at the altar (*Yoma* 22b). Thus it was permitted to count fingers. It appears clear that the prohibition against counting Jews in Exodus was restricted to counting heads. Fingers, ties, or some other matter was never prohibited.

A Jewish Informer

QUESTION: Jewish law considers the crime of informing upon a fellow Jew a most vile and odious sin. Why? What is the nature of the sin of the informer (*mosar*) that galvanizes such a negative reaction?

RESPONSE: The Ramban rules that an informer is not to be deemed as part of *k'lal Yisrael* (*Hilchot Mamrim* 2:2). In another section the Ramban notes that an informer is not to receive a share in the world to come (*Hilchot Teshuvah* 3:12). The rationale, says HaGaon Rav Hutner (*z"l*), is based upon the following theory of the Ramban: namely, that one who separates himself from the ways of the community (*ha'poraish mi'darkai tzibur*) "even though he does not sin . . . has no share in the world to come" (*Hilchot Teshuvah* 3:11). Thus, separation from communal standards is tantamount to exclusion from the Jewish people. This, moreover, does not relate to any specific sin. Informing upon Jews, contends HaGaon Rav Hutner (*z"l*), is an action that goes against the essence of Jewish communal standards. It is a behavioral pattern that is simply not Jewish. This is not what Jews do. As such, the informer (*mosar*) is excluded from *k'lal Yisrael* as a reaction to his refusal to observe the moral character of the Jewish people (Pachad Yitzchok Pesach, *Ma'amar* 63:5).

Halachic Diversity and Decisors

QUESTION: Does halachah condone diversity?

RESPONSE: Yes—in fact, it is endemic to the system itself. Two examples:

The prophet Amos warns the Jewish people, "Behold, days are coming, says the Lord, and I will send a famine in the land, not a hunger for bread nor a thirst for water, but to hear the word of God . . . and they will run about to seek the word of the Lord and shall not find it" (Amos 8:11, 12). Says Rav Shimon Bar Yochai, in the Talmud, "*Chas v'shalom*—Heaven forbid that Torah will ever be forgotten from Israel." If so, then what is the meaning of the above verse? It means that a time will come when halachah will not be monolithic. There will be no definitive halachah. There will be diversity (*Shabbat* 138b–139a).

The Maharal of Prague makes the following incisive comment: *Yisrael v'oraita chad hu*—"Israel and Torah are one" (*Zohar*, Parshat Acharai). Each impacts the other. The status of Israel—the Jewish people—is reflected in the status of Torah. Just as Jews are not physically united but dispersed throughout the world, so too is Torah not monolithic; it too is dispersed (*Tiferet Yisrael*, ch. 56; see also *Pachad Yitzchok Purim*, no. 31). As such, *galut*—the exile—has a spiritual component. As long as Jews are not physically united in Israel, diversity is a normal feature of the halachic process. As long as the *galut* exists, so too does diversity.

The Talmud records that Choni HaMagel was a Jewish Rip Van Winkle. After his legendary sleep, he visited the *Bet HaMidrash* and heard the scholars bemoan his death, contending that Choni had the ability to clearly resolve halachic problems: "Ah, if only Choni were alive!" they contended. Choni approached them and revealed himself, but the rabbis disbelieved him and he departed dispirited (*Ta'anit* 23a). Rav Chayyim Schmuelevitch, Dean of the Mir Yeshivah in Jerusalem, made the following poignant remarks: What is a Torah sage? Is he not one who has mastered Torah knowledge? Accordingly, Choni should have requested the rabbis to pose halachic questions to him. Choni's ability to resolve difficult Torah problems would have verified his status. Perhaps, suggests Rav Chayyim, certain problems cannot be resolved by sages of previous generations. Each scholar, in each era, must rule on the problems of the day. There must be a charismatic relationship between master and disciple. For this reason *Pirkei Avot* delineates the chain of tradition. Moshe, having received the Torah at Sinai, transferred it to Yehoshua, Yehoshua to the Elders, they to the Prophets, and they to the men of the Great Assembly. No era relied totally on the leadership of the previous generation; each had its own leadership (*Sichot Musar* 5731, p.

19). Accordingly, differences may emerge due to different eras' concerns and personalities.

It should be noted that halachic diversity is not synonymous with deviance. The latter is aberrant behavior outside the perimeter of halachic guidelines. Of interest is the halachic reaction to institutionalized deviant worship. The Talmud notes that in Alexandria, Egypt, contrary to halachic rules prohibiting animal sacrifice outside the Temple in Jerusalem, the *kohanim* practiced this ritual. The Mishnah cites Scriptures to prohibit those *kohanim* who ministered in the House of Onias from ministering in the Holy Temple (*Menachot* 109a), the implication being that such *kohanim*, though deviant, were devout Jews otherwise qualified to minister in Jerusalem. The congregants, or worshippers in the House of Onias, were not ostracized or delegitimated. This position seems to be the model for traditional reactions to nonhalachic Jewish clergy; their rabbis are not deemed rabbinic leaders, their services are ruled deviant, but the ordinary people (the worshippers) are not excluded nor condemned. The door is constantly open to all Jews to pray together and observe mitzvot.

Of major concern, therefore, is a question that goes to the root of Jewish power and influence, namely, who has the authority to establish halachah? This question has two major components: (1) Who has the right to go through the intellectual process of creatively providing the research, precedent, and logic to formulate halachah on specific issues? (2) Who has the authority to establish policy? To set policy requires a concern not only for the legal religious issues, but also for the ramification of the decision upon the status of *k'lal Yisrael*. Indeed, should a particular ruling be viewed as generating a negative impact upon the sphere of Torah, the observance of mitzvot, or the future status of the people, many rabbinic authorities would refrain from establishing a halachic practice. This suggests that an issue or practice that may be legally (halachically) permissible may be prohibited as a policy. Thus it is evident that the formulators of halachic policy influence the contours of religious life. Who are these people? We know that they are rabbis, but what type of rabbis? This presentation is an analysis of the *galut* rabbinate and in particular the pulpit rabbinate, namely, those rabbis who serve as leaders of congregations or synagogues.

The *galut* pulpit rabbi is not controlled by any formal hierarchical structure. There is no regional or national rabbinic supervisor to impact his freedom of action. Theoretically, his authority to formulate halachah is inherent in his position as a Jewish leader; he is equal to anyone. Yet, from a pragmatic viewpoint, the pulpit rabbi (especially in the United States) until recently has been perceived as the lowest figure of authority for the establishment of halachic policy. He may implement or execute halachah but was not deemed the proper vehicle to set policy itself. It was generally assumed that halachic policy was simply beyond the scope of such rabbis.

A popular maxim from *Pirkei Avot* (1:2) will help clarify the issue. It is reported that Shimon HaTzaddik (Simon the Just) frequently said: The world stands (or is based) upon three principles: Torah, *avodah, u'gemilat chasadim.* Torah is self-understood; *avodah* is religious, pious service of prayer; and *gemilat chasadim* is loving kindness. It should be noted that Jewish life has developed institutions to carry out (and, in a way, serve as the specialists of) each of the three endeavors.

1. The yeshivah serves as the bastion of Torah learning. It is in the yeshivah that one finds the greatest concentration of Torah scholarship and creative Torah excitement. As such, the Rosh HaYeshivah, the head of the yeshivah, logically should serve as the final decisor for Torah questions. He simply is the greatest reservoir of Torah knowledge. The head teacher of Torah and rabbis, it is assumed, simply knows more than others. Accordingly, policy has legitimacy when it emanates from such a source.

2. The hasidic *shtibel* generally serves as the repository for the manifestation of fervent pious prayer. The hasidic rebbe need not be the greatest Torah scholar but certainly he excels in *daven*ing. He is considered a holy Jew. He is, perhaps, a specialist in *avodah,* religious service. Service to God has legitimacy and so, therefore, do such specialists in piety.

3. *Chesed* and *tzedakah* (charity). In the Diaspora synagogues are a major religious source for the collection and disbursement of charity. The rabbis serve as leaders of congregations that number amongst their midst many philanthropists. Thus, pulpit rabbis are courted by *roshai yeshivah* and hasidic rebbes not because of the fact that such rabbis are great Torah scholars or unique, truly pious Jews, but because of the potential influence such pulpit rabbis may have over directing lay leaders to support specific Torah or hasidic institutions.

To the extent that the normal functions of synagogue life do not by their very nature require their rabbis to be great Torah scholars, the pulpit rabbis were by general understanding deemed not the proper, legitimate source for formulating halachah. As such, a new dimension was added to halachic policy. The quality of research or the scintillating creativity of the logic was of no paramount issue. The major question was the source of a halachic ruling: Who said it? The name of the rabbi who proclaimed policy was essential for engendering acceptance.

Concomitant to this was the emergence of a "yardstick" to measure the validity or legitimacy of halachic decisions. It is called *daat Torah.* This principle projects the concept that a group of rabbinic sages imbued with the sanctity of Torah are the sole, authentic interpreters of our religion, and spokesmen for daily decisions. Accordingly, all decisions require the imprimatur of great scholars. No one else has the Torah authority for halachic policy. Thus, a decision that several great rabbis in unison promulgate has validity even if sources are not delineated. As long as a group is recognized as *daat Torah* all decisions must be abided, regardless of rationale or scholarship.

The underlying, energizing aspect of this concept is the perception that *daat Torah* is not solely the viewpoint of one or but a few of our great rabbis, but rather the consensus position of a goodly number of rabbinic sages. If a practice appears to project the position of the world of scholarship and piety it becomes the "in and approved" rabbinic concern.

Though in theory such a position appears to have great

merit, pragmatically it generated a number of dysfunctional manifestations.

1. Torah Judaism is based on scholarship. Pronouncements and policies are traditionally rooted in talmudic and halachic expertise. Yet, in the era of *daat Torah,* the source or quality of scholarly research became secondary to the name of the person and position of the rav who formulated it. This permeated within the rabbinic community a tendency to dismiss the findings of scholarship. It was necessary to acquire a *gadol*—a sage who would back a specific policy. Such a position, moreover, would have respect regardless of the quality of the scholarship serving as the pinions for such a ruling. Torah discourse became exercises in futility, for nothing would become policy until a proper *gadol* sanctioned it. This crystallized the approach of scurrying around for a *gadol* to approve halachic policies.

2. The concept *daat Torah* gives the impression that it is a consensus position of numerous sages. Its dysfunction is that the process of seeking consensus generally tends to promote *chumrot,* or extreme orientations. It is generally easier for those who seek lenient rulings to agree to stringent positions than for extremists to accept lenient rulings. Accordingly, lenient positions do not emanate from a *daat Torah* philosophy; it simply does not take place. There appears to be, moreover, a built-in negative response to any creative moderation or "loophole," even if such is halachically correct. This generates public denunciation and scathing criticism of innovative halachic rulings. Thus independent, objective halachic enquiry is stifled by political pressure. Most scholars are simply not desirous of incurring criticism or controversy and generally favor discretion over valor. This projects the image that Torah policy caters to right-wing ideology. Of major concern is that the *daat Torah* of the pulpit or modern Orthodox rabbinate was disregarded.

As *daat Torah* became more popular, it became evident that no one was serving as a halachic leader for the vast numbers of Orthodox laymen in modern Orthodox synagogues. No one was the spokesman for the moderates. Indeed, it became necessary for *rabbonim* of congregations, who deal daily with major problems, to once again assume responsibility for establishing halachic policy. Chaucer wrote, "Truth will out." So too with halachah. It is not and cannot be the esoteric domain of a few select leaders. All Jews must be aware of its methodology and principles. Its logical system must be tested in the open sphere of dialogue and debate. Halachic policy is the result of positions finely honed through Torah scholarship. That is the way it used to be; that is the way it should be again. Rabbis should have the ability to openly develop halachic policy, whether or not it is innovative or stringent or lenient or not part of a consensus. The issue is and should be: Is it halachically sound? And if it is sound, will the rabbinate implement the position?

There have been changes in the pulpit rabbinate, changes that alter the role of pulpit rabbis and their ability to formulate halachah. As a result of the phenomenal growth of Torah and yeshivah education, most major congregations have large numbers of former yeshivah students as part of their membership. These former *b'nei Torah* are demanding that pulpit rabbis manifest Torah scholarship and erudition. As such, a new breed of scholars are occupying the leadership of pulpits. No longer may they be dismissed for lack of Torah standing.

In addition, many rabbis of pulpits and *roshai* yeshivah are around the same age level. This generates a new, mutual respect. When the rabbis were aged in their twenties and thirties and the *roshai* yeshivah were venerable sages in their seventies and eighties or more, the pulpit rabbis would subordinate themselves to others. But when the rabbis in the major congregations are more or less the same age or older than the *roshai* yeshivah, a different relationship applies. Indeed, many pulpit rabbis even recall learning together as equals or peers with *roshai* yeshivah while both were students. Accordingly, both groups feel a sense of kinship and do not defer to the opinions of the others.

Some time ago a noted Israeli Rosh Yeshivah and member of Knesset visited with me. In an attempt to assess his character and religious hierarchical orientations, I asked him, "Who is your rebbe? Who is your rabbi for crucial ideological problems?"

His response was simple, matter of fact, yet quite astute. "You know, Reb Simcha, that those of us over forty years of age have no living rebbe. We, sadly, are our own rebbes." He's right.

As a result of all of the above-noted dynamic factors—the concern for policy to represent the needs of congregations, the desire to reassert the stature and role of the pulpit rabbi, the concern that stringency is not necessarily the raison d'etre of *k'lal Yisrael,* the distaste for vilification of alternate policies, the simple lack of any commanding imposing giant to coalesce action, the concern for a moderate view—all these issues generated a support system for pulpit rabbis to reassert their role in formulating halachic policy.

A professor of mine, Albert Salamon, once said, "The image of the King topples before his throne." So too with halachic policy. The dysfunctions supported a need for change. Congregations wished that Torah leadership should reflect the consensus views of Torah laymen. This view may not be heeded by the yeshivah or hasidic worlds of influence; such spheres of thought may seek out their own decisors of Jewish law. That is their right—but so, too, do the modern Orthodox have the right to seek out rabbinic scholars to espouse their viewpoint. Hopefully, halachic policy will be the result of creative scholarship finely honed in the corridors of halachic discourse—where ideas and talmudic and halachic guidelines are the issues, not personalities or political machinations. In fact, that is what Torah is all about.

In *Pirkei Avot,* it is written (1:2): *Shimon HaTzaddik ha'ya mishyarei Keneset HaGadolah.* Shimon HaTzaddik was one of the last survivors of the Men of the Great Assembly. He lived with greatness and grandeur. He was a member of the Great Assembly, thus he personally knew the top leaders of a previous generation, amongst whom were numbered several prophets who spoke in the name of God. He was a *kohen gadol.* Legend has it that he influenced Alexander the Great, and the Abarbanel writes that he communicated with Aristotle. What a pedigree! Yet after his death, the leadership of Torah passed to Antignos Ish Socho (a man from Socho)—not a high priest, not a man of Jerusalem; a new leader who came out of the woodwork to become the singular spokesman for religion and the emissary to pass on the *mesorah* to yet another generation. This teaches us again the old maxim *Torah tziva lanu Moshe, Morasha Kehilat Yaakov,* "The Torah that Moses commanded us is an inheritance to the children of Jacob" (Deuteronomy 33:4).

Torah does not belong to any one group. It belongs to all. All Jews are to learn Torah. Every Jew is a potential Hillel or Beruria. *Pirkei Avot* delineates the transmission of Torah from one generation to another. Moshe and Yehoshua each served as the ultimate leader for their generations, yet afterwards no one person emerged to be so acclaimed by the Jewish people. There was a group called the "Elders" (*z'kainim,* wise men), and Torah leadership was transformed from a single Master to a group of scholars, each lacking the ability to represent the totality of *k'lal Yisrael*—maybe that is what will now take place again.

The Prevention, Reporting, and Prosecution of Crime: Halachic Ramifications

QUESTION: Does Jewish law impose a responsibility to prevent or to report crime? Is it permitted to testify against another Jew in a secular court? Is it permitted to be a prosecutor?

RESPONSE: The Ramban rules, "whoever is able to save another and does not endeavor to do so, violates [the prohibition of the biblical verse which states] *Lo Ta'amod* (do not stand idly) over the blood of your neighbor; (Leviticus 19:16) therefore, one who witnesses his friend drowning in the sea or brigands attacking him and he [the witness] has the ability to save him, or he heard that people seek harm to him . . . and he does not contact his friend to reveal this, he is in violation of the biblical prohibition of "do not stand idly over the blood of your neighbor" (Maimonides, Hilchot Rotzaich, 1:14, also, *Shulchan Aruch, Choshen Mishpat* 426:1). This obligation to prevent crime is not limited to life-threatening situations or even to acts of physical violence, but applies as well to pecuniary matters.

Indeed, the rabbis rule that it is even morally incumbent upon one to rectify an erroneous legal decision. This is noted in *Shevuot* 31a wherein it states: "How do we know that a disciple sitting before his master, who sees that the poor man is right and the wealthy man wrong, should not remain silent? Because it is said: 'From a false matter keep far'" (Exodus 23:7). This case teaches us that silence itself maybe a form of falsehood. In a circumstance where silence would result in an erroneous legal decision, it is obligatory to speak out and rectify the wrong. Even though a case is being judged by a master rather than a disciple, and normally it would be considered audacious to contradict one's teacher, still the biblical injunction requires one to reveal the truth. Personal qualms about ruffling the dignity of the master by contradicting his sagacity or ruling have no bearing on the issue.

Yet, not all efforts to report or prevent a crime are lauded. There are limitations. Indeed, there is a fascinating citation relating to this concept in *Pesachim* 113b. The Talmud reports that a man named Tuvia sinned. He committed adultery. A man called Zigud was aware of this sin and by himself, without another witness, he came to *bet din*, the rabbinical court, to testify against Tuvia proclaiming that Tuvia was an adulterer. Rav Papa, the senior Rav of the *bet din*, punished Zigud for testifying. Zigud was appalled. He called out in protest, "Tuvia sinned and Zigud is punished?" In other words, the *bet din* did not punish Tuvia for the alleged sin of adultery, so why was Zigud punished? The Talmud notes that Zigud was punished for he was guilty of the crime of *lashon hara* (talebearing or being slanderous about another).

In Jewish law, sins relating to adultery require the presence of a minimum of two qualified witnesses. *Bet din* will, therefore, not accept the testimony of a single witness in matters pertaining to adultery. Thus, Zigud should have known that he had no standing in court by himself without a second witness and that the *bet din* would not act upon his testimony; yet, he persisted in testifying. Zigud, therefore, was in effect merely spreading gossip about Tuvia. The fact that the allegation may have been true was of no concern. Zigud was punished for informing others of slanderous material. He should have kept knowledge of the immoral act to himself.

A contemporary issue is whether a person is required to place himself or herself in jeopardy in order to report or prevent a crime. Does Jewish law obligate a person to place himself in danger in order to save others? What about a situation wherein a person is threatened with financial pressure; should he testify against another? Is the sin of *lo ta'amod* operational in such circumstances? What says halachah in such a predicament?

When confronted with the cost of observing a mitzvah, the rule is that one is not required to expend more than one-fifth of one's income. As such, should an item required for the performance of a mitzvah cost more than one-fifth of one's income, the Jew would not be obligated to purchase such a costly item, even if, as a result, he would not observe the mitzvah. This rule relates only to the observance of positive mitzvot. When dealing with the violation of negative mitzvot, there is no financial limit imposed upon the Jew. All funds must be expended to forestall the violation of a biblical negative command (Rama, *Shulchan Aruch, Orech Chayyim* 656). If this be so, then fear of a loss of funds should not be an obstacle to any effort of preventing a crime. Since the rule obliging a person to prevent crime is a negative command *lo ta'amod*, "Do not stand idly by the blood of your neighbor," loss of funds—real, perceived or threatened—should not excuse inaction or silence.

Scholars, however, finely hone this rule. They contend that the issue of concern is not whether the cost of observing a mitzvah is either a violation of a positive or a negative mitzvah, but, rather, whether a positive action is necessary in order to violate the negative mitzvah, or whether a violation takes place by inaction (as termed in talmudic parlance: *shev v'al ta'aseh*) (Pitchei Teshuva, *Yoreh Deah* 157:4). As such, silence or an omission of action to prevent a crime may not be culpable. In other words, when the variable of loss of funds is imposed upon a witness, he may elect not to testify, and, instead may hide under the cloak of discretion.

In addition, halachah does not dismiss the potential negative ramifications that may impact a witness or individual who seeks to stop the sin of another. The Rama rules in *Shulchan Aruch*: "Even though it is an obligation to protest sin (by attempting even to avert the sin) and anyone who has the potential to do so and resists making such a protest is deemed as if he [himself] committed the transgression, yet one is not obligated to expend funds for this matter and, therefore, common custom is to be lenient and not protest against sinners for one may be apprehensive that they [the sinners] will retaliate both physically and monetarily" (*Yoreh Deah,* 334:48). A realistic fear of retaliation halachically mutes the mandate to testify or to avert the crime. The Rama states as a general rule that whenever retaliation is probable the best course is silence and inaction.

Thus, the mandate to prevent crime may depend upon the fulcrum of conscience and personal judgment. The key question is not necessarily what Jewish law mandates, but, rather can one live with oneself by the personal judgment of inaction. Namely, can one live with oneself by being silent in the face of crime?

Of major concern is the uniquely Jewish concept of *mesira* (the prohibition against one Jew informing the secular courts and/ or police of the crime of another Jew). Jewish law deems the act of informing against Jews to Gentiles to be such a negative, reprehensible crime, that the codes overtly note that anyone who violates this prohibition "loses his share in the world to come" (*Shulchan Aruch, Choshen Mishpat* 388:9). The need for the codes to specifically detail the religious punishment for this crime, apart from any internal Jewish physical reaction, emphasizes the moral communal repulsion. This concept places major obstacles on the previously articulated mandate to avert crime. Based upon the strictures of the *mesira* prohibition, a Jew should be withheld from testifying against another Jew in a secular court. Indeed, it would appear that one may even be prohibited to provide evidence of a Jewish person's crime to the secular authorities. Also at issue is whether the *mesira* rule may be used by Jewish criminals to intimidate witnesses against them. This means that a potential witness may possibly be told that should he testify against another Jew, the entire Jewish community will ostracize him for he will be classified as an informer.

The Rama rules that a person being physically abused by another may inform the secular government about the attacker (*Choshen Mishpat* 388:7). The halachic commentator the Shach notes that the laws of *mesira* simply do not apply when a victim seeks to extricate himself from an abusive situation (388:45). One may not inform about a Jew to punish him for acts of the past. However, to cease abuse, it is permissible.

Based upon this decision of the Shach, a great scholar, the Tzitz Eliezer (vol. 19:52), ruled that one certainly may inform the government in cases of child abuse. Thus, even without life-threatening conditions, it is deemed meritorious to report a parent who may be abusing his child. The Tzitz Eliezer cites two additional sources to support his ruling.

Firstly, the *Aruch HaShulchan* (*Choshen Mishpat* 388:7) comments that the original laws of *mesira* related to such governments ("like those in Africa") where the rule of law was not operational. Accordingly, the concept of *mesira* was set up to protect Jews from inequitable governments. It was not applicable, he contends, to a government like Great Britain. Based on this theory, one may report cases of abused children because the law of *mesira* was simply not in effect in a democratic society ruled by an equitable set of laws. (Not all scholars accept this position of the *Aruch HaShulchan*.)

The second supportive case cited by the Tzitz Eliezer also has contemporary ramifications. The Mabit in a responsum gives the impression that a Jewish court, a *bet din*, may refer a case to the secular courts in the event that they lack the authority or power to enforce a decision. For example, he deals with a case wherein *bet din* actually referred a problem to the secular government for enforcement (part 1: *Siman* 22). Thus, in child abuse situations, if *bet din* is made aware of a situation that cannot be properly handled by the rabbinical court, the rabbis would grant permission to seek out the protection of the secular courts and the police. The practical implication of this concept is the recommendation to consult a rabbinical *bet din* as to the propriety of reporting a crime or testifying against another Jew in the secular court system. Once *bet din* permits the utilization of the police or the secular courts, the individual reporting a crime should have no qualms about his actions. In this situation, the odious reputation applied to a person who informs upon another Jew to the secular police or courts would not apply.

In addition, the *Shulchan Aruch* rules that to prevent a public crime, or a number of individuals from becoming victims of a crime, it is also permissible to seek out the protection of the secular government (388:12).

Thus, to put a stop to abuse or to prevent a crime that would be committed against a large number of people, the laws of *mesira* would not be operational.

This indicates that, unless one held the position of the *Aruch HaShulchan*, the concept of *mesira* was not applicable in democratic societies, there does not appear to be any halachic permission to report to the police and the secular government a crime that already took place, even if the crime has impacted negatively a number of people.

Though halachah, as noted, does specify conditions in which it is permissible to report criminal action to secular authorities, clarification is necessary to determine whether an Orthodox Jew is permitted to serve as a prosecutor. Perhaps a Jew should not be the person representing the secular, non-Jewish legal system. Indeed, HaGaon HaRav Moshe Feinstein rules that it is wrong to turn in to the police a thief who robbed a Sefer Torah. He argues that a prison sentence is generally accepted as punishment by the American courts for robbery. This punishment of imprisonment for robbery is not noted in Jewish legal sources. As such, the secular governmental court system will give the criminal a greater punishment than that ordained by Jewish law. This, he ruled, cannot be permitted by halachah. The source for this is the talmudic citation (*Moed Katan* 17a) that relates a case where Raish Lakesh was in charge of guarding a garden of fig trees. A person without permission ate a number of figs. This person even disregarded all warnings to desist. Raish Lakesh, therefore, placed this man in excommunication. The person complained that Raish Lakesh was unfair in his treatment of the crime. His argument was that his sin generated a financial loss to the owner that he was willing to repay. At no time, contended this man, did he deserve the punishment of excommunication. Raish Lakesh sought the counsel of the sages and was told that the excommunication he rendered was excessive and, therefore, invalid. Based upon this citation, HaRav Moshe rules that turning a thief over to the police would generate a punishment in excess of that which Jewish law would set up and, therefore, was not permissible (Iggrot Moshe, vol. VIII: *Orech Chayyim* part 5: *Siman* 9:11). This ruling would prevent a prosecutor from seeking any punishment beyond that outlined by Jewish law.

This decision of HaRav Moshe appears to be challenged by a number of sources. Firstly, the previously mentioned responsum of the Mabit deals with a case in which the *bet din* referred a problem Jew to the secular government who placed the Jew in jail. The general rule derived from this situation is that when the Jewish court system cannot handle a problem case, it may be turned over to the secular government for enforcement, even though a punishment may be exacted that is more arduous or excessive than Jewish law would establish. Raish Lakesh's case may simply have been one in which his reaction was deemed excessive. Perhaps, though, in cases where Jewish enforcement is not practical, governmental action may be the only recourse.

The Talmud in *Bava Metzia* (83b–84a) clearly portrays Jews turning in Jewish criminals to a Gentile power who punished such offenders above and beyond that of Jewish law.

Rabbi Eliezer ben Rabbi Shimon met a Jewish policeman and queried him concerning his job: "Perhaps you take the innocent and leave behind the guilty?" The response was that he had no choice but to detect and report criminals contending, "It is the king's command." Rabbi Eliezer then gave him sound advice to help him detect criminals. When the government heard of this incident, Rabbi Eliezer himself was given the job of turning criminals over to the authorities and he performed his task with success. This disturbed other rabbis. In fact, Rabbi Yehoshua ben Karchah sent a message to him saying, "Vinegar, son of wine, how long will you deliver the people of our God for slaughter?" Rabbi Yehoshua disparaged Rabbi Eliezer. "Your father was like wine, you are vinegar. Vinegar is wine that is spoiled. Rabbi Eliezer, the traits of your holy father did not transcend to his son. You are guilty of informing on Jews and you should cease and desist." Rabbi Eliezer responded, "I am getting rid of the thorns from the vineyard." Namely, I am not turning over good or innocent people. They are offenders that should be punished. In response, Rabbi Yehoshua claimed, "Let the owner of the vineyard eliminate the thorns." In other words, it is not for you to do. Let others do it. There is no indication that Rabbi Eliezer changed his position or view. The Talmud further states that a similar situation happened to Rabbi Yishmael ben Rabbi Yosi. Eliyahu the prophet rebuked him for turning in Jewish criminals to governmental authorities. Rabbi Yishmael responded that he had no choice for "it is the royal command." Eliyahu directed him to flee to another area where he would not be commanded to turn in Jewish criminals.

Thus, an ancient debate about this issue exists. Of importance is that the Bet Yosef, in his commentary on the Tur *Shulchan Aruch*, discusses this talmudic citation. He notes that secular law does not follow concepts of Jewish law. Secular law will punish offenders based upon the testimony of relatives, a situation not accepted by halachah. Such punishment will be ordained even without proper warning as stipulated by Jewish law. Yet, the laws of secular governments are necessary. Otherwise, society will be overcome by people who do not tell the truth. (The implication is the fact that the rabbis cannot enforce ethical or moral behavior.) The Talmud, indeed, relates that great rabbis detected and turned in criminals to secular authorities. Though they were rebuked by Rabbi Yehoshua and Eliyahu the prophet, it should not be viewed that such rabbis were fundamentally in error about the permissibility of their actions. It was, rather, due to the great piety of such rabbis that they should have personally refrained from being the ones who helped Jews to be punished. In other words, people known for great sanctity and piety should not be involved in any way with the punishment of Jews. As a son of a noted pious rabbi, Rabbi Eliezer was called "son of wine." He, too, should conduct himself with the highest level of piety. Under no circumstances were Rabbi Eliezer or Rabbi Yishmael in violation of Jewish law. Indeed, in the event that such rabbis violated Jewish law, this violation should have been explicitly noted. Also, Rabbi Yishmael tells Eliyahu that he had a job to do. If the process was wrong, if they were in violation of halachah, then having a job to perform from the government would not be an excuse. Eliyahu should have responded by saying, "Who said your blood is redder than anothers?" (*Pesachim* 25b). That statement is utilized to prevent a person from killing another to save his own life. It should have been directed against Rabbi Yishmael. If Rabbi Yishmael was implying that he was in a life-threatening situation should he refuse to do the bidding of the king to apprehend criminals, then Jewish law would have ruled that one may not save one's life by killing another. The fact that the rabbis were not simply informed that their course of action was in violation of Jewish law teaches that there is nothing wrong with serving in a professional capacity to help the government eliminate criminals (Bet Yosef, citing the Responsum of the Rashba, *Choshen Mishpat* 388).

What is surprising is that HaRav Moshe cites this Bet Yosef in the previously noted responsum. He remarks that the case of Rabbi Yishmael does not contradict his ruling that one may not hand over a criminal to the police in a situation where the punishment will be greater than by Jewish authorities, for a person appointed by the government is in a different category. In other words, HaRav Moshe admits that the *Bava Metzia* case deals with punishments more onerous than by Jewish law. The actions were deemed permissible solely because the rabbis were agents of the authorities. Yet the rationale that one is an agent of the secular authorities relates only to Rabbi Yishmael. Rabbi Eliezar does not utilize this excuse. He felt that he was providing a proper, moral course of action by eliminating criminals from society. What was his rationale? How did he harmonize his position with the laws of *mesira*? Though this case, together with the Bet Yosef's analysis, seems to allow a prosecutor to continue in his profession, it is not clear as to why his role pragmatically does away with the entire concept of *mesira*. If an action is a violation of Jewish law, then it should be morally wrong to be involved in such action whether or not one had a job to perform.

I suggest that there is a concept of Judaism that is so important and so vital that it alters the very nature of the concept of *mesira* itself. The Ramban rules that the worst sin of the Jew is the crime of *chilul hashem* (the profanation of the holy name of God). As such, should this sin take place, atonement is not granted until the sinner repents, prays on Yom Kippur for forgiveness, is afflicted with pain, and finally dies. Death is the final atonement (Hilchot Teshuva 1:4). It would appear that a vital goal of the Jew is to prevent the public shame or embarrassment of the holy name of God. Such endeavors would certainly be a means of sanctifying the name of God. In a country known for its commitment to the rule of law, it is a form of public shame for a member of the Jewish community to violate the laws of the land. A Jewish criminal is a shame to the Jewish religion. A religious Jewish criminal is a form of *chilul hashem*. Judaism is an ethical, ritual code of law. Jewish criminals make a mockery of our ethical standards. They send the message to the general society that Jews care not for the rule of law. The more visible Jewish the offender is, the more it generates a degree of *chilul hashem*. This, I believe, was Rabbi Eliezer's rationale for detecting and turning in Jewish criminals. He was eliminating thorns. He felt that his role was the most pious and sacred function of a rabbi. He was keeping the reputation of the Jewish community high and dignified in the eyes of the world. His symbolic message was Jews are moral. Jewish criminals would not be tolerated by the leaders of the Jewish community. Accordingly, to uproot criminals may be viewed from this perspective as a sacred profession. Even those who disagreed did not believe that reporting criminals to authorities was a violation of Jewish law. Their position was one of sensitivity. They felt that sages should not be personally responsible for the punishment of Jews.

Thus, a person may utilize the principle of preventing *chilul hashem* as an understandable rationale for informing the government about another Jew. Just as it is permitted, as a means of preventing damage to the Jewish community, to turn over to the police someone who is attempting to bring about a public crime or perform criminal acts to many people, so, too, should it be permitted to forestall a public shame or embarrassment to the Jewish community at large. It could be designated as "religious damage control."

Indeed, there is a precedent for the utilization of such a concept. It is known that in cases dealing with an attempt to extract funds from another, Jewish law requires the presence of two witnesses, while secular law relies upon the testimony of a single witness. In the event that a Jew, by himself without any other witness, has testimony regarding extracting funds from another Jew for the benefit of a Gentile, Jewish law would not deem it proper to testify against the Jew in a secular court. The reason is that the testimony of a single witness would cause a Jew to lose funds via a procedure not acceptable by Jewish law. Should, however, the Gentile have relied upon the Jew to testify, then, even though funds would be extracted through a procedure not recognized by Jewish law, the Jew would be required to testify because his silence would be a form of *chilul hashem* (Rosh, *Bava Kama*, ch. 10, *Siman* 14, *Shulchan Aruch Choshen Mishpat* 28:3). Thus, the sin of *chilul hashem* overrides the injunction against testifying.

There are those, however, who may have grown up distrusting all governments. Many Holocaust survivors will find it difficult to grant sanctity to those who inform against Jews. Accordingly, reactions to the informer as well as to the prosecutor may be tinged with emotionally negative trauma. Emotions will color the contours of the Jewish reactions to such activities. I suggest that the reporting of Jewish criminals may, therefore, be classified as either an act of honor sustaining the rule of law or, dependent upon upbringing and social mores, deemed an act of treason. Whatever the personal judgement, Jewish law may not be utilized as the barrier against reporting crime. As presented, there are numerous positions substantiating a positive involvement with governmental authorities.

My position is that a firm observer of Jewish law must by his or her very nature subscribe to the sanctity of law in an equitable society. Any and all activities that prevent a *chilul hashem* are to be deemed meritorious.

Notes

1. *Highlights of the CJF 1991 National Population Survey*, p. 19.
2. The position that intermarriage is an *issur mid'oraita* is maintained by many authorities. See Deut. 7:3; *Avodah Zarah* 36b; Rambam, *Hil. Issurei Bi'ah* XII:3, *Bet Shmuel, Even HaEzer*, 16:4; *Resp. Maharam Schick, Even HaEzer*, nos. 37 and 155. See, however, *Tur, Even HaEzer*, sec. 16.
3. *Resp. Seridei Esh*, II, no. 6.
4. *Orech Chayyim* 55:11. Regarding the various terms of excommunication, see *Yoreh Deah* 334.
5. *Orech Chayyim* 55:12.
6. Cited in *Mishneh Berurah*, ad loc., subpar. 46.
7. Or, more correctly, were. From the Emancipation onward, with the dismantling of the corporate structure of society and the transformation of the European communities into purely "voluntary" groups, the use of excommunication as a weapon of social control was made illegal in many places. Similar conditions, for different reasons, obtained in Eastern Europe as well. See *Aruch HaShulchan, Yoreh Deah*, 354: Introduction.
8. The ruling is noted, with approval, in Rabbi Yitzhak Y. Fuchs, *Tefillah B'Tzibbur* (Jerusalem, 1978), V:28. This work, an anthology of rules guiding synagogue practice, generally reflects common halachic usage.
9. Cf. R. Bonfil, *The Rabbinate in Renaissance Italy* (in Hebrew), Jerusalem, 1979, ch. II.
10. With the ironic, though prominent, possible exception of Jews from Orthodox or even highly traditional backgrounds.
11. Recall that Rabbi Weinberg himself was inclined to see the intermarried Jew as a *mumar letei'avon.*
12. 334:1.
13. Based upon *Terumat HaDeshen* 138.

14. Ibid.
15. *Yoreh Deah,* ibid., subpar. 1.
16. *Nekudat HaKesef,* ad loc.
17. See also *Aruch HaShulchan,* ibid., par. 5, who notes that while most authorities side with Rema, nevertheless such a drastic step should only be taken after careful consideration.
18. *Yoreh Deah,* 345:8.
19. While it is also true that the *Aruch HaShulchan* does state that most cases of *niddui* that were in response to transgression did include exclusion from a minyan, this is not automatic but requires the aforementioned deliberation and decision of the court.
20. *Hullin* 5a. See the discussion in *Darchei Teshuvah,* I, sec. 2, subpar. 75, as to whether this disqualification is biblical or rabbinic in origin.
21. *Hullin,* ibid., s.v. *ela lav.*
22. See the opinions cited by Rabbi David Z. Hoffman, *Resp. Melamed L'Ho'il, Orech Chayyim,* no. 29.
23. Ibid. (end).
24. *Binyan Tziyyon HacHadashot,* no. 3. Cf. in a different context *Resp. Iggrot Moshe, Yoreh Deah,* I, no. 160.
25. These positions were not, however, universally accepted by their contemporaries and succeeding generations. The Chatam Sofer advocated the expulsion of *Shabbat* desecrators from the community, irrespective of degree of incidence (*Resp. Chatam Sofer, Choshen Mishpat,* no. 195). The Munkaczer Rav, moreover, explicitly rejected Rabbi Ettlinger's argument by ruling that the sin of *Chillul Shabbat* was not in the least bit muted by the formality of the recitation of *Kiddush* (and by implication, any other non-*melachah* related *Shabbat* observance) (*Resp. Minchat Elazar,* I, no. 74). Finally, the contemporary authority Rabbi Moshe Stern, former Chief Rabbi of Debrecyn, endorsed the stance of *Seridei Esh,* that a *mechallel Shabbat* may not be counted as part of a minyan (*Resp. Be'er Moshe,* V., nos. 90–94).

    At the same time, the center of gravity among halachic authorities seems to lean in the direction of the position of the *Binyan Tziyyon* and those like him. This contention is borne out by a lengthy analysis of the issue by the former Rishon L'Tziyyon, Rabbi Ovadiah Yosef. In an encyclopaedic overview, Rabbi Yosef clearly defends Rabbi Ettlinger's analysis and cites numerous later authorities who ruled likewise (*Resp. Yabi'a Omer*, I, *Yoreh Deah* no. 11). Indeed, Rabbi Moshe Feinstein appears to have sided with the lenient position when he ruled that in an instance where there is reason to believe that an act of *Chillul Shabbat* was not committed solely for theological reasons, then the principle of delegitimation does not apply (*Resp. Iggrot Moshe*, I, *Orech Chayyim*, no. 33). (These and other sources are extensively discussed in Moshe Gorelick, "The Status of the Non-Sabbath Observer: The Rabbinic Response to Non-Conformity," unpublished paper, Yeshiva University. Thanks to Rabbi Gorelick for making a copy available.)

26. *Pesach, Ma'amar* III(2).
27. Cf. *Mishneh Torah, Hilchot Mamrim*, III:1–2.

    See also the famous comment of the Chazon Ish, (*Yoreh Deah*, sec. 2, pars. 16 [end] and 23) that in an age of *hester panim* one cannot view lack of belief and observance as the result of willful rebellion against God. In fact, obduracy in this regard would be counterproductive. The implications of this statement for our issue, and for *kiruv* generally, are clear.

    Rabbis Yosef Adler and Haskel Lookstein, have stated that they were informed by Rav Joseph B. Soloveitchik that, in his opinion, the punitive side of *mechallel Shabbat b'farhesiah* does not apply in the overwhelming majority of cases in America. The Rav based his judgment on his experience that Jews who knowingly desecrate *Shabbat*, will not do so openly and without inhibition in front of rabbis and other *Shabbat* observers. The identical point was made by Rabbi Shalom Schwadron in *Resp. Maharsham*, I, no. 121.
28. One could equally maintain that even if the majority of Jews presently marrying were *not* wedding non-Jews, still the existence of exceedingly large, Jewishly attenuated population doing so also would negate viewing their action as one of rebellion.
29. Another instance where this reevaluation will be increasingly relevant is that of the proper procedure for attending to the funeral and internment of one who had intermarried. The burial given to the financier and philanthropist Robert Maxwell, which was attended by both lay and rabbinic figures in Israel, brings home most strongly the implications of this question.
30. Cf. Rav Ben-Zion Meir Hai Uziel, *Piskei Uziel*, Jerusalem, 1976, pp. 249ff.

31. Morris Adler, "A Long Look Ahead," *Jewish Heritage*, Winter 1963/1964, pp. 8–9.
32. Milton Himmelfarb, "The Vanishing Jews," *Commentary* 36, no. 3 (September 1963), pp. 249–250.
33. *Yevamot* 48b, statement of Rabbi Yosi, *Tana*.
34. *Yevamot* 24b.
35. *Sanhedrin* 36.
36. *Baba Mezia* 58b.
37. Cecil Roth, *History of the Jews*, p. 131.
38. Solomon Grayzel, *History of the Jews*, p. 205. See also Louis Ginzberg, *The Legends of the Jews* vol. I, trans. J. Szold (Jewish Publications Society of America, Philadelphia, 1954), p. XXI. He maintains that the teachers of the Aggadah were not folklorists from whom a faithful reproduction of legendary material could be expected. They were primarily homelists whose object was to "establish a close connection between the Scriptures and the creation of the popular fancy, to give the latter a firm basis and secure a long life for them."
39. Midrash *B'Rayshit Rabba* (BaR) 13, 14–16
Midrash *Tanchuma, VaYakhayl* 8
40. *Mechilta Exodus* 22, 20 No. 178
Yalkut Shemot 349
B'Rayshit Rabba 46.2
Mechilta Nezikin 18, 95
41. Shemot Rabba 3.1
Tanchuma, Shemot 19
Mechilta R.S. 167
42. Yerushalmi *Berachot* 4, 8,b
Yerushalmi *Sanhedrin* 10, 28b–28c
43. The terms "biblical" and "Bible" shall refer in this study only to the Pentateuch.
44. See Jeremiah 7:6, and Jeremiah 22:3.
45. See Zechariah 7:10.
46. See Malachi 3:5.
47. See Ezekiel 22:9 and 22:7.
48. Exodus 12:49 (Translation from the *Soncine Chumahs*, edited by A. Cohen, The Soncino Press, London).
49. Exodus 22:20 (Soncino translation).
50. Exodus 13:9 (Soncino translation).
51. Leviticus 17:10 (Soncino translation).

52. Leviticus 19:10 (Soncino translation).
53. Leviticus 19:34 (Soncino translation).
54. The term used in the Bible to connote a proselyte.
55. See *Rayshit Chochmah*, ch. 4, dealing with modesty. It is stated, without giving a reference, that the prohibition concerned with observance of the Sabbath is repeated in the Bible twenty-eight times; the injunction against idol worship is reiterated twenty-eight times; and the laws requiring fair treatment for proselytes is also repeated twenty-eight times. The author, therefore, maintains that the laws dealing with the treatment of proselytes are as vital and important to Judaism as those relating to the observance of the Sabbath and the belief in monotheism.

    See *Yalkut Shimoni, Parshat Mishpatim* 349, wherein it states that Rabbi Eliezer HaGadol said that the injunction against proselytes is mentioned in the Bible thirty-six times. "Others" are quoted as saying it is mentioned forty-six times. See *Tosfot Baba Mezia* 59b. There it is said that the number forty-six includes phrases where the word *ger* (proselyte) is mentioned in the Bible but not in the form of a command. See *Tosfot Kedushin* 70b. Here a source is quoted that maintains that the word *ger* is only repeated twenty-four times. See *Sefer Hachinuch*, commandment 63, of R. Yitzchok of Barcelonia, who states that the injunction relating to proselytes is repeated twenty-one times.
56. *Kedushin*, ch. 4, Mishna 6:7.
57. *Sifre*, Deuteronomy 159.
58. *Sifre*, Deuteronomy 129 (Deuteronomy 26:3).
59. *Sifre*, (Deut. 22:19).
60. *Niddah* 13.
61. *Tanchuma Emor, Piskah* 11 (Exodus 32).
62. *Yevamot* 109b.
63. *Pasikta Aseret Hadebrit* 22:4.
64. A. Z. Marcus, *Le-Toldot Dat Natseret* Part I, Gerim, Jerusalem: 5697 (1937), p. 58.
65. Ibid., p. 60. See ibid., p. 23, wherein it is maintained that proselytes themselves created favorable legends about conversion.
66. *Kedushin* 4, Mishnah 6:7.
67. *Sifre* Deuteronomy 129.
68. *Sifre* Deuteronomy 94.
69. Tractate *Horayut* 3, Mishneh 8.

70. See G. R. Driver and John C. Miles, *The Babylonian Laws*, (Oxford: The Claredon Press, 1952) for copy of Hammurabi's code. See trial by ordeal, ch. 2, 132.
71. See ibid., ch. 8, 206.
72. Morris Jastrow, *The Civilization of Babylonia and Assyria* (Philadelphia & London: J. B. Lippincott Company, 1915), p. 284.
73. Edward Chiera, *They Wrote on Clay* (Chicago: The University of Chicago Press, 1938), pp. 77–78.
74. *Ketubot* 16b and 17a and Exodus 23:7.
75. Exodus 12:48.
76. *Sanhedrin* 74a, statement of Rabbi Dimi.
77. *Sanhedrin* 74b, statement of Rabbi Jacob in Rabbi Johanan's name.
78. Rashi, *Sanhedrin* 73b.
79. *Shabbot* 49a and 130a.
80. Tosafot *Shabbot* 49a. For other discussions of matter see Code of Maimonides, Chapter 5, Book of Fundamental Beliefs.
81. See *Shabbot* 130a.
82. *Ketubot* 62b and Midrash Rabba, Leviticus 21:8.
83. *Shabbot* 33b.
84. *Pesikta D'R. Kahana* 88b.
85. *Yalkut* Exodus 349.
86. In the event one merely announces an event at the synagogue, HaGaon HaRav Moshe (*z"l*) notes that such probably would not be a case of incitement.
87. *Orech Chayyim* 308:45.
88. *Tos. Betza* 12a s.v. *hachi garsinan.*
89. *Yam shel Shlomo, Betza,* I:34.
90. *Orech Chayyim* 518:4.
91. *Orech Chayyim* 518:2.
92. *Orech Chayyim* 518:9. Mishneh Berurah does not mention Rashal's ruling in *Hilchot Shabbat* (308:158).
93. Magen Avraham cites *achronim* who contend that those who permit ball playing do so only on *Yom Tov* and not on *Shabbat* [Magen Avraham, *Orech Chayyim* 308:73]. *Aruch HaShulchan,* though, rejects any distinction between *Shabbat* and *Yom Tov* on this question [ibid., 308:70]. The position of Magen Avraham may be rooted in a distinction between *Shabbat* and *Yom Tov.* The observance of the latter (unlike *Shabbat*) contains within it room for personal enjoyment, each according to his preference (*chetzyo*

lachem). Hence, it is possible to say that even according to those authorities who permit ball playing on *Yom Tov*, such would still be prohibited on *Shabbat*. Whereas, if ball playing were allowed on *Shabbat*, a fortiori it would be allowed on *Yom Tov*. (See *Betza* 15b and *Shulchan Aruch, Orech Chayyim* 529:1.)

94. *Orech Chayyim* 518:8. *Aruch HaShulchan* may reflect the opinion of *Terumat HaDeshen* (no. 61) that *Oneg Shabbat* contains a subjective element.
95. Rabbi Yitzhak Yosef, *Sefer Yalkut Yosef* IV, pp. 388–389.
96. *Yerushalmi, Ta'anit* 4:5. See *Korban HaEda*, ad loc., and *Midrash Eicha* II.
97. Cf. *Tur, Orech Chayyim* sec. 308. *Aruch HaShulchan* (*Orech Chayyim* 308:70) also cites this tradition.
98. *Badei HaShulchan* 109:16.
99. *Orech Chayyim* 308:96. This is not to say that ball playing (or any other athletic activity) is inherently not Jewish. The issue is whether it is halachically appropriate as a *Shabbat* activity.
100. *Orech Chayyim* 308:83.
101. 308:157. "It is like a stone that is *muktzah*, per se."
102. This is in contradistinction to the view of Rav Yosef Chayyim Sonnenfeld that ball playing is forbidden even to soothe a crying child (*Resp. Simat Chayyim* 1:71). His opinion, however, is based upon his advocacy of the position of Bet Yosef, who considers the ball *muktzah*. We who accept the position of Rema as modified by Rashal could allow this as well.
103. See the summary in *Encyclopedia Talmudit*, 16 (Jerusalem, 1980), pp. 167–169.
104. Careful attention should also be paid to the type of playing field upon which ball playing may be pursued. Rema, for example, rules that playing with nuts on an earthen floor is prohibited out of concern that one might smooth holes (*masveh gumot*). Hence, ball playing on a non-paved or non-seeded ground is not permitted [*Orech Chayyim* 338:5 and *Mishneh Berurah* 308:158].

    As Rav Na'eh notes in his discussion, even those authorities who permit ball playing do so only on an ad hoc basis, but certainly not as a scheduled event (*Badei HaShulchan*, ibid.).
105. *Orech Chayyim* 308.
106. *Darchei Moshe*, ad loc.
107. Shibbolei HaLeket makes no distinction between *Shabbat* and

Yom Tov. Sefer HaAgur makes a point of emphasizing this lack of differentiation.

108. This is the stated opinion of the Gaon of Vilna (*Bi'ur HaGra, Orech Chayyim* 308:96).
109. Rabbi Moshe Mat, *Sefer Mateh Moshe* (Jerusalem, 1982), sec. 477. In our text *Tosafot* does not mention *Shabbat.*
110. Ibid., sec. 485.
111. *Midrash, Devarim Rabbah, Parshat VaYelech,* sec. 9.
112. Rosh, *Pesahim,* 10:3.
113. In addition, even according to those who disagree with Rosh, this license cannot refer to *Yom Tov*. Accordingly, on *Yom Tov* it would always be prohibited to play ball. Thus, Mateh Moshe's position is at variance with that of *Tosafot,* who explicitly allowed ball playing on *Yom Tov.*
114. *Orech Chayyim* 518 subpar. 1.
115. Ibid., subpar. 4.
116. *Orech Chayyim* 518:12.
117. The above analysis of Shibbolei HaLeket and Rashal strongly indicates that ball playing is prohibited on *Shabbat* and *Yom Tov* irrespective of the type of ball used. This view is in contradistinction to the oral report of the view of HaGaon Rav Yosef Shlomo Eliashiv cited by Rav Yechiel Goldhaber that contemporary balls have the status of a *keli,* even according to Rav Yosef Karo; though most Sephardic authorities continue to ban ball playing to this day. This view, contends Rav Goldhaber, is contradicted by Shibbolei HaLeket himself, for the type of balls used at Tur Shimon were probably Greek in origin or derivation and created exclusively for ball playing [*Bi'ur . . . b'din Kadur* etc., *Kovetz Beit Aharon v'Yisrael,* 6(4) 5741, p. 89 n. 34].
118. Leviticus 23:2 s.v. *Daber.*
119. Ibid.
120. Exodus 23:12 and Rashi, ad loc. The fullest exposition of this idea is to be found in the commentary of Ramban to Leviticus 23:24.
121. Cf. Ramban, *Drasha L'Rosh HaShanah, Kitvei Ramban,* II, ed. H. D. Chavel, (Jerusalem 1964), pp. 217–219. See also *Orech Chayyim* 328:42 and Mishneh Berurah, ibid.
122. Exodus 20:8.
123. Ibid. See also the comments of Sforno, ad loc.
124. See *Shmirat Shabbat K'Hilchata* 16:1.
125. Cf. *Yalkut Yosef* ibid., pp. 387–391. A prominent demurral to this

position is offered by Rabbi Hayim David HaLevi, Sephardic Chief Rabbi of Tel Aviv. He contends that a careful reading of the Shibbolei HaLeket suggests that the issue relating to ball playing is not one of the *muktzah*, but rather a concern for *kavod* and *zilzul Shabbat* [*ShuT Aseh Lecha Rav* 11, (Jerusalem), pp. 94–96].

126. Commonly assumed to be the lowest age of *chinuch*. See the discussion in *Shmirat Shabbat K'Hilchata* 16:3, note 11, that according to Rabbi Shlomo Zalman Auerbach, banging stones with a child below the age of *chinuch* in order to pacify him/her *is* permitted. Other authorities permit this when done in a bizzare fashion, i.e., *kelacher yad*. Under such circumstances, according to Rabbi Auerbach, the rocks would not be considered *muktzah*. It is reasonable, therefore, to conclude that playing ball with a child of this age would be permitted, certainly if done *kelacher yad*.

127. The Bach's rationale for standing for *Yishtabach* suggests that all preparations should take place during the recitation of *Yishtabach*. Accordingly, those who do not cover their heads with the *tallit* during *Pesukai d'zimra* but do so prior to *Barchu* preferably should complete the process during *Yishtabach*.

Glossary

a laz. A rumor.
achronim. Rabbinic sages, generally from the sixteenth century and afterwards.
af al pi ken. Nevertheless.
Aggadah. Narrative section of the Talmud.
Ain ma'avirim al hamitzvot. One does not pass over mitzvot.
aivarim. Limbs of sacrifices.
akalalot. Perverseness.
akira. Picking up a stationary object with the intention to move it to another area, for example, from a private home to a public area.
akkel. Bale.
Aleinu. Prayer at conclusion of morning, afternoon, and evening prayers.
Al Ha'aretz. Literally, "for the land." The concluding phrase of the second blessing of Grace after meals.
al pi din. According to the letter of the law.
aliyah. Literally, "to go up." To emigrate to Israel. To be called to read in the Torah.
amira l'akum. Requesting a Gentile to perform an act on *Shabbat* or *Yom Tov* that Jews are forbidden to do.
Am Yisrael chai. "The nation Israel lives for ever."
Amidah. Literally, "standing." Silent prayer (*Shemoneh Esrai*).
amud. Podium.
anan sadi. General presumption.
ani'nut. Status of bereavement prior to burial.
a'nus. Unintentional, accidental.
apikoros. Apostate; nonbeliever.
aron. Ark.
Aron HaKodesh. Holy Ark.
arvut. Communal responsibility.

Asher natan lanu. Literally, "which you gave us." Phrase of blessing for the Torah.

Ashkenazim. European Jews; followers of the Rema.

ata. You.

Atah chonantanu. Literally, "You have graced us." First phrase of prayer added to evening service to signify conclusion of *Shabbat.*

Av. Hebrew month in which the Holy Temple was destroyed.

availut. Mourning.

avodah. Service in the Holy Temple.

avodah zarah. Literally, "strange worship." Idolatry.

Ayn m'kablin oto. "We do not accept him."

azara. Sanctuary.

baal koreh. Reader of the Holy Scroll (*sefer Torah*).

baal teshuvah. (pl. *baalei teshuva*). Penitent.

bainonim. In between, neither righteous nor wicked.

Bameh madlikin. Literally, "With what do we light?" First phrase of talmudic section dealing with the kindling of the *Shabbat* candles, which is recited in the synagogue on Friday nights.

Bar Mitzvah. Age of male religious maturity: thirteen years.

Barchu. First word of the phrase *Barchu et HaShem* (Bless God).

Baruch She'amar. "Blessed is He" (first words of prayer).

Baruch she'chalak. "Blessed is He that shared (His Torah with man)."

Baruch she'natan. "Blessed is He that gave (us the Torah)."

Bat Mitzvah. Age of female religious maturity: twelve years.

ba'yom hashevi'i tishbot. Rest on the seventh day.

b'dieved. After the fact.

becher. Goblet.

bechor. Firstborn son.

bedavka. Specifically (because).

Be'ezrat HaShem. "With the help of God."

ben Torah. Literally, "son of Torah." Scholar.

berachah. (pl. *berachot*). Blessing.

berachah levatalah. Unwarranted blessing.

Berov am hadrot melech. "In the multitudes of people, the king's glory" (Proverbs 14:28).

besurah tovah. (pl. *besurot tovot*). Good tiding.

bet din. Rabbinic court.

bet hakisai. Lavatory.

Bet HaMikdash. The Holy Temple.

bet mishteh. House (place) dedicated for drinking alcoholic beverages.

bezah haderech. In such a manner.

bima. Platform in synagogue near Ark.

Birkat HaChodesh. Blessing for the new (lunar) month.

Birkat HaMazon. Grace after meals.

Birkat Kohanim. The blessing of the *kohanim* (those Jews that descend from Aaron, the High Priest).

birshut hakohanim. With permission of the *kohanim*.

bittul aseh. Violations of a positive commandment.

bittul Torah. Waste of precious time.

b'nai Torah. Students of Torah.

Boneh berachamav Yerushalayim, Amen. Literally, "rebuilds Jerusalem with His mercy, Amen." Third blessing of the Grace after meals.

Boneh Yerushalayim. Literally, "He who builds Jerusalem." Third blessing of the Grace after the meals without any reference to "mercy."

berachah she'eina tzricha. An unnecessary blessing.

Brich Hu. "Blessed be He."

brit milah. Covenant of circumcision.

bizui mitzvah. Violation of a commandment.

Chabad. Hasidic sect (Lubavitch).

chabadnik. Member of the Chabad sect.

chachmei Yisrael. Jewish sages.

chachmim. Sages, wise men.

chaiyecha kodem. Your life takes priority.

challah. (pl. *challot*). Twisted, braided loaves of bread served on *Shabbat* and holidays.

Chamisha asar b'Av. The fifteenth day of the Hebrew month of Av.

chas v'shalom. "Heaven forbid."

chayai she'ah. Short period of time to live.

Chazak, chazak, v'nitchazaik. "Be strong, be strong, and be strengthened."

chesed. Kindness.

chetzyo lachem. One half (of the holiday time) should be spent caring for pleasurable, human needs.

chibuv mitzvah. Expression of pure love for the performance of a mitzvah.

chilul HaShem. Profanation of God's Name.

chinuch. Education. Torah study and observance of mitzvot of minors.

chiyuv. Obligation.

Chol HaMoed. Intermediate days between first and last days of such holidays as Sukkot and Passover.

choleh. A sick person.
Chumash. (pl. *Chumashim*). Pentateuch.
chumrah yetera. Excessive stringency.
churban. Destruction.
chutzpah. Audacity; unmitigated gall.
daat Torah. Consensus or perspective of Torah scholars.
da'ato hashfaila. Lowly spirit.
daven (davening). Pray (praying).
Dayan ha'emet. Literally, "Blessed be the true judge." Final phrase of blessing recited upon hearing of the death of a close relative.
derashah. Sermon.
din. (pl. *dinim*). (Letter of the) law.
duchen (duchening). Blessing of the *kohanim*.
dvar Torah. A Torah message.
ein berai'ra. No alternative choice.
Eretz Yisrel. Land of Israel.
Eretz Yisrael le'am Yisrael al pi torat Yisrael. "The land of Israel belongs to the Jewish people according to the Torah."
erev. Eve (of Sabbath or *Yom Tov*).
erev Shabbat. Friday evening.
eruv. (pl. *eruvim*). Symbolic enclosure to permit carrying on the Sabbath.
et la'asot. Time for action.
etrog. Citron (part of the ceremony observed with the palm branch of Sukkot).
ezrat nashim. Women's section of synagogue.
frum. Very observant.
frumkeit. The state of scrupulous observance.
gabbai. Agent, surrogate.
gadlu. Declare the greatness.
gadol. Adult. Great in stature.
gadol habayit. Head of household.
gadol hador. (pl. *gedolai hador*). Outstanding sage of the generation.
galut. Diaspora.
Gan Eden. Paradise.
Gaon. Title granted to great rabbinic sages.
Gehemon. Purgatory.
gematria. Process of comparing Hebrew words of similar numerical values. (Hebrew letters have specific numerical values.)
Gemorah. Talmud.

ger. Convert.
ger toshav. Special, semi-convert in ancient Israel who committed to believe in God and perform certain commandments.
ger tzedek. Altruistic, sincere convert.
gerushah. Divorced woman.
ge'ulah. Redemption.
gezairah. A rabbinic ban or ordinance.
hachnasa. Act of carrying item into a private domain from a public domain.
Haggadah. Guide for the rituals of the first night of Passover.
HaGaon. Title for a great rabbinic sage.
Hakadosh Baruch Hu. "The Holy One, Blessed be He."
Hakail hakadosh. Literally, "the Holy God." Last phrase of the third blessing of the *Amidah*.
halachah. (pl. *halachot*). Jewish law.
halachic. Jewish legal (concept).
Hallel. Prayer of thanksgiving and praise.
Hamatchil b'mitzvah omrim lo gemor. "Whoever commences a mitzvah, should conclude."
Hamotzi. Literally, "who brings forth." Main portion of blessing for bread.
hanacha. Consciously placing an item in a stationary position.
hanhaga. Behavior.
ha'poraish mi'darkai tzibur. One who separates himself from community practices.
HaRav. Rabbi.
Hashata avdai. "This year we are slaves."
HaShem. God.
hashva'at gumot. Filling in and smoothing holes.
hasid. (pl. *hasidim*). Pious follower of the Baal Shem Tov and his disciples.
Hatikvah. Literally, "the hope." Israel (Zionist) national anthem.
Hatov shimcha. Literally "good is Your Name." Last phrase of the next-to-last blessing of the *Amidah*.
Hatov u'maitiv. Literally "who is good and bestows good." Last phrase of blessing recited upon hearing good news.
Havdalah. Concluding prayer of *Shabbat*.
Hazon. Literally, "Who sustains." Last phrase of the first blessing of the Grace after meals.
hazzan. (pl. *hazzanim*). Cantor. Hazzanut—The music of cantors.

hechsher mitzvah. Preparation for a mitzvah.
hefker. Belonging to no one.
hefsid merubah. Major financial loss.
hefsik. Undue interruption.
herem. Excommunication.
hester panim. Era wherein God's glory is not manifested.
hiddur mitzvah. Beautification of a mitzvah.
hiddush. Novel, creative concept.
hillul Shabbat. Violation of *Shabbat.*
Hinai kail yeshuati. Literally, "Behold, God is my salvation." First phrase of *Havdalah* ceremony.
hotza'a. Act of consciously carrying an item out of a private domain to a public domain.
humra. (pl. *humrot*). Stringency.
ikar. Primary; fundamental.
Iyar. Hebrew month after Nisan.
kabbalah. Mysticism, tradition.
kabbalat hatorah. When the Torah was received on Mt. Sinai.
kabbalat mitzvot. Acceptance of mitzvot.
kabbalat ol malchut shemayim. Acceptance of the yoke of heaven.
kabbalat Shabbat. Onset of *Shabbat.*
Kaddish. Memorial prayer.
kashrut. A product observing Jewish dietary rules.
ketoret. Fragrances, spices.
Kadosh, kadosh, kadosh. "Holy, Holy, Holy."
kafui tova. Ingrate.
kalut rosh. Excessive levity.
kal v'chomer. Argument from minor to major.
karmelit. Open courtyard, deemed neither private nor public domain.
kavana. Intention.
kavod. Honor, homage.
kavod HaShechina. Homage to God.
kavod hatorah. Homage to Torah.
kedoshim. Holy people.
kedushah. Holiness.
Kedushat Shabbat. The sanctity of *Shabbat.*
kehilla. Community.
kelacher yad. Not a normal mode of action or behavior.
keli. Utensil.
keriat hatorah. The public reading of the Torah.

kesher resha'im. Confederacy of wicked.
ketuvim. Holy writings.
kevi'ut. Permanency.
kezayit. The size of an olive.
kibaid. Honor.
kibud. Honor.
kibud av. Honoring a father.
Kiddush. Sanctification of *Shabbat* and *Yom Tov* via prayer over wine.
Kiddush HaChodesh. Sanctification of the (new) lunar month.
Kiddush HaShem. Sanctification of the Holy Name of God.
Kiddush h'Shem. Sanctification of God's Name.
kippah. Skullcap (yarmulka).
kiruv. Enabling Jews to become closer to Judaism.
kisai shel Eliyahu. Chair (seat) of Elijah.
k'lal Yisrael. The Jewish people.
kohen. (pl. *kohanim*). Priest; descendent of Aaron, the High Priest.
kohen gadol. High Priest.
kol b'isha evrah. Woman's (singing) voice is licentious.
kol hatorah kulo. The entire Torah.
korban. (pl. *korbanot*). Animal sacrifice.
kos. Goblet.
kos shel berachah. Goblet used for the performance of a mitzvah (i.e., *kiddush*).
kosher (noun: koshrut). Jewish dietary laws.
kotel. Western Wall of Holy Temple; Wailing Wall.
Kri'ya. Mourner's obligation to rend garment.
Kudsha Brich Hu. "The Holy One, Blessed be He."
Kuti. Sect of Judaism that did not subscribe to all mitzvot.
Lachem. "To you."
Lag b'Omer. The thirty-third day of the counting of the omer. A date celebrated as a semi-holiday.
laishev basukkah. To sit (dwell) in a *sukkah*.
lashon hara'nik. Gossipmonger.
l'chumra b'alma. For the sake of being stringent.
leayla. Beyond.
lechat'chila. Ab initio.
lechem mishneh. Two whole twisted Sabbath loaves of bread.
ledor vador. For all generations.
lehachis. To incite hateful behavior.
lehorot. To instruct.

leshana haba. Next year.
Leshana haba b'nai chorim. "Next year we shall be free."
Leshana haba b'Yerushalayim. "Next year in Jerusalem."
Lashem shamayim. "For the sake of heaven."
letei'avon. Personal pleasure.
levi (p. levi'im). Member of the tribe of Levi.
l'fi re'ot eynei HaMorah. Within the purview of the judge.
Lifnai iver lo titain michshol. "Do not place a stumbling block before a blindman" (Leviticus 19:14).
lishmore v'la'asot. To observe and to do.
Li'yot am chofshi b'artzeinu. "To be a free people in our own land."
Lo ta'teh mishpat ger yatom. "Do not twist the rights of the convert (and) orphan" (Deuteronomy 24:17).
lo tisnah. Do not hate.
Lo tosef. (pl. *lo tosefu*). "Do not add (to the mitzvot)" (Deuteronomy 4:2).
luach. Calendar; guide for synagogue service.
lulav. Palm branch.
Ma'ariv. Evening prayers.
ma'aseh bet din. Official action of *bet din.*
Machzor. Holiday prayerbook.
maftir. The *Shabbat* Torah portion is divided into seven parts. After seven people are called to the Torah, part of the last portion is repeated and is called *maftir*. The one called to *maftir* also reads the prophetic section.
mai'sit u'maidiach. Incite another to commit idolatry.
maizid. Willingly violating Jewish law.
makom HaMikdash. Site of the Holy Temple.
mapolet. Collapse of walls.
mashgiach. Supervisor.
mashgiach ruchani. Supervisor of (student's) religious values.
masveh gumot. Smooth holes.
matzah. Unleavened bread used on Passover.
mechallel Shabbat befarhesiah. One who publicly desecrates the Sabbath.
Medinat Yisrael. State of Israel.
mee toch. Since.
Megillah. Scroll.
Megillat Esther. The Scroll of Esther.
mekabel Shabbat. Assuming the sanctity of *Shabbat.*

mekabel tuma. Contract ritual impurity.
mekudash. Sanctified.
melachah. Act prohibited on *Shabbat* and/or *Yom Tov*.
menorah. Candelabra for Chanukah (eight lamps).
meraglim. Spies.
mesai'a. Assisting (a sinner).
mesorah. Tradition.
mid'oraita. Biblical.
midrash. Biblical legends.
mikra'ai kodesh. Sacred assembly.
mikvah. (pl. *mikva'ot*). Ritualarium.
milah. Circumcision.
min. From.
min hashamayim. From heaven.
Mincha. Afternoon prayers.
minhag. (pl. *minhagim*). Custom.
minhag ra. Bad custom.
mishmar. Division of *kohanim* and/or *levi'im* in the Holy Temple.
minyan. Quorum of ten Jews.
mishkan. Tabernacle.
Mishnah. Oral traditions edited by Rav Yehudah HaNasi.
mishteh. Drinking party.
mitzvah. (pl. *mitzvot*). Commandment: good deed.
mitzvah d'rabbim. Public mitzvah.
mizbei'ach. Altar.
mizmor LeTodah. A psalm of thanksgiving.
Mizmor Shir Leyom HaShabbat. "A psalm, a song for the day of *Shabbat*."
modim. Appreciation.
mohel. Circumcision specialist.
mosar. Informer.
Moshe keebal Torah mi Sinai umsaruha le Yehoshua. "Moses accepted the Torah from Sinai and gave it to Joshua."
motzi. Include another.
muktzah. Item forbidden to move on *Shabbat* or holidays.
mumar. Apostate.
my chazit. Idiomatic phrase indicating that one has no right to kill another to save one's own life.
myrtle. A spice.
Na'aseh v'nishma. "We shall act and we will listen."

nachash hakadmoni. Original serpent.
nahagu. People took upon themselves a custom.
nasi. Leader, president.
netilat yadayim. Ritual washing of hands.
nazir. Person prohibited to shave or drink alcoholic beverages.
ner tamid. Eternal light.
nesi'at kapa'im. Manner in which *kohanim* hold their hands during the priestly blessing.
nevi'im. Prophets.
nidah. Menstruant.
niddui. Excommunication.
omer. Offering brought to the Holy Temple on the sixteenth of Nisan, subsequent to which the new harvest was permissible to eat.
oneg. Pleasure, enjoyment.
ones. Accidental; beyond human responsibility.
ora. Light.
panim el panim. Face to face.
parsha. (pl. *parshiyot*). Torah portion.
parshat hashavua. Torah portion of the week.
parshat parah. Special Torah reading dealing with the red heifer.
parshat zachor. Special Torah reading recalling the war with Amalak.
pasul. Flawed.
perutah. (pl. *perutot*). Minor ancient coin.
Pesach. Passover holiday commemorating the Exodus of the Jews from Egypt.
pesak. Halachic decision.
pesikta. Name of ancient work.
pikuach nefesh. Life-threatening condition.
posek. (pl. *poskim*). Decisor of Jewish law.
p'sukai d'zimra. Section of morning prayers dealing with praise to God, prior to *Barchu*.
pur'anuyot. Tragic events.
Purim. Holiday commemorating the victory of Mordechai and Esther and the Jews of ancient Persia over their enemy, Haman.
Rabbenu. Our teacher, our Rabbi.
raishit tzmichat ge'ulatainu. The precursor of redemption.
rasha. Evil person.
Rav. Rabbi.
rebbe. Hasidic rabbi; teacher, mentor.
rebbono shel olam. Master of the universe.
Retzai. "Be favorable." Phrase prior to *modim* section in the *Amidah*.

Rev'i. "Support me."
revi'it. One quarter (a measure).
ribit devarim. Oral interest.
rishonim. Early sages; after the period of Gaonim until the fifteenth century.
rishut. Evil.
rishut harabbim. Public thoroughfare.
rodef. Pursuer.
Rosh Chodesh. First day of Hebrew (lunar) month.
Rosh Chodesh Av. First day of the Hebrew month of Av.
Rosh HaYeshivah. Head of rabbinical academy.
Ruach acheret imo. "(He) had a different spirit in him."
Rubo kekulo. Majority deemed comparable to entirety.
safek derabbonim l'kula. Doubt of rabbinic law, decided leniently.
safek safaikah. Double doubt.
sakana. Danger.
sandak. Person holding child during circumcision.
Sanhedrin. Supreme Jewish court of law.
s'chach. Covering of Sukkah.
secheeta. Squeezing.
Seder. Literally, "order." Passover eve service.
sefer. (pl. *sefarim*). Book.
sefer Torah (pl. *sifrai Torah*). Torah scroll.
Sefirah (also Sefirat HaOmer). The counting of the *omer* commencing the second night of Passover and continuing for forty-nine days.
seudah. Meal.
seudat Rosh Chodesh. Rosh Chodesh meal.
sevara. Logic.
Shabbat. Saturday, Sabbath.
Shacharit. Morning prayers.
shamash. Sexton.
shaveh lakol. Behavior practiced by most people.
Shavuot. Holiday commemorating the giving of the Torah.
She'asani kirtzono. "That You made me according to Your will."
She'hecheyanu. Literally, "Who kept us alive." Phrase of blessing recited upon acquiring new items or hearing good news.
Shem. Holy Name.
Shemoneh Esrai. Silent prayer; *Amidah.*
Shem U'Malchut. Name of God and reference to His kingdom.
sheva berachot. Seven blessings (recited for bride and groom).

shevi'it. Sabbatical year.
shidduch. Matrimonial match.
shivah. Seven; generally the seven days of mourning.
shliach. Agent, surrogate.
shliach tzibur. Agent of the congregation that leads services; *hazzan*.
shlichut. Process of serving as an agent.
Shlita. Acronym signifying "May he live to a long and good life."
Shlomo Hamelech. King Solomon.
shloshim. Thirty. The first thirty days from burial.
shofar. Ram's horn.
shogaig. Unintentional.
shokel. Quiver, shake.
shtibel. Informal place of worship.
Sh'yibaneh bimhaira b'yameinu. "That will be built speedily in our time."
siddur. Prayerbook.
siman. Sign, omen.
siman tov. Good sign, omen.
siman berachah. Omen of blessing.
simchat Yom Tov. Joy of holiday.
sukkah. (pl. *sukkot*). Tabernacle, frail booth. Holiday after Yom Kippur.
S'u yedaichem kodesh, u'varchu et HaShem. "Lift up your holy hands and bless God."
ta'anug. Pleasure.
Tachnun. Daily prayer of confession.
tafel. Secondary importance.
tallit. Prayer shawl.
tallit gadol. Large prayer shawl.
tallit katan. Literally, "Small prayer shawl." *Tzitzit* worn under garments.
Talmud. Repository of oral Torah traditions and debates.
Tammuz. Hebrew month prior to the month of Av.
tefila. Prayer.
tefila b'tzibur. Public prayer.
tefillin. Phylacteries.
teshuvah. Repentance.
tevilah. Immersion in a ritualarium.
tinok she'nishba. A child captured by Gentiles who never becomes aware of Jewish traditions.

tirchah. Excessive, burdensome.
tirchah d'tzibur. Excessive public burden.
Tishah b'Av. Literally, "Ninth of Av." Fast day commemorating the destruction of the Holy Temple.
Tishrai. Hebrew month of Jewish New Year.
tiyol. Recreation.
Toda. "Thank you."
Torah. Jewish bible, written and oral tradition.
Trai koli lo mishtami. "Two simultaneous voices are of no concern."
traifah. Not kosher.
tzaddik. (pl. *tzaddikim*). Saintly, pious person.
Tzadka mi'meni. "She is more righteous than me."
tzedakah. Charity.
tzibur. Community, congregation.
Tzitzit. Religious fringes on four-cornered garment.
tzorech iyun. Requires further research.
tzorech ma. A minor or insigificant need.
u'gemilat chasadim. Lovingkindness.
Uva l'tzion. "And shall come to Zion (the redeemer)." Prayer directly prior to *Aleinu*.
uvda d'chol. Not a proper *Shabbat* activity.
V'ahavta l'raiachu. "And you shall love your neighbor."
V'atem lo teitzu mipetach baito. "And you shall not leave the opening of your home."
VaYavaraich David. "And David blessed." Prayer in *Shacharit* (*p'sukai d'zimra*).
V'chai bahem. "And you shall live by them."
V'dabar davar. To limit speech on *Shabbat* to concepts of *Shabbat*.
Ve'horashtem. "And you shall dispossess."
V'hodatem levanecha v'livnai vanecha. "And you shall make known to your sons and to their sons."
V'imru amen. "And let us say Amen."
Viyeshavta ba. "And dwell in it."
v'kidashto. "And you shall make him holy."
V'shamru. "And you shall observe."
V'tzivanu. "And commanded us."
V'yas Kalev et ha'am. "And Kalev stilled the people."
Ya'aleh v'yavo. "Go up and come." (Section containing reference of prayers for a blessed month.)
yahrzeit. Anniversary of death.

Yamim Nora'im. Days of Awe.
yayin. Wine.
Yechi hamelech. "Long live the king."
yaish omrim. Some say.
yerushah. Inheritance.
yeshivah. (pl. *yeshivot*). Institution for Torah and rabbinic study.
yeshivat sukkah. Dwelling in the *sukkah*.
Yesh lachem al ma lismoch. "They have an halachic authority upon which to rely."
yetzer hara. Inclination for sin; evil impulse.
yetzer tov. Inclination for good.
yetzer tov shoftan. Guided by the good inclination.
Yevarech'che'cha. "(May God) bless you." First word of priestly blessing.
Y'hai Shmai Raba. "Let His Name be great" (or "Let His great Name").
yichus. Pedigreed lineage.
Yishtabach. "Praise." First word of daily morning prayer prior to *kaddish* and *Barchu*.
yishuv eretz Yisrael. Settling the land of Israel.
yishuv HaAretz. Settling the land (of Israel).
Yisrael v'oraita chad hu. "Israel and the Torah are one."
Yom Kippur. Fast of Atonement.
Yom Tov. Holiday.
Yom Tov ketzat. Semi-holiday.
Yom Yerushalayim. Day Jews gained access to the Western Wall.
zacheh. Worthy.
zayit (pl. zaytim). Olive (size of measurement).
zechut. Privilege, advantage.
zemirot. Sabbath songs.
zilzul Shabbat. Disrespect for *Shabbat*.
Zimun. Introductory prayer added to Grace after meals when three or more males are in attendance.
z'kainim. Elders, sages.
z"l. *Zichrono levracha*—"May his memory be a blessing."
z'man. Time.
z'nut. Sexual promiscuity.
zonah. Prostitute.
z'rizim. Zealous; doing a mitzvah at the earliest time available.

References

Aaron ben Yaakov Hakohen of Luniel, codifier of Jewish law, (*Orchot Chayyim*). Narbonne (end of thirteenth to first half of fourteenth century).

Arieli, R. Yitzchok. See *Einayim LeMishpat.*

Aruch HaSchulchan, novellae and halachic rulings on the Codes. R. Yechiel Michal Epstein. Belorussia (1829–1908).

Asher ben Yechiel, Rabbeinu (Rosh), talmudist and codifier of Jewish law. Germany (1250–1327).

Ateret Zekeinim, R. Menachem Mendel Orbach, halachic decisor. Vienna, Kracow Kurishtan (1620).

Avodat HaGerhuni, R. Gershon ben Yitzchok Ashkenazy, Germany. Metz, France 1693. Disciple of Bach, Halachic scholar.

Avnei Nezer, responsa, R. Avraham ben Ze'ev Nachum Bornstein. Sochaczew, Poland (1830–1910).

Baal Haitur, Codes of law, R. Yitzchok b. Abbaa Mari, Marseilles, France; Spain (1120?-1190?).

Babbad R. Yosef. See *Minchat Chinuch.*

Bach, commentary on Codes of R. Yaakov b. Asher (Tur), R. Yoel Sirkes. Poland (1561–1640).

Badei Hashulchan, HaRav Chayyim Naeh, contemporary halachic sage, Jerusalem. Commentary on Shulchan Aruch HaRav, entitled *Ketzot HaShulchan, Badai Hasculchan* contains sources and footnotes.

Bai'er Moshe, R. Moshe Stern, Debrinitziner Rav (Boro, Brooklyn, N.Y.) *Responsa*, contemporary hasidic leader and Posek.

Baruch HaLevi Epstein, R. Bible commentator. *Torah Temimah, Tosefot Berachah*, also commentary on the prayer book and Avot, *Baruch She'Amar*. Russia (1860–1942).

Baier Heitiv, commenary on *Shulchan Aruch*, R. Yehudah Ashkenazi. Frankfurt, Germany (1730–1770).

Bet Ephraim, responsa, R. Ephraim Zalman b. Menachem Mannes Margolis. Brody, Russia (1760–1820). *Shar Ephraim on Keriyot HaTorah.*

Bet Shmuel, R. Shmuel b. R. Or Sshraga Faivish, commentary on Codes. Lvov, Shidlov (d. 1694).

Bet Yosef, commentary on Codes of R. Yaakov b. Asher (Tur) (R. Yosef ben Ephraim Caro, author, *Codes of Jewish Law* (*Shulchan Aruch*), which is divided into four sections: *Orech Chayyim* (prayers and holidays); *Yoreh De'ah* (Kashrut, Torah, Mourning); *Even HaEzer* (marriage, divorce); *Choshen Mishpat* (torts, jurisprudence). Spain; Safed, Israel (1488–1575). Also commentary on codes of Maimonides, *Kesef Mishneh.*

Binyan Sholomo, responsa R. Shlomo, Chief Rabbi, Vilno, halachic sage, b. 1820, d. 1908.

Binyan Tzion, halachic responsa. R. Yaakov Etinger. Manheim, Altuna, Germany, (1788–1862).

Birkai Yosef, R. Chayyim Yosef David Azulai (Chida), halachist, kabbalist. Glosses to *Shulchan Aruch.* Jerusalem (1838–1933).

Bnai Yesachar, Rav Zevi Elimelech Shapira, *Dinov*-hasidic essays Shabbat and Holidays, Rav Munkatch Dinov.

R. Yosef Caro. See *Bet Yosef.*

Channiel b. Chushiel, Rabbeinu, talmudic commentator and halachic scholar. Rome (d. 1056).

Chanukat HaTorah, R. (Avraham) Yehoshua Heshel Rav, Lublin, Kracow, Brisk; author homiletic volume, Rebbe of the Shach.

Charaidim, R. Elazar Azkari Constantinople (b. 1533, d. 1600) analyses of *mitzvot.*

Chatam Sofer, R. Moshe Sofer, halachic scholar, *responsa, Torat Moshe,* Pentateuch. Pressburg, Czechoslovakia (1763–1830).

Chatan Sofer, HaRav Shmuel be R. Simcha Bunon Ehrenfeld, Rav Mittisdorf (Mattersberg, Austria). Grandson of the Chatam Sofer (1835–1883).

Chav'at Yair, responsa, R. Yair Chayyim b. Moshe Shimshon Bachrach. Germany (1638–1702).

Chayyei Adam, code on *Orech Chayyim,* R. Avraham Danzig(er), also author of *Chachmat Adam,* code on Yoreh De'ah. Danzig, Vilna (1748–1820).

Chayyim Sonnenfeld, R. Yosef, *responsa, Simcaht Chayyim.* Jerusalem (1849–1932).

Chelkat M'Chokaik, commentary, *Codes Even Haezer*, Rav Moshe Lina (1605? -1658). Rav, Brisk and Vilna.

Chidah, halachic scholar, kabbalist, R. Chayyim Yosef Dovid Azulai. Jerusalem (1724–1806).

Chofetz Chayyim. See *Biur Halachah.*

Daat Torah, commentary on Codes, R. Shalom Mordechai b. Moshe Shvadron (Maharsham-Moreinue Rav Shalom Mordechai). Galicia (1835 -1911).

Darkei Teshuvah, Commentary on Codes, R. Tzvi Hirsch Shapira. Munkach (1850–1914).

Derech HaChayyim, Codes, R. Yaakov ben Yaakov Mose Lorberbaum of Lissa, Poland (1760–1832). Published in prayer books.

Drishah uPrishah, commentary on Codes of the Tur, R. Yehoshua ben Alexander Hakohen Falk. Lublin, Poland; Lemberg, Germany (1555–1614).

Druk, R. Zalman, Contemporary Rav of Great Synagogue in Jerusalem, halachic scholar, *Mikrai'ai Kodesh, Laws of Keriyat HaTorah.*

Eiger, R. Akiva, talmudist and halachic sage Eisenstadt, Austria; Posen, Poland. Lithuania (1761–1837).

Einayim LeMishpat, talmudic commentaries. R. Yitzchok Arieli, contemporary dean, Yeshiva Merkaz HaRab. Jerusalem (published 1947).

Aishel Avraham, commentary on Codes (*Mahadura Tenina*). R. Avraham Wharman, Butchatch, Ukraine (1859–1920).

Engel, R. Yosef, halachic and talmudic scholar, *Gilyonai HaShas*, Bet HaOtzur. Kracow, Poland (1859–1920).

Epstein R. Baruch. See R. Baruch.

Feinstein, R. Moshe, renowned contemporary halachic scholar, *responsa, Iggerot Moshe*. Russia, New York (1895–1986).

Frank, R. Tzvi Pesach, halachic scholar (*Eretz Tzvi*, also *Mikra'ei Kodesh*), former chief rabbi, Jerusalem (1873–1960). *Har Tzvi, responsa.*

Gershon b. Yehudah, Rabbeinu. Major German talmudic scholar (960–1028).

Grodszensky, R. Chayyim Ozer, rabbinic leader and sage, *responsa, Acheizer*. Vilna, Lithuania (1863–1940).

H'Admor of Lubavitch, Rabbi Menachem Mendel Schneerson, international spiritual leader of Chabad hasidim. Brooklyn, New York. (1902–1993). *LiKutai Piskai Halacha U'Minhag.*

HaGra (Vilna Gaon), halachic scholar (*Siddur, Likutei Dinim, Glosses on Codes, Divrei Eliyahu* (Prophets). R. Eliyahu b. Shlomo Zalman. Vilna (1720–1797).

Halevi, R. Chayyim David, Sefardic Chief Rabbi, Tel Aviv, *responsa, Aseh LechaRav.*

HaMaor, contemporary rabbinic journal (United States).

Hapardes (1981). Contemporary rabbinic journal, published by R. Simcha Elberg (*z"l*), New York.

HaRah, R. Aaron HaLevi (Barcelona, 1235–1300).

Haviv, R. Moshe b. Shlomo ibn, talmudic commentator, Turkey (1654–1696). Tosafot *Yom HaKippurim.*

Hazon Ish, halachic scholar (Israel). R. Avraham Yeshiayah Karlitz (1878–1953).

Henkin, R. Yosef Eliyahu, halachic decisor: *Eidut LeYisrael, Lev Ivrah* (synagogue Luach); Belorussia and New York (1880–1973).

Hirsch, R. Samson Raphael, German Orthodox leader; biblical commentaries, *Responsa Shamesh Marpeh*; Frankfurt (1808–1888).

Hoffman, R. Dovid Tzvi, Rosh Yeshivah, Heldesheimer Seminary; Halachic authority; *Responsa Melamid LeHo'il*; Berlin (1843–1921).

Hurowitz, R. Pinchas b. Tzvi Hirsh HaLevi (*Haflah* and *HaMakneh*) Talmudic commentary, *Panim Yafot*, Bible commentary; Frankfurt, Germany (1730–1805).

Hutner, R. Yitzchok, contemporary Rosh Yeshivah, Rabbi Chaim Berlin Rabbinical Academy (Pachad Yitzchok); New York (1905–1980).

Kesef Mishneh. See *Bet Yosef.*

Kitzur Shulchan Aruch, R. Shlomo ben Yosef Ganzfried. Popular abridged Codes; Ungar, Hungary (1804–1886).

Kluger, R. Shlomo, halachic scholar: Responsa, *Tuv Taam v'Daat, HaElef Lecha Shlomo*, Haggadah; Brody, Russia (1785–1869).

Kol Ram, Rabbi Avraham Fishelis, biblical interpretations cited in the name of his rebbe, Rav Moshe Feinstein; contemporary author; New York.

Korban HaEda, Rav Mirlish Frenkel, Halachic sage; Rav Frankfurt, Berlin (1703–1762).

Landau, R. Yechezkal **b. Yehudah**, Halachic authority: *Responsa, Noda B'Yehudah, Dagul Mervavah, Tzlach* (commentary on the Talmud); Prague, Czechoslovakia (1713–1793).

Luria, R. Shlomo **b. Yechiel (Rashal)**, Talmudic commentator and

Halachic scholar; *Yam shel Shlomo* and *Chachmat Shlomo*; Poland (1510?–1574).

Likutai Ma'harich, R. Yisrael Chaim Friedman, compendium of halachot and customs pertaining to prayers; Rav Rechov, Hungary (late nineteenth century–early twentieth century).

Luach Dinim L'Chayalai Tzahal, religious guide, prayers, and observance for members of the Israel Armed Forces; services compiled by Rav Gad Navon, Chief Rabbi of Tzahal (1989).

Ma'alot HaTorah, Rav Avraham, Brother of the Vilna Gaon; essays on the value of Torah learning; Vilna (eighteenth century).

Mabit, R. Moshe b. Yosef Mitroni, Responsa, *Kiryat Sefer* also commentary on Rambam; Safed (1505–1585).

Machatzit HaShekel, Rabbi Samuel haLevi Kolin, commentary on the *Magen Avraham*; Bohemia (1720–1806).

Madani Shmuel (commentary on Codes of Passover) and *Minchat Shabbat* (Laws of *Shabbat*), R. Shmuel HaKohen Burstein, author's paternal grandfather; Shatava Ukraine (1860–1920).

Magen Avraham, R. Avraham Abeli Gombiner, Halachic commentator on *Shulchan Aruch*; Poland (1637–1683).

Magid Mishneh, R. Vidal Yom Tov of Tolosa, commentary on Rambam's codes; Spain (second half of fourteenth century).

Maharal of Prague, R. Yehuda Loew b. Bezalel; Halachic scholar and kabbalist; *Tiferet Yisrael*; Prague, Czechoslovakia (1525–1609).

Maharam Shick, R. Moshe b. Yosef Shick, Rabbi and Halachic scholar; Hungary (1807–1879).

Mahari Berunah, Rabbi Yisrael ben Chayyim, German rav, Berunah and Regensburg (1400–?).

Maharil, Rabbi Yaakov ben Moshe, head of German, Austrian, and Bohemian Jewish communities (1340?–1427).

Maharsha, R. Shmuel Eliezer Halevi Aydels, Commentator, Talmud; Poland and Austria (1555–1631).

Maharsham. See *Daat Torah*.

Margolit HaYam, HaRav Reuven Margolit (*z"l*). Commentary on Sanhedrin; contemporary Israeli sage.

Mateh Levi, Rav Mordechai HaLevi Horowitz, Responsa; Rav, Frankfurt (published 1891).

Mateh Moshe, Rav Moshe ben R. Avraham. Collection of customs, disciple of Rashal; Poland.

Matikai Shmuah, Yitzchok Zev HaLevi. Collection of Torah thoughts of the Brisker Rav, HaGaon R. Soloveitchik, last Rav, Brisk; Jerusalem (1886–1960).

R. Meir Simcha HaKohen, Talmudic and Halachic sage; *Meshech Chachmah* (biblical commentary), commentary on Rambam; Dvinsk, Lithuania (1843–1926).

Meiri, R. Menachem b. Shlomo Meiri (HaMeiri), talmudic commentator; *Bet Habechirah*; Provence, France (1249–1316).

Mechilta, R. Shimon Bar Yochai, Halachic *midrash*, Exodus.

Mechilta, Tannaic commentary of Shemot.

Midrash Rabbah, oldest Amoraic classical *midrash* on the Pentateuch and the *Megillot.*

Minchat Chinuch, commentary on *Chinuch* (list of biblical mitzvot), R. Yosef Babad. Tarnopol, Russia (nineteenth century).

Minchat Elazer, R. Chayyim Elazar Shapira, Responsa; *Minchat Elazer, Darchei Chaim V'Shalom*; Munkach (1882–1947).

Minchat Pitim, Rav Meir ben Aaron Judah Arik, Halachah responsa; Tarnow (1855–1926).

Minchat Shabbat. See *Madani Shmuel.* (Sha'ar HaTzion).

Minchat Shlomo, R. Shlomo Zalman Auerbach (*z"l*) Responsa; Contemporary sage; Rosh Yeshivah, Kol Torah Jerusalem.

Mishnah, Compendium of Oral Torah, redacted by R. Yehudah HaNasi (later half of the second century and beginning of third century C.E.).

Mishneh Berurah. See *Biur Halacha (Sha'ar Hatziyon).*

Rabbi Mordechai b. Hillel HaKohen, German rabbinical authority (1240–1298).

Naeh, R. Avraham Chayyim. Contemporary Jerusalem halachic scholar; *Ketzot HaShulchan, Badei HaShulchan*, commentary on codes of *Shulchan Aruch HaRav*; Israel (b. 1925).

Netziv, R. Naftali Tzvi Hirsch. Talmudic and Halachic scholar; Berlin; Volozhin, Russia (1817–1893).

Or HaChayyim, R. Chayyim Michel, Bible commentator; (1792–1846).

Peri Megadim, R. Yosef b. Meir Teomim. Commentary on Codes; Lvov, Russia (Ukraine) (1727–1792).

Pirkei D'R. Eliezer, Eighth century aggadic work.

P'nei Yehoshua, R. Yaakov Yehoshua. Talmudic commentary; Lvov, Berlin, Frankfurt (1681–1756).

Prishah. See *Drishah u Prishah.*

Ramban, R. Moshe b. Maimon, halachic authority; *Yad Chazaka, Sefer HaMitzvot*; Egypt (1135–1284).

Ramban, R. Moshe b. Nachman, Bible commentator and Halachic scholar; Verona, Italy (1194–1270).

Ran, R. Nissim b. Reuven Gerondi. Halachic scholar; Barcelona (fourteenth century).

Rashal. See R. Shlomo Luria.

Rashba, R. Shlomo ben Aderet, Talmudic commentary and responsa; Rav Barcelona (1235–1310).

Rashi, R. Shlomo b. Yitzchok, Bible and Talmud authority; Troyes, France (b. 1040).

Rema, R. Moshe b. Yisrael Isserles, halachic scholar; Kracow, Poland (1525- or 1530–1572).

Rif, R. Yitzchok b. Yaakov Alfasi, talmudic and halachic scholar; Fez, Morocco (1013–1103).

Ritva, Rabbi Yom Tov ben Avraham Ishbili, Seville, Spain (1250–1330).

Rivash, R. Yitzchok, b. R. Shaishet; Barcelona, Spain; Algiers, Algeria (1362 to 1407).

Rosh. See Rabbeinu Asher ben Yechiel.

R. Yehudah Roznis, author; *Mishneh LeMelech*, commentary on the Rambam; Turkey (1658–1727).

Schwarz, R. Yosef HaKohan, *Responsa, VaYitzbar* Yosef; Grosvardin, Czechoslavakia.

Sha'arei Teshuva, R. Chaim Mordechai Margolies (completed by his brother, R. Efrai'im Zalman Margolies), *Responsa* arranged to the *Shulchan Aruch*; Rav Dubno, Russia.

Sedei Chemed, Rabbi Chayyim Chezekiah b. Raphael, Halachic encyclopaedia; Sephardic author; Constantinople (1832–1904).

Sefat Emet, R. Yehuda Aryeh Leib Alter, Gur Rebbe; Talmudic commentary and responsa (1847–1903).

Shach, R. Shabbetai. b. Meir HaKohen, commentary on Codes, *Nekudat HaKesef*; Lithuania (1621–1662).

Shelah HaKodesh (The Holy Shelah), R. Yeshia b. Avraham Halevi, Kabbalist, rabbinic leader; Frankfurt, Prague, Jerusalem (1565?–1630).

Sheternbuch, Rav Moshe, Contemporary sage; *Ta'am Ve'Daat*, Bible commentary; Johannesburg and Jerusalem.

Shibolei Haleket, R. Zedkiyahu HaRofeh, Compendium of halachic decisions and customs; Rome (thirteenth century).

Shita Mekubetzet, R. Bezalel b. Avraham Ashkenazi, Digest of talmudic commentaries; Safed, Israel; Egypt (1520–1591).

Shmirat Shabbat K'hilchata, R. Yehoshua Yeshia Noibert, Published Jerusalem, 1979; compendium of laws of *Shabbat.*

Shmuelevitz, R. Chaim, Contemporary Rosh Yeshivah, Mir, Jerusalem; *Sichot Musar.*

Shulchan Aruch—See *Bet Yosef.*

Shulchan Aruch HaRav, R. Shneur Zalman of Laidi, Codes of Jewish law; founder of Chabad hasidism (Baal HaTanya); Belorussia (1745–1813).

Sifre, halachic *midrash* to the Books of Numbers and Deuteronomy, first printed in Venice, 1545.

Soloveitchik, R. Aaron, contemporary Rosh HaYeshivah, Yeshivah University and Yeshivat Brisk, Chicago.

Soloveitchik, R. Chaim (Brisker), Talmudist, Brisk; Brest Litovsk (1853–1918).

Soloveitchik, R. Yosef Dov, Contemporary Rosh HaYeshivah, Yeshivah University; *B'Sod HaYachid V'Hayachad* (1903–1993).

Spector, R. Yitzchok Elchonon, Rabbinic author; responsa, *Bet Yitzchok*, Kovna, Lithuania (1817–1896).

Sridei Eish, R. Yecheil Weinberg, Responsa; last Rosh Yeshivah, Berlin Rabbinical Academy (1885–1966).

Talmud, Babylonian, The interpretation and elaboration of the *Mishnah* (first half of third century C.E. to the end of the fifth century).

Avodah Zarah (idolatry)
Arachim
Bava Kamma (damages)
Bava Metzia (torts)
Berachot (blessings)
Hulin
Kiddushim (marriage)
Ketubot (wedding contracts)
Megillah (Purum)
Menachot
Nedarim (vows)
Peah
Pesachim (Passover)
Rosh Hashanah
Sanhedrin
Shabbat (Sabbath)
Sotah (woman suspected of adultery)
Sukkah
Ta'anit (fast days)
Zevachim

Talmidai Rabbenu Yona, Disciples of Rabbenu Yona, Spain (thirteenth century).

Taz (Turei Zahav), R. David b. Shmuel Halevi, Commentary on *Shulchan Aruch*; *Mishptzot Zahav*; Kracow, Poland; Posen, Poland-Lithuania; Vohynia, Russia (1586–1667).

Terumot Hadeshen, R. Yisrael Iserlun, Halachic sage; Bomberg, Germany (1390–1460).

Tiferet Yisrael, R. Yisrael b. R. Gedalya Lipshitz, Commentary on *Mishnah* ; community rabbi, scholar; Danzig (d. 1840).

Tosafot, Commentators on *Talmud* ; France and Germany (1100–1300).

Tur, R. Yaakov b. R. Asher, Codes on Jewish Law; *Baal HaTurim* Germany; Toledo, Spain (1270–1340).

Tzemach Tzedek, R. Menachem Mendel, Halachic authority and leader of Chabad; Russia (1789–1866).

Usiel, R. Ben Zioni Hai, Former Sephardic Chief Rabbi of Israel; halachic authority; *Piskei Usiel*; Tel Aviv (1935).

Vilna Gaon—See HaGra.

Yisraeli, R. Shaul (*z"l*), Contemporary Rosh Yeshivah, Mercaz HaRav, Jerusalem; dayan; halachic sage; responsa; *B'Mareh HaBezek*.

Yonah, Rabbeinu, R. Yonah b. Avraham Gerondi, Commentator, Talmud; halachic scholar, *Sha'arei Teshuvah* (Gates of Repentance); Toledo, Spain (1200–1263).

Yosef, R. Ovadia, Contemporary scholar, former Sephardic Chief Rabbi, Israel (b. 1920); *Responsa Yabia Omer*.

Yosef, R. Yitzchok, Halachic contemporary scholar; son of R. Ovadya Yosef; *Yalkut Yosef*.

Index

About the Author

Rabbi J. Simcha Cohen is the Rav of the Melbourne, Australia Mizrachi community, a network of five synagogues, an elementary and high school as well as a *koshrut* supervising agency. He is the descendant of eighteen generations of rabbis and was ordained by the renowned Gaon, Rav Yitzchok Hutner. Rabbi Cohen attended the Yeshiva and Kollei of the Rabbi Chaim Berlin Rabbinical Academy. He has a number of university degrees and is a member of Phi Beta Kappa. His weekly column, "Halachic Questions" appears in the *Jewish Press*. Rabbi Cohen is the author of five previous works: *Intermarriage and Conversion, A Halachic Solution, The Jewish Heart, Timely Jewish Questions: Timeless Rabbinic Answers, The 613th Commandment*, and *How Does Jewish Law Work? Vol. 1.* He has served at the helm of major Jewish organizations and his writings have been acclaimed as "remarkable achievements" that "succeed in creating genuine Torah excitement."